Captain Cook's War and Peace

Captain Cook's War and Peace

THE ROYAL NAVY YEARS, 1755–1768

JOHN ROBSON

Seaforth
PUBLISHING

Copyright © John Robson 2009

First published in Great Britain in 2009 by
Seaforth Publishing,
Pen & Sword Books Ltd,
47 Church Street,
Barnsley S70 2AS

www.seaforthpublishing.com

British Library Cataloguing in Publication Data
A catalogue record for this book is available from the British Library

ISBN 978 1 84832 033 8

Typeset and designed by JCS Publishing Services Ltd, www.jcs-publishing.co.uk
Printed and bound in Great Britain by Cromwell Press Group, Trowbridge

Contents

Abbreviations   vi
Acknowledgements   vii

Introduction   1

1   Captain Cook's War, 1755–1762   7
2   Joining the Royal Navy, 1755   14
3   HMS *Eagle*, 1755–1757   19
4   HMS *Solebay*, 1757   40
5   HMS *Pembroke*, 1757–1758   46
6   Louisbourg, 1758   51
7   Surveyor, 1758   60
8   Quebec, 1759   74
9   HMS *Northumberland*, 1759–1761   95
10 St John's, Newfoundland, 1762   112
11 Captain Cook's Peace, 1763–1768   123
12 Newfoundland, 1763   127
13 Northern Peninsula, 1764   140
14 South Coast of Newfoundland, 1765   156
15 South-west Coast of Newfoundland, 1766   164
16 West Coast of Newfoundland, 1767   172
17 HMB *Endeavour*, 1768   182

Conclusion   190

Appendix 1: Cook's Ships, 1755–1767   193
Appendix 2: Masters' Regulations and Instructions
       (from *c*1750)   194
Notes   195
Bibliography   201
Index   210

Abbreviations

AB	Able seaman
ATL	Alexander Turnbull Library, Wellington
BL	British Library
CO	Colonial Office
HLHU	Houghton Library, Harvard University
NLA	National Library of Australia
NMM	National Maritime Museum, Greenwich
PRO	Public Records Office
SLNSW	State Library of New South Wales, Sydney
TNA	The National Archives, Kew
UKHO	UK Hydrographic Office
W	The Royal Collection, Windsor Castle
WO	War Office

Acknowledgements

In the United Kingdom, thanks to:

Cliff Thornton for reading the text and providing ongoing support; Guy Hannaford in the Hydrographic Office at Taunton; Nigel Rigby at the National Maritime Museum, Greenwich; staff in the Caird Library, National Maritime Museum, Greenwich; Bruno Pappalardo and other staff at National Archives, Kew; Derek Morris for much information about and a wonderful tour of Mile End Old Town; Ruth Boreham for undertaking extra research at Kew on my behalf; and Jessica Cuthbert-Smith for an excellent job of copy-editing.

A special word for the British Library at St Pancras. Tom Harper in the Map Room at the British Library, St Pancras, provided excellent assistance. Unfortunately, the same cannot be said for his colleagues. I was prevented from using the library during my visit in late 2007 because of the draconian rules introduced to make it difficult for readers to renew their tickets. On three occasions staff were rude and unhelpful. The irony is I have to lodge copies of this book with them!

In Canada, thanks to:

Donald Graves for information about Quebec and allowing me to quote from his revised edition of CP Stacey's book on Quebec. What was already a good book is now a marvellous one; Derek Hayes; Dave Fisher for photos of Louisbourg; Shannon Parker at the Art Gallery of Nova Scotia in Halifax; Daniel Vickers for his scholarship on Ashley Bowen; and Lynda Silver, librarian at the Maritime Museum in Halifax.

In Newfoundland, many thanks to:

Olaf and Ellen Janzen, Selma Barkham and Bernie Conran for wonderful hospitality. The beauty of their island is no longer a secret. To Olaf and Selma especially, thanks for enabling me to see places on the west coast where Cook surveyed; and Bernie Conran and Joan Ritcey at the Library of Memorial University of Newfoundland have continued to provide great assistance with resources.

In the USA, thanks to:

Karen McInnis of the Marblehead Historical Society for permission to reproduce text and drawings of Ashley Bowen; Denison Beach at the Houghton Library, Harvard University for help in acquiring a copy of Cook's sailing directions for Louisbourg; and Donald Olson for permission to use his map showing Wolfe's passage down the St Lawrence River.

In New Zealand, thanks to:
Megan Symes for proofreading the text; Lesley Wilson for providing the index; Max Oulton for redrawing and computerising all the maps; William Jennings for French translations; and my work colleagues in the New Zealand Collection at the University of Waikato Library – my mind has been elsewhere somewhat for the last two years or so.

Special thanks to Julian Mannering at Seaforth Publishing in the UK for agreeing to publish the book and providing ongoing encouragement and support.

Given that some events covered in the book have been described by soldiers and officials using civil time and by sailors using nautical time I have changed all dates and times (where they can be established) to civil time to avoid confusion.

Unless otherwise referenced, all quotations from logs and journals are from manuscripts held at the National Archives in Kew (TNA) and the National Maritime Museum in Greenwich (NMM). All quotations from logs are taken from Cook's logs, unless indicated otherwise.

As ever I thank my corgis, Hector and Cullen, for their patience throughout the process of assembling this book.

Finally, in late 2007 I discovered that a namesake of mine had sailed with Cook on HMS *Pembroke*. This earlier John Robson suddenly appeared one day while I researched in the Caird Library at Greenwich. I had previously been unaware of his existence but I now had another personal reason for being interested in Cook. I do not know what happened to him or whether we are related but I dedicate the book to him.

Introduction

James Cook's exploits in the Pacific are well known, having been covered by countless books. Cook, however, was already thirty-nine when he set out for the Pacific, and most of those books skip over Cook's earlier career in the Royal Navy if it is even mentioned at all. Flann O'Brien in his novel *At Swim-Two-Birds* had a character who 'was born at the age of twenty-five', and, in a similar vein, many of the authors of books about Cook have him 'born at the age of thirty-nine. For them, he was a ready-made explorer with no previous, personal history, just waiting to set off to discover peoples, lands and fortunes.

It is the intention of this book largely to ignore Cook's time in the Pacific but instead to focus on his career in the Royal Navy before his great adventures on *Endeavour* and *Resolution*. Similarly, only a brief overview will be presented of Cook's childhood and the time he spent sailing on colliers in the North Sea. For more detail on that part of Cook's life you are referred to the works of Cliff Thornton (*Captain Cook in Cleveland*) and Julia Rae (*Captain James Cook Endeavours*). Cook spent thirteen years in the Royal Navy before sailing to the Pacific, having joined in 1755. This book aims to show that most of the qualities that led to Cook being chosen to command *Endeavour* were developed during this period. His progress from able seaman to ship's master capable of drawing hydrographic charts will be shown using examples from logs, journals and letters.

Cook's career over this time has been presented before, not least in an overview by JC Beaglehole in his *The Life of Captain James Cook*, but new information has come to light since the publication of that book in 1974. A few other authors have covered the period in part: Victor Suthren dealt with the Canadian aspects in *To Go Upon Discovery*; William Whiteley wrote about Cook in Newfoundland; and writers such as Raleigh Skelton and Andrew David have discussed Cook's development as a surveyor-hydrographer, which took place during this time.

The thirteen years under consideration divide neatly into two, providing an explanation for the title of this book. The first part, here called 'Captain Cook's War', was taken up with Cook's service in the Seven Years' War. The second part, 'Captain Cook's Peace' covers the six years during which he was occupied surveying the coast of Newfoundland. Each offered Cook opportunities to learn and develop new skills, which he did with quiet determination.

So who was James Cook and how did he come to be in the Royal Navy? He was born in Marton-in-Cleveland in the north-east of England, the second son of a farm labourer. His father, James Cook senior, who was originally from Ednam in Roxburghshire, south-east Scotland, had moved south to Cleveland some time in the 1720s. The details and reason for the move remain unknown but there he met Grace Pace, a local woman from Thornaby-on-Tees, and the couple were married in Stainton Parish Church on 10 October 1725 when the groom was thirty-one and the bride was twenty-three. Farm work was seasonal and temporary, so labourers attended the hirings held in local market towns and moved as necessary to wherever they could get work . The Cooks moved regularly around the Cleveland district over the next few years, albeit a few kilometres each time. Their first child, John, was born in 1727 when they were living in the Morton district. Shortly after, they moved a few kilometres to Marton, where Cook senior had secured work for George Mewburn.

The explorer, James Cook, was born in Marton on Sunday 27 October 1728 and was baptised a week later in Marton's parish church, St Cuthbert's, on 3 November. What little we know of Cook's early life is a mixture of fact, hearsay and legend, blended together over the years by biographers. The Cook family was poor and the children were expected to work as soon as they were able. It is believed, therefore, that young James was already tending stock, watering horses and running errands by the age of five for a local family, the Walkers. One story has it that, in return, Dame Walker is supposed to have taught him his alphabet and how to read. Two daughters followed James: Christiana in 1731 and Mary, born in 1733 (this Mary died in 1736).

It is thought that the Cooks lived in two separate homes in Marton but nothing remains of either of them. In 1736 the family left Marton to live at Aireyholme Farm on the slopes of Roseberry Topping near Great Ayton, six kilometres to the south-east. Aireyholme was owned by Thomas Skottowe, the lord of the manor of Great Ayton. The move was a promotion for Cook senior, who was the new hind or foreman on the farm. It also represented security for the family as it meant their travelling days were over, and they would stay at the farm until 1755, a period of nineteen years. At Ayton four more children were born: Jane in 1738 (died 1742); another Mary in 1740 (died 1741); Margaret in 1742; and William in 1745 (died 1748).

James, by now eight years old, went to the Postgate School in the village as well as working on the farm. It is thought that he was an average student though proficient in mathematics. He was a loner and obstinate but had the respect of the other boys. He attended the school until he was twelve, when he began full-time work, probably for the Skottowe family. This brought him to the attention of Thomas Skottowe, who would prove to have a considerable influence on Cook's life.

Skottowe was also a justice of the peace for the North Riding of Yorkshire and attended sessions at Guisborough, where it is probable that he met William Sanderson. Sanderson was a merchant and shopkeeper from Staithes, on the coast between Redcar and Whitby, who also acted as a constable in that district. The two men were friends and became related later on, when their sons married sisters named Gill. In 1745, when James Cook was sixteen and ready to leave home and get a job, it was arranged that he should work for Sanderson in his haberdashery and grocery shop at Staithes.

Staithes is a small, cramped, fishing village nestled at the foot of cliffs where Roxby Beck enters the sea. Always a very close community, newcomers took a long time to be accepted and, for a young boy like Cook, away from home for the first time, it would have been a strange and lonely place. However, Staithes did introduce Cook to the sea and Sanderson, realising that Cook was unsettled, used his connections and influence to introduce the boy to the Walker family in Whitby.

In 1746, Whitby, twelve kilometres to the east of Staithes at the mouth of the river Esk, was a port of over five thousand people, which presented a new experience for the seventeen-year-old Cook. The town already had a long history, mostly associated with the abbey, which dominated the town from high on East Cliff. The town's prosperity came from its involvement in the North Sea coal trade and Whitby families owned and operated over two hundred ships on the North and Baltic Seas. The Walkers, John and Henry, were Quakers who operated several ships and were always in need of crew, so James Cook was a welcome addition. He was taken on either as an apprentice or as a servant and lived in John Walker's house in Grape Lane when not at sea.

It is not known in which ships he sailed during his first year, but in 1747 a new Act of Parliament was passed that decreed that all ships must keep muster rolls. From that time, therefore, there is a near-complete record of the Whitby (and other) vessels on which Cook sailed. Cook is known to have sailed on *Freelove* (1747–8), *Three Brothers* (1748–51) and *Friendship* (1751–5), all owned by the Walkers. After his apprenticeship finished in 1749 he also spent some months on other vessels, *Mary* and *Hopewell*.

The North Sea coal trade had developed to meet the ever-expanding need that London had for coal. The South Northumberland coalfield, close to the coast and with good port facilities at the mouth of the river Tyne, had been best able to satisfy that need and fleets of ships sprang up to transport the coal down the east coast to the capital. Whitby became an important point along this trade route. Each round-trip could take over a month: a week to load the coal at North Shields, a week to unload at Wapping on the Thames and a week each way sailing along the east coast. The winter weather and conditions in the North Sea could be treacherous, and so the crew would be given a break of two to three months over that season. The coal trade gave Cook his introduction to London as the colliers sailed up the Thames to discharge the coal at the wharves along the north bank of the river, east of the Tower of London. The Walkers dealt with other Quaker families in Wapping and Shadwell and it is probable that Walker arranged accommodation for his crew in the area. Cook possibly stayed at the Bell alehouse near Execution Dock in Wapping, which was owned and run by the Batts family. In 1762 the daughter of the family, Elizabeth Batts, married James Cook.

While the majority of Cook's experience was on the Tyne–Thames coal route he also visited Norway on *Three Brothers* and he sailed into the Baltic Sea on *Mary*; he may have even reached St Petersburg. Cook was also on board *Three Brothers* when it was commandeered to take British troops and horses from Middelburg in Zeeland to Dublin and Liverpool.

This period was crucial in Cook's life as it was then that he learned the skills in seamanship that would serve him well in the future. Cook was prepared to study and learn, which obviously impressed Walker, so that a lasting friendship developed between the two men. Later, Cook would write to Walker on his voyages and visited him in Whitby between voyages. Cook's abilities singled him out and enabled him to progress from seaman to mate; he would probably have become a master of one of Walker's ships had he not surprised everyone by volunteering for the Royal Navy. On 17 June 1755 James Cook joined the Royal Navy at Wapping in East London.

Being a sailor on the North Sea had already taken Cook away from his family in Cleveland. His move into the Royal Navy distanced him further from them as he was now based in the naval ports of Plymouth, Portsmouth and London – all in the south of England. Opportunities for visits to the north-east became fewer, although it is thought that Cook possibly saw his family before and after his time on *Solebay* in 1757. After his marriage to Elizabeth Batts in 1762, there was even less imperative to go north as he now had family in London.

Thirteen years after joining the Royal Navy there was another surprise involving Cook. He was selected to lead an expedition to the Pacific. Some writers have asked the question, 'Why was James Cook chosen to lead the *Endeavour* expedition?' I hope that after reading this book people will ask different questions: 'Why would the Admiralty have chosen anyone else to lead the expedition?' and 'Who else could they have chosen?'.

COOK IN EUROPE
1755 – 1758

SHETLAND

NORWAY

ORKNEY
1757

SCOTLAND

NORTH
SEA

Edinburgh
Ednam
Newcastle
CLEVELAND
Marton
Whitby

1747–1755

IRELAND
Dublin

ENGLAND

Cape   1755
Clear

London

Portsmouth

Plymouth

ENGLISH CHANNEL

1755-8

NORMANDY

ATLANTIC
OCEAN

Ushant   Brest

BRITTANY

FRANCE

1756-7

BAY OF BISCAY

Cape
Ortegal

Cape
Finisterre

SPAIN

N

0   100   200
kilometres

Max Oulton

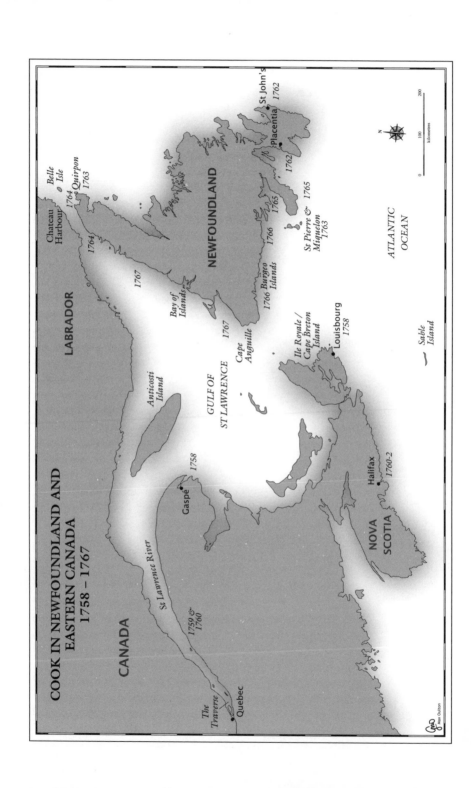

COOK IN NEWFOUNDLAND AND
EASTERN CANADA
1758 – 1767

CANADA

Quebec

The
Traverse

St Lawrence River

1759 &
1760

1758
Gaspé

Anticosti
Island

LABRADOR

Chateau
Harbour

1764

1767

Belle
Isle
1764 Quirpon
1763

GULF OF
ST LAWRENCE

Bay of
Islands

1767

Cape
Anguille

NEWFOUNDLAND

1766 Burgeo
Islands

1766
1765
1765 St John's
1762

Placentia
1762

St Pierre & 1765
Miquelon
1763

Ile Royale /
Cape Breton
Island

Louisbourg
1758

Halifax
1760-2

NOVA
SCOTIA

Sable
Island

ATLANTIC
OCEAN

N

0   100   200
kilometres

Alex Oulton

❧ I ❧

Captain Cook's War, 1755–1762

James Cook joined the Royal Navy in 1755, exchanging life as mate on a collier in the North Sea for life as an able seaman on a ship of the line. He did so just as the Seven Years' War (or Captain Cook's War, as I will call it), which had been simmering for some time, was beginning in earnest. The war would dictate the events in Cook's life for the next few years. The principal protagonists, the major European nations, had been lining up to begin another in the series of wars that marked the eighteenth century and which regularly interrupted the short periods of peace. The previous war, the War of Austrian Succession had finished in 1748 and the Treaty of Aix-la-Chapelle that formally ended that war had resolved little. For many of the nations involved, the treaty only represented a temporary truce. In this way, the Seven Years' War may be viewed as a continuation of the earlier war.

Fighting took place beyond Europe, on other continents, and some commentators in the late twentieth century began to portray this war as the first global conflict. The war is actually known by several different names. The overall name by which it is known in Britain and France is the Seven Years' War (lasting there from 1756 to 1762). However, the duration of the war varied, depending on the location and, in North America, where fighting lasted from 1754 to 1760, the war is known as the French and Indian War. The war in Central Europe is known by some as the Third Silesian War, and for part of the war in India the term Third Carnatic War is used. Given William Pitt's role in directing the British effort, some British historians referred to it as Pitt's War. Captain Cook's War is therefore another in a long line of appellations.

France and Britain were invariably on opposite sides during the eighteenth-century wars and, similarly, Austria and Prussia usually opposed each other. King Frederick II of Prussia had gained the rich province of Silesia in 1748 and Empress Maria Theresa of Austria had agreed peace terms only in order to rebuild her army and to form new alliances. Nations often formed alliances with different partners and so Austria – which had been allied with Britain before 1748 – this time formed a new alliance with France, and a pact was signed at Versailles in May 1756. Prussia was at odds with most of its neighbours and Russia, Sweden and Saxony soon sided with Austria and France against Prussia.

George II of Britain was still Elector of Hanover and retained strong interests there, so Britain signed the Convention of Westminster with Prussia in January 1756 – in anticipation of the Austrian move – believing that Prussia would assist in the protection of Hanover. The French–Austrian–Russian alliance might have much larger numbers of fighting men but Britain had the best navy and Prussia had the most effective army

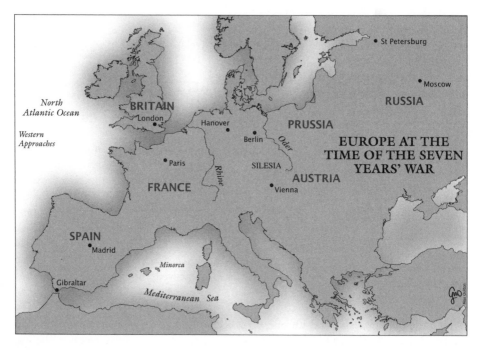

and commanders. This agreement allowed Britain to concentrate on control of the seas and on land actions in North America and India, leaving Prussia to handle things in Continental Europe. The war began formally in Europe in May 1756 when Britain and France declared war on each other. Frederick of Prussia then invaded Saxony in August, thus starting the war in Central Europe.

The other spark for war came from the rivalry between Britain and France over land and new territory, especially in North America and India. Skirmishes and small actions had been taking place in these locations for some time before 1756. In North America, events began in 1754 and George Washington, the future first President of the United States, was at the centre of things. The French had entered the Ohio valley and Washington was dispatched from Virginia to investigate. Relations deteriorated, fighting broke out and soon full-scale warfare began. Britain dispatched troops under Edward Braddock to Fort Duquesne (Pittsburg) in 1755 but they were roundly beaten. The much smaller population of French Canada could not sustain an army to fight the superior numbers assembled by the British and, though the French continued to win further encounters over the next three years, they were never able to gain total victory. For their part, the British could afford to suffer those defeats before inflicting two significant blows at Louisbourg and Quebec that ended all French hopes.

India was the third theatre where fighting broke out as old rivalry between the British and French East India Companies escalated. Both sides had alliances with local Indian rulers and the ensuing battles often involved Indian troops fighting alongside Europeans.

In central Europe, Frederick II (or Frederick the Great, as he was often known), the King of Prussia, had invaded Silesia in 1740, the same year that he took power. The ensuing First Silesian War (1740–2), part of the War of the Austrian Succession, resulted in Prussia retaining the province. Austria attempted to recover Silesia in the Second Silesian War (1744–5), but Frederick was victorious again. In 1756, Austria, keen to recover Silesia, sided with France, even though they had been traditional enemies, and began conspiring against Prussia. Frederick, aware of developments, acted first by entering Saxony on 29 August. This was the first action in the Third Silesian War (1756–62).

Russia, under Empress Elizabeth, entered the conflict on the side of Austria, and a series of inconclusive battles were fought over the next six years. Huge numbers of men were killed or wounded in these clashes. Each side won some encounters and then lost some, and territory was similarly gained and lost. Prussia's army was able to survive even in the face of more numerous enemy because it was much better trained and organised. It also had, in Frederick, a leader of exceptional ability.

Frederick was helped by Ferdinand, Duke of Brunswick-Lüneburg, who assumed command of the allied Hanoverian army in November 1757 after that army's defeat under the Duke of Cumberland at Hastenbeck. Ferdinand skilfully led his army against the French for the next four years, tying the French down so that they were unable to assist Austria against Prussia. The Austrian army was led by Leopold Josef, Graf Daun. He was a cautious general and let slip several opportunities where he could have pressed home an advantage that might have defeated Prussia. Prussia was also fortunate in that Austria rarely worked in unison with the Russian army, commanded by Count Pyotr Semyonovich Saltykov.

Britain originally declined to commit its forces on the Continent, where it depended on Prussia and Hanover to carry on the fight. It did, however, help fund the Prussian army and later committed some troops to help the Hanoverian army fight the French near the Rhine. Britain's war aims, largely directed by William Pitt (see section 'William Pitt and the Seven Years' War'), were to control the seas and thereby destroy the French navy and merchant fleet. France would then be in no position to assist its colonies; Britain's empire would grow and France would no longer be a rival. Britain's situation was helped greatly by France concentrating its efforts in Europe to fight Prussia and Hanover.

Pitt was prepared to order naval attacks on selected French ports, which would irritate the French and cause them to retain troops in France that would otherwise have gone to fight on France's eastern front. Attacks were made against Rochefort, St Malo and Cherbourg, though not with much success.

In other areas British sea power was one of the telling factors in the war. Despite being short of ships and experienced crews when the war began, Britain quickly built up its fleet and was soon able to use it to stifle French efforts. Anson, as first lord of the Admiralty began reorganising the Royal Navy. He promoted capable admirals such as Boscawen, Hawke and Saunders to counter the existing group of elderly and incapable ones. The seas around Britain were to be regarded as British territory, needing constant protection. Soon the British navy was larger than the French and Spanish combined.

Anson developed the idea of the Western Squadron operating in the Western Approaches to the English Channel and in the Bay of Biscay. The following quote is attributed to Anson from 1756:

> Our colonies are so numerous and so extensive that to keep a naval force at each equal to the united force of France would be impracticable with double our Navy. The best defence therefore for our Colonies as well as our coasts is to have such a squadron always to the Westward as may in all probability either keep the French in port or give them battle with advantage if they come out.[1]

Fleets of British ships were soon patrolling off Brittany to effect a blockade of Brest, the major French port, while other British ships based at Gibraltar prevented French vessels leaving the Mediterranean. In this way French colonies were cut off from support and were at the mercy of the British forces able to attack them. The French government was mostly powerless to help and left its colonies to fend for themselves. The French attitude to Canada at the time was summed up by Voltaire: 'You are perhaps aware that these two nations [France and England] are at war over a few acres of snow near Canada although they could buy up the whole of Canada with the money they are spending on the war.'[2] France persuaded Spain, which until then had been neutral, to join the French side in 1761. This only served to widen the war and Britain quickly responded. In 1762 British forces attacked and captured the Spanish cities of Havana in Cuba and Manila in the Philippines.

In Europe the normal method of fighting major battles involved the two armies facing each other on an open expanse and then attacking with infantry, cavalry and artillery. The armies of Central Europe fought a whole series of battles along these lines but the results were indecisive as first one side won and then the other gained a temporary victory. Throughout the war the Prussians were greatly outnumbered and were attacked on two fronts by Russia and Austria, but their superior leadership – especially Frederick's – ensured that they remained in the fight. Both sides lost such large numbers of men that a draw was inevitable.

In North America a more irregular form of warfare developed; this new method of fighting was a novel experience for the British, which they took time to come to terms with. Much of North America was still covered in forest, and open spaces where European-style battles could be fought were uncommon. Much of the fighting took place in wooded areas, rendering cavalry and artillery largely ineffective. The French Canadians and their Native American allies had perfected a form of guerrilla warfare and often harried and ambushed British forces, each time inflicting small-scale losses that accumulated over time. The British were unfamiliar with these conditions and continued to wear their traditional uniforms, which were unsuitable for the new type of warfare. Many battles involved besieging forts, which also required different tactics. The scale of operations was also very different in North America from that in Europe. Battles in Europe often involved armies with thirty thousand men or more on each side, while even at Quebec, one of the largest battles in North America, the armies only totalled about four and a half thousand men on each side. The battle at Quebec was the first fought in the European manner and the British were in their element there. The French Canadians opposite them were undisciplined and untrained to face enemy fire so, when the first fusillade devastated their lines, the survivors turned and ran.

James Cook's experiences during the Seven Years' War were quite varied. He was occasionally at the centre of things but more often he was involved in routine work away from the action. During the first two years of the war Cook was on HMS *Eagle*, which undertook patrols off the Irish coast, took part in the blockade of Brest and patrolled the Normandy and Brittany coasts to prevent invasion. *Eagle* often stopped and captured small vessels but it was only near the end of Cook's time on the ship that *Eagle* was engaged in a major action, when a French Indiaman was attacked. Most of the time was spent sailing back and forth in cold and often stormy conditions, which took their toll on the ship and the crew. Despite the apparent lack of activity, the blockade of which *Eagle* was a part was a major contributing factor in the overall British victory.

Cook was promoted to master in 1757 and transferred onto HMS *Solebay* for a couple of months. The ship undertook an incident-free patrol from Leith to Shetland and back. Later that year Cook joined HMS *Pembroke* and, after a few more months of taking part in another blockade, sailed to North America. During 1758 and 1759 Cook was present at two of the most decisive battles of the war. He was largely an observer at the siege of Louisbourg in 1758 but played a significant part during the siege of Quebec the following year. Louisbourg introduced Cook to surveying and he became proficient so quickly that he was able to put his new skills into practice in the St Lawrence River near Quebec.

The French loss at Quebec was effectively the end of the war in North America, although the French held out until September 1760, when they eventually surrendered at Montreal. By then Cook was master on HMS *Northumberland* and based at Halifax, Nova Scotia. The war in Europe continued and the British could not afford to leave Canada unprotected so Cook and *Northumberland* were part of a squadron left to prevent the French from making an attempt to retake the country. It was a time of routine and boredom as Cook's ship did not leave port for nearly two years before responding to a French attack that took place in mid-1762. In one of the last acts of the Seven Years' War, a French force captured St John's, the capital of Newfoundland; Cook was part of the British force that retook the island in September 1762. This marked Cook's introduction to the island that became the centre of his activity for the next five years. *Northumberland* then crossed the Atlantic to find a Britain ready for peace.

Thus ended Captain Cook's war. That he had survived was no mean feat. Death or injury such as loss of limb was common through naval battles, but many more men succumbed to scurvy and other diseases prevalent on Royal Navy ships of the time. Cook could even be said to have prospered during the war. Having started on the lowest rung, he had been promoted to emerge as a ship's master, the senior warrant officer ranking. He had developed other abilities and his surveying skills had marked him out so that he was soon appointed to undertake a survey of the largely unknown coastline of Newfoundland. To complete matters, he married.

The war in Europe had also drawn to a weary close. Fighting had ended in Central Europe in November 1762 and the conflict there was formally concluded by the Treaty of Hubertusburg on 16 February 1763. Territorial boundaries remained as they had been in 1756, and Prussia retained Silesia. In Western Europe, William Pitt, who was responsible for much of the planning behind Britain's success, had been forced from office and his successor, the Earl of Bute, wanted peace – as did the majority of the population. Peace negotiations began between Britain, France and Spain in late 1762 and a treaty was signed at Paris on 10 February 1763. Among the clauses were three that impinged on Cook in his future role:

IV. . . . His Most Christian Majesty cedes and guaranties to his said Britannick Majesty, in full right, Canada, with all its dependencies, as well as the island of Cape Breton, and all the other islands and coasts in the gulph and river of St. Lawrence . . .

V. The subjects of France shall have the liberty of fishing and drying on a part of the coasts of the island of Newfoundland, such as it is specified in the XIIIth article of the treaty of Utrecht; which article is renewed and confirmed by the present treaty.

VI. The King of Great Britain cedes the islands of St. Pierre and Macquelon, in full right, to his Most Christian Majesty, to serve as a shelter to the French fishermen.[3]

WILLIAM PITT AND THE SEVEN YEARS' WAR

William Pitt dominated the British political scene during the mid-eighteenth century. He was a formidable orator and showed great ability as a wartime leader during the Seven Years' War. Born 1708, the son of Robert Pitt, William Pitt entered Parliament in 1735, aged twenty-seven, after attending Oxford. He gained prominence through his opposition to Prime Minister Sir Robert Walpole, and by his association with Frederick, Prince of Wales. These actions gained him the enmity of King George II.

Pitt was paymaster general from 1746 in the governments of Henry Pelham and his successor, the Duke of Newcastle. By late 1755, he was making it known that he felt he should be a secretary of state so he could run foreign policy and was asserting the need for action in North America.

The events of 1756, including defeats in North America, led to the downfall of Newcastle's government. In November, the king was forced to agree to a new government led by the Duke of Devonshire at the Treasury and with Pitt as Secretary of State for the Southern Department. The duke was the figurehead who guaranteed support, while Pitt soon emerged as the man in charge. He did not change policy immediately, though: while stressing the need for action in North America, Pitt now accepted Britain's role in Europe, including paying subsidies for Prussia, which had been agreed under the Treaty of Westminster.

Pitt had long been out of favour with George II for criticisms he had made of the monarchy. He now pleaded for mercy for Admiral Byng, who had been sentenced to death, but the king enforced the execution in March. The king dismissed Pitt on 6 April 1757. The Devonshire government fell shortly after and the Duke of Newcastle resumed his position as first lord of the Treasury in June. Pitt took up his as secretary of state again, enjoying a similar relationship with Newcastle as he had with Devonshire.

Things did not begin well. The Hanoverian army under Cumberland was defeated at Hastenbeck and Cumberland was forced to sign the Convention of Klosterseven, demobilising his army. However, Britain refused to recognise the treaty and instead agreed to subsidise the Hanoverian army and even contributed British troops to it. In April 1758, a second treaty of Westminster was signed with Prussia.

Pitt's policies began to show results outside Europe. He used advisers such as Anson on naval matters and Ligonier for the military. He also dealt directly with commanders in the field, issuing them very precise instructions. His promotion of the navy's role and the effective stifling of French access to North America led to changed fortunes in North America, beginning with Louisbourg in August 1758. In India, British forces gradually won dominance in Bengal and in the Carnatic region around Madras.

For Pitt, 1759 was probably his greatest year, with British successes, especially naval, around the world at Quebec, Lagos, Quiberon Bay and in India. Horace Walpole wrote: 'Our bells are quite worn threadbare with ringing for victories. Indeed one is forced to ask every morning, what victory there is? for fear of missing one.'[4]

George II died in late 1760 and his successor, George III, wished to end the war as soon as possible. He was also no friend of Pitt and described him as: 'the most ungrateful . . . most dishonorable of men, a true snake in the grass'.[5] The new king's adviser, the Earl of Bute, became Secretary of State for the Northern Department in May 1761. As Bute's influence grew, so that of Pitt diminished. Peace negotiations began with France in May. Pitt was all for keeping everything that had been gained during the war but Bute and his colleagues felt some appeasement of France was necessary. The French were offended by Pitt's stand, even though the French minister, the Duc de Choiseul was already trying to bring Spain into the war through a Bourbon family compact. When news of this compact became known, Pitt advocated action against the annual Spanish treasure fleet from America. None of his cabinet colleagues agreed and Pitt, now totally isolated, resigned from office on 5 October. After his resignation, Newcastle wrote: 'With all his faults, we shall want Mr Pitt; . . . I know nobody, who can plan, or push the execution of any plan agreed upon, in the manner Mr Pitt did.'[6]

Now in opposition, Pitt was severely critical of the terms of the peace treaty signed in 1763. In July 1766, Pitt was asked to lead a coalition government; Pitt was created Earl of Chatham, but his government was a failure and he fell into depression and resigned in October 1768. He remained in Parliament and continued to speak out against British policy in the colonies and to fight for parliamentary reform. He collapsed in the Lords in 1778 and died a month later at the age of seventy. Pitt was popular with the people and especially with London merchants. However, he made few friends among politicians and was disliked by both Georges II and III.

2

Joining the Royal Navy, 1755

We know that James Cook joined the Royal Navy at Wapping in East London on 17 June 1755. What we do not know is why he joined, as he left no explanation for his move. Why he chose to join at all and why he chose that particular time and place have puzzled researchers, and it is interesting to speculate as to what might have caused Cook to take the step he did.

In June 1755, James Cook was twenty-six years old with eight years' experience on colliers sailing in the North Sea between the river Tyne and the river Thames. He had made some other short voyages that had taken him to the Baltic and Irish Seas but his experience had been mostly off the east coast of England. Cook had learned to sail on ships belonging to the Walker family of Whitby and, gradually, he had acquired skills and abilities that impressed the Walkers sufficiently for him to be promoted to mate on one of their ships, *Friendship*. By then he must have known the rudiments of seamanship and navigation, and have shown the potential for leadership. It is believed that, in 1755, Cook was close to being offered his own command on one of the Walkers' ships, possibly *Friendship*. However, having arrived in the Thames on 14 June, Cook resigned from the Walkers' employ and, three days later, joined the Royal Navy instead.

The Royal Navy used the 'Impress Service' to recruit men both as volunteers and as impressed men. Naval officers, often termed 'regulating captains', were allocated to ports and usually set up their headquarters in a local public house. The headquarters was known as the Rendezvous, or more familiarly as the 'rondy'. The regulating captains employed groups of men known as 'press gangs' to round up likely men who were then pressed into service in the navy. Many of the men found this way were not and never would make seamen, but numbers were what mattered. The population despised the press gangs and did all they could to hinder their work. Cook, though, was not being pressed and entered the Rendezvous in Wapping as a volunteer.

So why might he have resigned a relatively secure position and future career with the Walkers? From the little we know of Cook's personality, he continually strove to stretch himself and to experience new things. It was these traits that contributed to his success later in the Pacific; in 1755, these tendencies might have urged him to leave the merchant service and join the Royal Navy. The colliers he had sailed on delivered coal to wharves on the Thames in and around Wapping, and Cook stayed close by. Wapping was a place where one would meet seamen with experience on all the known seas and oceans of the world and Cook would have heard stories about places that would have fired his imagination. For a man such as Cook, the thought of sailing to the East and West Indies would have proved much more exciting than the prospect of repeating the same journey between the Tyne and Thames countless times for the rest of his working life. Although Cook had become close to the Walker family, there was no guarantee that he would benefit financially to the extent that he might own his own vessel or be able to dictate his own destiny. More probably, he faced a future where he would be a master of a vessel but remain an employee serving in the Walkers' or someone else's fleet.

While places such as the East Indies might sound enticing, Cook would have been aware that various diseases were common in overseas waters and, in Royal Navy ships, you also ran the risk of dying in combat. However, the North Sea was not without its own risks and colliers were regularly wrecked on England's east coast.

Another possible reason for Cook's move may have been that he was running from somebody or something. However, there is no apparent evidence that that was the case. James Cook remained close friends with John Walker and other people in Whitby after he joined the Royal Navy, so there appears to have been no problems with his former employer. Similarly, he kept in touch – as much as he could – with his family in Cleveland, so a rift there is unlikely. What we know of his character does not suggest he had fallen foul of the law. It is, therefore, highly unlikely that he was running away.

Cook saw the Royal Navy as a means of extending his experience and offering new challenges. Kippis reports that Cook was 'determined to take his future fortune that way.'[1] Beaglehole, in his biography of Cook, quotes John Walker, Cook's previous employer, as saying: 'He had always an ambition to go into the Navy.'[2]

What may have tipped the scales for Cook and caused him to enlist when he did was the very active recruitment undertaken by the Royal Navy in the first part of 1755. Recruitment officers were prominent throughout the country and especially at all ports in an attempt to increase manpower for the anticipated war. That war, the Seven Years' War, had not formally started (it was only officially declared by Britain on 17 May 1756 and a few weeks later by France, in June), but a war of sorts had begun the previous year in 1754 in North America, and some actions had already occurred at sea. Those naval actions had been initiated largely by the Royal Navy, even though, ironically, the Royal Navy was in a very poor shape and, at the beginning of 1755, did not have the ships, men or resources to undertake a war. Manpower and resources had been run down by the British government since the end of the War of Austrian Succession in 1748.

Henry Pelham, first lord of the Treasury (the equivalent of prime minister) from 1743 until his death in 1754, had assumed power during the War of Austrian Succession (begun in 1739), which was concluded with the signing of the Treaty of Aix-la-Chapelle in 1748. Once the war was over, Pelham began cutting government expenditure drastically to reduce interest on the national debt and so that he could reduce taxation. The navy was a principal sufferer and Pelham rejected the Admiralty's request to maintain naval forces at something like wartime strength. The number of men employed by the navy thus fell from 50,596 in 1748 to 8,346 in 1753. Admiral George Anson, then first lord of the Admiralty, had asked the government to establish a naval reserve of 3,000 men but the government bowed to pressure from others and nothing was done. The number of ships dropped similarly and the state of those ships that were retained worsened.

In March 1754, Henry Pelham was succeeded by his brother, Thomas Pelham-Holles, the Duke of Newcastle. Newcastle had been a secretary of state since 1746 and part, therefore, of the ruling administration. He had been a party to its policies, and he did little to change them. Over the next two and a half years, Newcastle proved to be an ineffective leader and he resigned in November 1756.

Fighting between British and French forces began in North America in 1754, when border disputes in the Ohio valley erupted into war. France had moved into the region, which brought it into conflict with the claims of the British colonies, especially Virginia. During the spring of 1754, George Washington was ordered to take Fort Duquesne at the confluence of the Allegheny and the Monongahela rivers, a position held by the French. In May, en route to the fort, Washington and his three hundred Virginian militiamen attacked a reconnaissance party, killing ten members, including a French emissary. Washington and his men took refuge in Fort Necessity, where they were surrounded by a larger French force. Washington surrendered on 4 July 1754.

News of these events reached London later in July. Newcastle wanted to confine the war to North America and, after much hesitation and confusion, his government resolved to send troops to North America. In the autumn of 1754, Major General Edward Braddock was given command of an expedition charged with putting the British colonial troops on a war footing and removing the French from the Ohio valley. Fort Duquesne would be captured and the French sent back north into Canada and south to Louisiana.

Braddock sailed from Cork in December 1754 and disembarked at Hampton, Virginia. Finally, on 10 June 1755, Braddock and a force of British troops and colonial militia marched from Wills Creek, Maryland. However, on 9 July 1755, the British were caught in a French ambush after crossing the Monongahela River on their way to Fort Duquesne. Braddock was among the casualties and he died on 13 July 1755.

A French squadron under Admiral Dubois de la Motte sailed from Brest early in 1755 with supplies and reinforcements for French settlements in North America. The Royal Navy quickly dispatched Vice Admiral Edward Boscawen from Portsmouth on 27 April 1755 with eleven ships, to follow the French. Boscawen sailed into the Atlantic with orders to reinforce British interests in North America and to intercept the French attempts to reinforce their side. Though Boscawen missed most of a French fleet en route to Louisbourg, he did encounter a small part of the fleet near the Grand Banks in June 1755. In capturing two ships, Boscawen's actions helped trigger war in Europe; the British were soon also intercepting and capturing French vessels returning to French ports. Britain was moving onto a war footing and recruitment and impressment had started in earnest.

On 13 September 1755, two months after joining the navy, Cook reported in his log:

At 4pm sent out a tender with a lieutenant and men to impress seamen.

Impressed men would look for a chance to escape and on the same day Cook reported the desertion of one of the crew:

At 11 ditto swam ashore and ran away Robert Gordon seaman.

'Ordinary citizens' could obtain rewards if they reported men suitable for recruitment. Members of the gentry even placed adverts in regional newspapers offering financial inducements for men to volunteer to enlist. Clifford Thornton has suggested that Cook's enlistment may have come in such a way. Cook's father was then on the point of retirement; his employer, Thomas Scottowe, made land available in Great Ayton and helped the Cooks build their own new cottage, which bears the date 1755. The deed transferring the land to Cook senior was completed on 16 June 1755 and Cook junior signed on in London two days later. Thornton suggests this timing was not coincidence. Scottowe might have helped finance Cook's father and in return received the 'bounty' when Cook enlisted.[3]

However, among the suitable men who would make good sailors were many unemployable men and criminals. The navy and the imminent war were seen as easy ways of disposing of undesirable members of society as cannon fodder. The navy, for its part, did not welcome just anyone, because agricultural labourers and other non-sailors required a great deal of training before they could be deemed seamen. They were usually termed landsmen and were employed pulling ropes and other duties on deck until they gained skills to go aloft. To offset the landsmen and misfits, the navy also impressed many seamen from merchant ships. While a few merchant seamen had protection from being pressed, many did not. In his log on *Eagle* for 9 August 1755, Cook described the stopping of a merchant ship and taking some of the crew on board:

> 1pm Brought to and examined a ship from Barbados bound for London out of which we impressed 4 men. Passed by HMS Blandford who spoke with us.

Four days later *Blandford* was the first British ship captured by the French.

It was against this background that Cook enlisted in June 1755. He was, in fact, one of 20,175 men who joined the Royal Navy in the first six months of 1755. Such numbers were necessary for, as well as the initial shortage, acute sickness was rife in the navy. When Boscawen returned to Britain late in 1755 after chasing the French fleet, he reported that two thousand men had either died or were too sick for service. Admiral Hawke was also experiencing great difficulty at Portsmouth in manning another fleet to go out on patrol in the July.

Diseases of various types were common in the navy at the time and more men died from disease than died in combat. The cause of the diseases was not always known or understood; human life was not valued very highly anyway, so many captains paid little attention to the problem. Scurvy, caused by a lack of vitamin C as a result of poor diet, would affect seamen after they had been away at sea for just a few weeks. It was not yet recognised that fresh fruit and vegetables were essential in the sailors' diet to combat this. The cramped and dirty conditions on most ships also allowed other diseases such as typhus to incapacitate crews. Cook would see many examples first hand and his crews' health became one of his main concerns when he had his own commands.

The food provided for seamen on Royal Navy ships was actually quite reasonable, both in quantity and quality, given all the problems of victualling a large ship full of several hundred men for a period of several weeks at sea. Many seamen would be eating better than they had on land – few would have enjoyed four meals a day at home. The diet was plain and repetitive but it offered the men sufficient calories with which to do their work. As a voyage wore on, though, the raw materials deteriorated, often badly, and the men's health suffered accordingly. Water for drinking was a major problem as there was no way of keeping it fresh. Most water stowed on board was used for cooking. For drinking, seamen were issued with a ration of eight pints of beer a day, meaning that many men were relatively inebriated for much of their time at sea. This was condoned as long as it did not prevent them carrying out their duties effectively. The length of a voyage was often determined by how long the beer was drinkable and how long it lasted.

There was no immediate financial benefit for Cook in joining the Royal Navy in that the bounty paid on enlistment for a man like him with naval experience was only £3. He would also have received two months' wages in advance and travel expenses to Portsmouth to join his first ship (there is no guarantee that he did receive his wages then as the navy was notorious for being very behind in paying seamen). In the short term Cook's actual wage would have dropped. An able seaman on a merchant ship would have earned £1 4s a month at that time and a mate would have earned more than that. New Royal Navy volunteers with naval experience were rated accordingly, but Cook was, no doubt, aware that he would not remain an able seaman for very long. In this Cook was correct as, within weeks of enlisting, on 24 July 1755, he was promoted to master's mate (£2 7s 10d a month).

Cook's opportunities for promotion were numerous. He was competing with men, of whom many had never been to sea before, many had been impressed and resented being there, and many were sick and not in a condition to serve. Added to that, Cook was experienced and possessed obvious abilities, so what might have seemed a risky move was really more of a calculated gamble. What perhaps Cook could not have realised at this stage was that any promotion would only be through the petty and warrant officers' ranks. Becoming a commissioned officer was much more difficult and rare.

Though Cook joined at Wapping he was sent south to Portsmouth, where Admiral Edward Hawke was struggling with his shortage of fit and able men. Cook was allocated to His Majesty's Ship *Eagle*, anchored at Spithead.

Cook may have been contemplating his move for some time, but the catalyst appears to have been the recruitment drive by the Royal Navy in early 1755. He would have been aware that on colliers he was not necessarily safe from impressment and that, as a volunteer, he would be treated more favourably than a pressed man. Cook's chances for advancement were high given the limited opposition both in quantity and quality. It was a gamble that may, in the short term, have seen very limited success but, in the long term, was a masterstroke.

❧ 3 ❧

HMS *Eagle*, 1755–1757

After joining the Royal Navy, Cook was immediately sent to Spithead to join HMS *Eagle*, as part of the move to redress the shortage of seamen in the Portsmouth area. He appeared on the records of that ship on 25 June 1755, having been entered on the muster on 17 June 1755 as #161 at the London Rendezvous and rated able seaman (AB). We are fortunate that Cook immediately started keeping a log, albeit a basic one, which records where he was at most times between the end of June 1755 and when the log finishes in December 1756. The front of the log states that Cook was a master's mate; the log covers the period of the 'phoney' war before Britain (in May 1756) and France (in June 1756) formally declared war, it then continues when the war proper had begun in Europe.

Cook's ship, *Eagle* (see Appendix 1), had seen action at the end of the War of Austrian Succession and was the fourth Royal Navy ship to carry this name. Launched in 1745, the ship was recommissioned in May 1755. When Cook joined the ship at Spithead, she had just come out of Portsmouth dockyard after recommissioning; she had also needed some repairs after a storm damaged her while in the dockyard. The captain of *Eagle* was Joseph Hamar (see section 'Joseph Hamar'), an officer with a sound, if somewhat undistinguished, record. Hamar had overseen the recommissioning and *Eagle* was his first command in the new campaign.

Cook probably had little direct contact with Hamar and his lieutenants and would have had far more with Thomas Bisset, the ship's master. It is probable that Bisset had a deep and positive effect on Cook, setting an example of how to behave as a warrant officer and how to run a Royal Navy ship.

For the first few weeks, Cook's log, which began on Friday 27 June 1755, recorded the routine of the ship as it prepared itself for service. It is probable that Cook copied many of the details from another log, possibly the master's. The weather featured every day, while the taking on of provisions and business to do with sails, rigging and so on were regular entries. Cook mentioned the movements of other ships, while interspersed with these more routine entries were occasional pieces relating to out of the ordinary or special events.

28 JUNE. At 5pm came on board longboat with water and boatswains stores.

29 JUNE. am Employed scraping the masts and paying of them. At 12 noon sailed hence His Majesty's Ship Sphinx.

On 3 July, Lord Anson, the first lord of the Admiralty, and other Lords Commissioners inspected the fleet assembled at Spithead.

JOSEPH HAMAR – COOK'S FIRST CAPTAIN

According to his lieutenant's passing certificate issued on 9 February 1737, Joseph Hamar was born in 1714. He had seen early service on *Otter*, *Dolphin*, *Deal Castle* and *Suffolk*. He was later on board the storeship *Deptford* and the yacht *Royal Exchange* before joining HMS *Flamborough* in 1741.

During the mid-1740s, Captain Joseph Hamar commanded *Flamborough* in South Carolina and Georgia waters, helping to protect the communities there from the Spanish. (*Flamborough* was a sixth rate, built at Woolwich in 1707 and rebuilt at Portsmouth in 1727). There are records of Hamar having built a wharf at Port Royal Island, South Carolina; his will refers to a silver cup and cover given to him by the merchants of Carolina, presumably in thanks. He must also have had dealings with the Bahamas as the will refers to assets connected with Providence Island there. There is a Hamar Street in Beaufort, South Carolina, named after him – in 1748 he was assigned two lots of land on the street.

He was in command of *Adventure* from 1746. In 1753, on 5 July, Hamar married Elizabeth Limeburner at St Dunstan's Church in East London. The following year a daughter, Margaret Elizabeth, was born at Greenwich on 4 June 1754.

In early 1755, Hamar recommissioned HMS *Eagle* at Portsmouth. The paths of Hamar and James Cook crossed here, but it is unlikely that they had much actual contact. A gale damaged the ship in September 1755 and Hamar, believing the main mast was broken, took the ship into Plymouth. Inspection proved him wrong and he left the ship in September, apparently relieved of his duties by an unhappy Admiralty. He became a superannuated rear admiral in 1758 under a scheme introduced in 1747 to remove incompetent officers or officers not likely to be given another active command.

Hamar's wife Elizabeth died and he remarried. His second wife, Ann, or Anne, was the widow of William Berry and she already had a son, also called William. Hamar's will, written in late 1773 in Manchester, refers to his house in Hampstead, North London. His wife Ann, daughter Margaret Elizabeth and stepson William are all mentioned in the will. Hamar must have been ill before his death as he died in early 1774, the will being proved in March of that year.

3 JULY. At 12 noon Admiral Anson with some of the Lords of the Admiralty viewed the fleet and then went on board the *Prince*.

While war with France had not been formally declared, the skirmishes that had taken place in North America caused the British government to prepare its forces. In previous wars, a tactic had been to position a flotilla of warships off the French port of Brest to monitor the movement of French shipping and blockade the port if possible. Anson had decided to resurrect this tactic and the ships assembling at Portsmouth were to be the Western Squadron.

Anson's visit to the fleet was a prelude to another inspection two days later by the

THOMAS BISSET

Thomas Bisset, or Bissett, occupied a special position in shaping James Cook's career but remains one of the least known of Cook's colleagues. He was master of HMS *Eagle* for the majority of the time Cook served on the ship. It is probable that as his first Royal Naval master, Bisset was a strong influence on Cook's development and set an example for Cook to follow.

A warrant was issued in 1737 for a Thomas Bissett as a ship's carpenter and another in 1751 as master of HMS *Surprise*. He joined *Eagle* on 21 July 1755. In April 1757 Bissett left *Eagle* to help commission a new ship called HMS *Pembroke* that was being finished in Plymouth dockyard. In October of that year he left *Pembroke* and was replaced by his protégé James Cook. Bisset instead went on board *Stirling Castle*, under Captain Michael Everitt. Two years later, Bisset was able to work with Cook again during the siege of Quebec as *Stirling Castle* was part of Admiral Charles Saunders's squadron. Saunders transferred his flag to *Stirling Castle* for the duration of the siege and Bisset would have had an opportunity to bring Cook to the admiral's notice.

There is a story about a master out surveying in the North Channel being attacked and only just managing to escape. It supposedly happened to James Cook but, if it happened at all, it is far more likely to have involved Bisset.

Bisset died in Barbados on 4 May 1761 while with *Stirling Castle*; his will was proven in the August of 1762. In it he left everything to his wife Jannet, who lived in the parish of New Church in Plymouth. The will makes no mention of children.

Duke of Cumberland. Admirals Edward Hawke and Temple West were in command of the ships assembling off St Helens on the Isle of Wight. On 24 July, the two squadrons departed, their initial aims being to find the fleet of Admiral Du Quay and the North American fleet under Admiral Dubois de la Motte. *Eagle* was still not ready for sea and remained anchored at Spithead off Gilkicker Point.

24 JULY. At 6pm sailed from St. Helens Admirals Hawke and West with the ships under their command.

25 JULY. am Employed scrubbing the ship's bottom.

Two major events happened at the end of July. Thomas Bisset, who would prove a mentor to Cook, arrived on board as *Eagle's* new master. Bissett recorded:

21 JULY. This day I made my appearance on board being appointed Master to Navy warrant.

Three days later, on 24 July, perhaps not coincidentally, Cook was made master's mate.

Finally, on 3 August, *Eagle* weighed anchor and came to sail. The ship was not to be a part of the main squadrons but, instead, was to sail further north acting as a lone cruiser patrolling off the south-west coast of Ireland. It set off west along the south coast of England and the log changed to record the activities of a ship at sea:

> 4 AUGUST. 1pm Tacked to the westward. 2pm Close reefed each topsail. Took in mizzen topsail. 3pm Brailed up the sails and hoisted up the longboat.

Eagle was charged with stopping and inspecting any ship at sea, which the crew carried out near the Lizard:

> 8 AUGUST. 6am Fired a shot and brought to and examined a ship from Antigua bound to London out of which we impressed 3 men.

Eagle rounded the Scilly Isles on 9 August and was off the Irish coast on the 11th. Hamar and his men had exchanged the routine of port for the routine of patrol. For the next few weeks they would ply back and forth near the coast, chasing and stopping vessels. At the end of the month the weather worsened and on 1 September *Eagle* was hit by a storm in which its main mast was sprung (split or warped):

> 1 SEPTEMBER. 3am Brought to under a main sail. 6am A very hard gale. Lost the driver boom overboard. 7am Reefed the fore sail and balanced the mizzen. 9am Brailed up the main sail and wore and brought to under fore sail and balanced mizzen. 10am Found the main mast to be sprung in the lower partner.

Hamar was sufficiently concerned that he decided to return to port and, on 4 September, *Eagle* anchored in Plymouth Sound. The master mast-maker from the dockyard went on board and inspected the mast. In his view, given on the 6th and again on the 13th, the mast was not sprung, but Captain Hamar showed no inclination to return to sea and *Eagle* slowly made its way in to anchor in the Hamoaze on 21 September. Hamar's actions seriously displeased the Admiralty and he was removed from his command.

In the meantime, *Eagle* was tied up alongside *Leopard*, an old ship, and all stores and ballast were transferred to allow the lightened *Eagle* to go into the dock:

> 24 SEPTEMBER. pm Employed in getting out the ballast. At 6 ditto cast off from the Leopard to go into the dock. At 8 got in having put all our men with proper officers on board the Leopard.

> 25 SEPTEMBER. At 8am having got her bottom cleaned and tallowed came out of the dock and made fast alongside the Leopard.

Then began the process of reloading everything back onto *Eagle*. Hugh Palliser took over command of the ship as the new captain on 1 October – an auspicious day for James Cook. Palliser would prove to be an influential colleague and close friend to Cook over the years as their lives and careers crossed.

> 1 OCTOBER. am Cast off from the *Leopard* and warped over and made fast to a mooring upon the wethering shore. Ditto came on board Captain Palliser and took possession of the ship.

Eagle was able to return to sea on 8 October. Hawke had returned his squadron to port already, complaining about the state of his ships and his crews, who were suffering from

OFFICERS ON *EAGLE*, 1755–1757

Captains
Joseph Hamar – May to September 1755 (see section 'Joseph Hamar').
Hugh Palliser – October 1755 to February 1758 (see section 'Hugh Palliser').

Lieutenants
Hamilton Gore – first lieutenant; Gore (1719–75) was descended from several well-
    to-do Irish families. His father, William Gore, was dean of Down, prebend of
    Timothan and chaplain to the Irish House of Commons. Gore made commander
    on 20 June 1765 but had no subsequent naval career of record.
John Milligan – second lieutenant; Milligan (?–1788) made lieutenant on 28 June 1746
    and captain on 26 May 1768. His last command was *Dunkirk* from 1778 until 1782.
Walter Griffith – third lieutenant; Griffith (1727–79) was from Montgomeryshire
    in Wales. He had a successful naval career until he was killed in command of
    Conqueror on 18 December 1779 at Port Royal Bay, Martinique, during a skirmish
    with the French. There is an entry for Griffith in the *Oxford Dictionary of National
    Biography*.

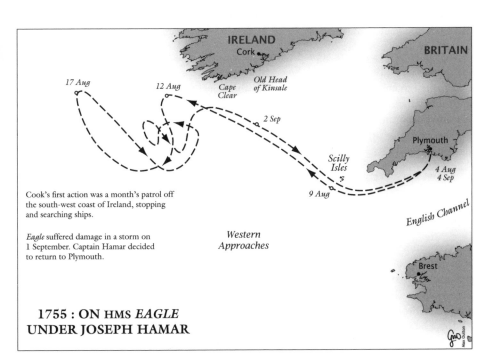

Cook's first action was a month's patrol off
the south-west coast of Ireland, stopping
and searching ships.

Eagle suffered damage in a storm on
1 September. Captain Hamar decided
to return to Plymouth.

**1755 : ON HMS *EAGLE*
UNDER JOSEPH HAMAR**

scurvy and other ailments: 'Had I stayed out a week longer, there would not have been men enough to have worked the large ships, they fell down so fast.'[1]

Admiral John Byng was now assembling a replacement squadron of which *Eagle* was a member. *Eagle*'s duties were similar to before but this time it was to patrol further south in the Western Approaches to the English Channel and monitor Brest. However, Byng's squadron was in position by mid-October but was too late to prevent all of Dubois de la Motte's ships re-entering Brest.

Given that war had not been officially declared, it was unclear what could and what could not be done. The British had orders to detain French ships of the line but they should not fire first. HMS *Blandford* had been captured in August (and released in September) by the French, which provided a vague excuse for British actions. Then, in August 1755, the British were ordered to capture French merchant ships and take them into British ports.

Eagle was soon in action when a French banker (a fishing vessel), returning full of fish from the fishing grounds on the Grand Banks off Newfoundland, was captured on 12 October. *Eagle* took on board 149 prisoners, while a prize crew went on the banker to sail it to Britain. A week later, this action was repeated when a French snow (a small sailing vessel resembling a brig) was taken. In the meantime British and neutral ships were inspected and sent on their way. Saturday 18 October proved a dramatic day:

> 18 OCTOBER. At 6pm Handed the topgallant sails. ½ past the main topmast went by the board. Wore in order to save as much of the wreck and lay to under the foresail and mizzen. The topmast broke the main cross trees ... Was obliged to cut away the rigging to save the main yard. 8pm Employed getting in what we could of the wreck.

Eagle's crew was now occupied with replacing the broken topmast, yards and rigging. *Monmouth* appeared and joined *Eagle*, its carpenters assisting with the repairs. The two ships sailed in company and chased several ships over the next few days. On 2 November another French ship returning from Newfoundland was captured and forty-five more prisoners accommodated on *Eagle,* while another crew took over the prize.

The wintry weather conditions were taking their toll on *Eagle*, which suffered more damage:

> 4 NOVEMBER. Very fresh gales with strong squalls. In chase. ½ past noon found the fore topmast sprung about 2 foot above the caps. Got the fore topgallant yard and mast down and handed the fore topsail. Employed in unrigging the topmast and getting to hand and fitting the spare one.

Again repairs were effected. On 9 November, *Eagle* encountered Admiral John Byng with his squadron of five ships. About seven months later, Byng would make an unsuccessful defence of Minorca in the Mediterranean and was court-martialled and executed, a scapegoat for the British loss. *Eagle* next met, on the 12th, Admiral Temple West with his small squadron and a French ship, *Esperance*, which had been captured the night before.

Esperance, under Captain Louis Jubert de Bouville, was a French ship of seventy-four guns, which had sailed as part of a fleet from Brest on 3 May 1755 across to Louisbourg on

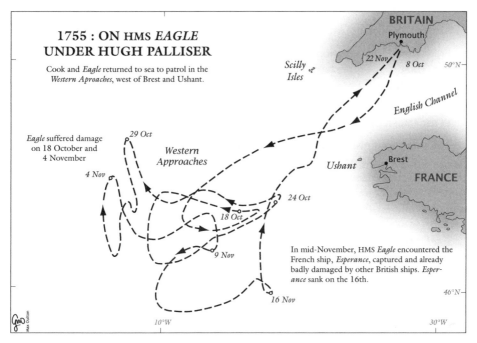

**1755 : ON HMS *EAGLE*
UNDER HUGH PALLISER**

Cook and *Eagle* returned to sea to patrol in the
Western Aproaches, west of Brest and Ushant.

BRITAIN

Plymouth

Scilly
Isles

22 Nov

8 Oct   50°N

English Channel

Eagle suffered damage
on 18 October and
4 November

29 Oct

4 Nov

Western
Approaches

Ushant   Brest

FRANCE

24 Oct

18 Oct

9 Nov

16 Nov

In mid-November, HMS *Eagle* encountered the
French ship, *Esperance*, captured and already
badly damaged by other British ships. *Esperance* sank on the 16th.

46°N

10°W   30°W

Cape Breton Island. The fleet was under the command of Dubois de la Motte and part
of it had been harried by Admiral Boscawen's squadron. *Esperance,* which had carried
troops to reinforce the fort, left Louisbourg on 17 October to return to France, when
it was intercepted on 11 November. *Orford* led the attack that left *Esperance* on fire and
sinking. Heavy seas, though, hindered the removal of the French crew.

14 NOVEMBER. At 9am the Esperance fired a gun and made a signal in distress. ½ past
set the foresail. At 11 wore ship. Set main topsail. The Esperance fired 2 guns in distress
but no possibility of relieving her the sea running so high.

All the crew were eventually removed and distributed among the watching British
ships before the French ship sank. Admiral Byng wrote: 'The French Ship of War that
Admiral West brought into the squadron ... was in the most distressed condition I ever
saw a ship, extremely leaky and not able to carry any sail, having only her lower masts
standing and foretopmasts ...'

Worsening conditions and the state of the ships and crews caused Byng to order the
British to sail back to home ports, and *Eagle* made for Plymouth. On 22 November,
the ship anchored off Penlee Point in Plymouth Sound and began unloading French
prisoners. It then began the journey round into the Hamoaze and anchored there
alongside the gun wharf on the 30th. Further sorties were not expected that year and the
slow process began of cleaning, repairing and restocking the ship.

2 DECEMBER. Employed in examining the rigging and sending what we found bad on
shore to go there with some of the sails.

19 DECEMBER. Fidded the main topmast and seized in the dead eyes futtock shrouds. And rattled the topmast shrouds.

Fresh stores and provisions were taken on board and water was obtained from South Down. There was no break for Christmas or New Year festivities and work continued right through. As *Eagle* needed to go back into the dock, *Panther* was brought alongside and the crew began transferring material across to the other ship to lighten the load.

28 DECEMBER. am Transported the Panther alongside to take in our stores and lumber.

The year 1755 finished, therefore, with Cook and *Eagle* in port at Plymouth. Cook had completed his first six months in the Royal Navy and had experienced two short patrols off the Western Approaches to the English Channel, interspersed with the somewhat boring routines of shipboard life in port at Spithead and Plymouth. He had also encountered Thomas Bisset and Hugh Palliser, who would feature prominently in his life.

Eagle was hauled into the dock on 1 January 1756 and out again the next morning. Over the next three weeks, as cleaning and repairs continued, all the material was slowly reloaded into *Eagle* from *Panther*. Cook's log, interestingly, makes reference to the brandy and fish rooms:

2 JANUARY. am Got the brandy and dry provisions out of the *Panther* and stowed them away. Stowed also in the brandy room 26 pigs of ballast taken out of the fish room.

The brandy (or spirits) room was located in the hold to contain the spirits that would be drunk by the crew. It was always secured. Between the brandy room and the after-hold was the fish room where all the salted fish was stowed. Ballast was heavy bulk material carried in the hold to help stabilise the ship. Some of it was iron cast in oblong blocks known as pigs.

For Cook personally, 22 January 1756 was an important day. In his log he wrote:

22 JANUARY. am Had a survey on boatswains stores when succeeded the former boatswain.

The previous boatswain, Jonathan Atkinson, had died. Cook's elevation to boatswain appears to have been temporary and unofficial as he was never recorded as holding the position. On 7 February 1756, Cook was discharged from the muster and went into hospital at Plymouth. The nature or severity of his illness was not mentioned but Cook was able to rejoin ten days later on 17 February, again as master's mate. He was now #486 on the muster. By February, Cook was reporting on the provisions being taken on board. They provide a good summary of the food served in Royal Navy ships of the day:

5 FEBRUARY. am Received on board 10 casks of pease, 25 casks of flour, and 10 hogsheads of brandy. Also fresh beef for the Ship's company.

7 FEBRUARY. am Received on board 54 puncheons and 42 hogsheads of water.

9 FEBRUARY. am Received on board 10 barrels of oatmeal, 11 ditto of suet, 4 of raisins, 4 casks of vinegar and 4 jars of oil, 42½ firkins of butter and 188 cheeses.

The Regulations of the time stipulated that:

I. There shall be allowed to every man serving in His Majesty's ships a daily proportion of provisions according as in expressed in the table:

	Sun.	Mon.	Tue.	Wed.	Thu.	Fri.	Sat.
Biscuit (pounds avoirdupois)	1	1	1	1	1	1	1
Beer (gallons, wine measure)	1	1	1	1	1	1	1
Beef (pounds avoirdupois)			2				2
Pork (pounds avoirdupois)	1				1		
Pease (pint Winchester measure)	½			½	½	½	
Oatmeal (pint Winchester measure)		1		1		1	
Butter (ounces)		2		2		2	
Cheese (ounces)		4		4		4	

Being in port, *Eagle* was an observer of and a participant in all that was happening in Plymouth. Cook's log noted signals and the movements of other ships in and out of the harbour. The deaths of two crewmembers were also recorded. Several courts martial took place on other ships, leading occasionally to drastic sentences:

23 FEBRUARY. am A midshipman punished with 20 lashes alongside of every ship for sodomy, by the sentence of a court martial.

A more mundane activity took place every Thursday with the visit of the clerk of the cheque. This elaborate title was applied to a senior member of the dockyard staff who visited the ship to carry out the muster of the ship's company.

Many of the ship's crew had been pressed and were not, therefore, experienced seamen. So, the men were trained when opportunities arose, and then given practice in performing their duties. At the end of February Cook recorded:

24 FEBRUARY. pm Exercised small arms. At sunset got down topgallant yards and lowered down lower yards.

25 FEBRUARY. At sunrise got them up again and so continued by way of exercise.

After Admiral Byng had ordered *Eagle* and other ships back to port in November he had left four ships patrolling over the New Year. Admiral Osborne took out fourteen more ships in January, but no incidents of note had taken place. Early in 1756, the British received reports that the French were planning an invasion. This required a modification of the British tactics, and ships were to be deployed in the English Channel to watch for activity in French ports along that coast. Meanwhile, Hawke returned with the Western Squadron to be off Brest in February.

Finally, on 12 March, *Eagle* left the Hamoaze and sailed into Plymouth Sound and, the next day, the 13th, put to sea. The orders this year were to patrol in the English Channel off the north coasts of Normandy and Brittany. By 19 March, *Eagle* was patrolling north of Cap (Pointe) de Barfleur, the north-east point of the Cotentin peninsula of Normandy.

At the beginning of April, *Eagle*, in company with HMS *Windsor* (John Gore, later to sail with Cook, was a master's mate on *Windsor* at the time) and HMS *Isis*, moved west to patrol off the Brittany coast near Morlaix and the Île de Batz. On 5 April, another important event in James Cook's career took place:

> 5 APRIL. 10am Brought to on the starboard tack. When I went on board the Cruizer cutter to take command of her with men, arms and ammunition. 12 noon In company with Eagle, Falmouth, Greyhound and Ferret ships.

This was Cook's first command in the navy. His vessel was a cutter named *Cruizer*, not to be confused with a sloop of the same name built at Deptford in 1752 and based, at the time, at the Downs. Cook refers to his vessel as a cutter but in the Royal Navy of the time the terms sloop and cutter were sometimes interchangeable. Lieutenant John Milligan recorded in his log:

> 4 APRIL 1756. Joined by two armed cutters.

> 6 APRIL. At 1pm the Greyhound and a cutter parted company.

Cook's log for 7 April includes his first known coastal view, albeit a very cramped and naive sketch. It shows Roscoff and the Île de Batz, close to the mouth of the Morlaix River. Cook and *Cruizer* began patrolling off the coast of Brittany, concentrating near the Île de Batz. The cutter was ideal for the conditions, being able to sail close to shore

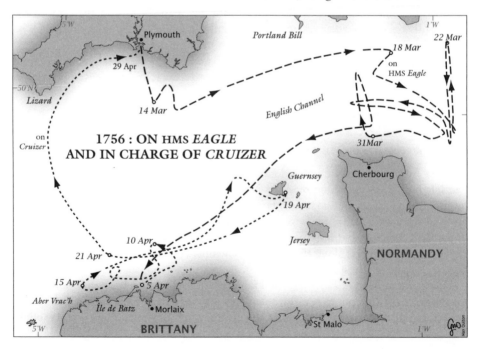

in the shallows and rocks. This type of vessel would later be used by customs officers and became known as a revenue cutter.

Cruizer chased, fired on and stopped several vessels, sometimes in company with the sloop *Ferret* and the cutter *John and Robert*. They operated as far west as the Aber Wrac'h Rocks, but on 17 April put in to St Peter Port, Guernsey, to repair leaks in the cutter's bottom. Cook was now reporting to and obtaining provisions from HMS *Falmouth* as *Eagle* had returned to Plymouth on the 16th. *Cruizer* briefly returned to patrol but sailed north on 22 April to enter Plymouth Sound on the 24th.

Having safely returned *Cruizer* to port, Cook and his crew were then taken on board HMS *St Albans*, captained by William Gordon, and, on 30 April, left Plymouth to rejoin their ship, *Eagle*. *St Albans* was part of a squadron with *Elizabeth*, *Romney*, *Bedford*, *Swiftsure* and *Colchester*, all of which gave chase to vessels as the squadron sailed towards the French coast. They were heading for the island of Ushant (French: Ouessant). The high rate of mortality at sea can be demonstrated as Cook records the death of three seamen, Thomas Hayman, Richard Smith and James Atkinson over the next few days.

Cook's regular ship, *Eagle*, commanded by Captain Hugh Palliser, was already at sea patrolling off the west of Brittany near Brest, part of Admiral Edward Boscawen's squadron. On 2 May, *St Albans* joined the fleet off Pointe du Raz, one of the western tips of Brittany. At some point during the next day, Cook transferred to *Eagle*, though he does not record the move in his log other than by changing the name of the ship at the top of his remarks column.

Eagle spent a few days plying back and forth before Boscawen's squadron was joined by those of Admirals Edward Hawke and Francis Holburne on 6 May. After meeting with other officers, Hawke sailed home to Britain with seven ships the next day, leaving Boscawen in command of the Western Squadron with nineteen ships. On the 9th, *Eagle*, together with *St Albans* and *Romney*, parted company with the fleet and sailed south to patrol in the Bay of Biscay closer to the Spanish coast.

Various small ships were sighted, with some being chased and a few being stopped and captured as prizes. On 12 May, after a French ship bound for Martinique was taken, *Eagle* received prisoners on board and sent three of its crew on board the prize to sail it back to Britain. By 13 May, they had sailed so far south that Asturias, the central region on the north coast of Spain, could be seen and Cook recorded:

13 MAY. 9pm Middle of the high land of Asturias distance 9 or 10 leagues.

On 17 May 1756, Britain declared war on France, which soon reciprocated. The two countries were to all intents already at war and had been on a war footing for about a year. *Eagle* now began working north again, but encountered a few days of light airs and the three ships, still in company, made little progress. However, on 19 May, *Romney* chased and captured a French ship sailing from St Domingue, a French colony on the island of Hispaniola (which in 1804 became independent and known as Haiti).

The next day three more ships were seen and the British dispersed in pursuit. *Eagle* chased and captured a ship that also turned out to have sailed from St Domingue. This ship was *Triton*; Cook's log recorded:

21 MAY. 4pm Brought to the chase, which proved a ship from Santo Domingo, lead [laden] with sugar and coffee. Employed transporting the prisoners on board. 6pm I went on board to take command of the Triton prize. 8pm Moderate and fair. In company with the Eagle and other prize.

Walter Griffith, one of the *Eagle's* lieutenants, recorded:

21 MAY. At 3pm the chase brought too. Proved to be a French ship from St. Domingo bound to Bourdeaux.

Cook, though still a junior warrant officer, was chosen to sail the prize back to Britain, probably because Captain Palliser could not spare any of his three lieutenants for such a task. Another prize crew had already been dispatched a few days earlier and Palliser,

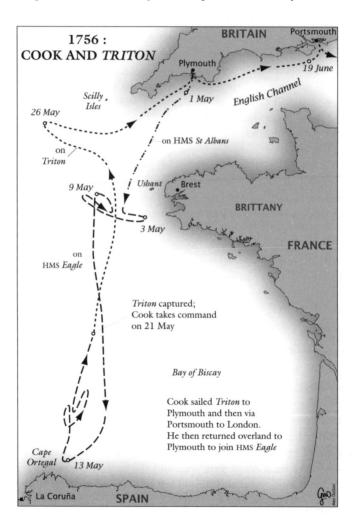

1756: COOK AND TRITON

Triton captured;
Cook takes command
on 21 May

Cook sailed *Triton* to
Plymouth and then via
Portsmouth to London.
He then returned overland to
Plymouth to join HMS *Eagle*

being aware by now of Cook's background in the North Sea and his ability, would not have hesitated to use him.

Cook and *Triton* sailed north at first with *Eagle* but parted company on the 23rd. They experienced a few days of stormy weather and very rough seas, forcing Cook to sail north-west before he could turn on 26 May and head for Britain. Land's End and the Lizard were sighted on the 29th and *Triton* stopped in Cawsand Bay to collect a pilot. Cook anchored *Triton* in the Catewater by Plymouth on 31 May 1756.

Cook had the crew begin unbending the sails and repairing the rigging. However, in the uncertain period before war was officially declared, prizes were taken to London so that their contents could be assessed by the Commissioners for the Sale of Prizes taken before the Declaration of War. Cook, therefore, began preparing to return to sea in order to sail *Triton* to the Thames.

2 JUNE. Received on board a fortnight's provisions for six men.

Finally, *Triton* left Plymouth as part of a small fleet under the protection of several frigates.

16 JUNE. am Came to sail, the Arundel having made the signal for weighing.

Also sailing with *Triton* was another prize, *St Mark*. By 19 June, *Triton* was off the Isle of Wight but had trouble anchoring off Culver Cliff and lost its kedge anchor and a hawser. A pilot was taken on board near South Foreland to take the ship into the Thames and by the evening of the 22nd they had arrived at Long Reach. HMS *Aldborough*, a new ship that had just come out of Perry's shipyard at Blackwall in May, loaned them a replacement kedge anchor, and another pilot – this time a river pilot – went on board to take the ship up to the Pool, originally the stretch of the Thames by the City of London, but the name later covered that part of the river below London Bridge as far as Cherry Garden Stairs in Rotherhithe.

Cook, a good monarchist, fired salutes as he passed Greenwich and in the Pool, as 23 June was the anniversary of King George II's coronation in 1727. He moored *Triton* alongside the other prize, *St Mark*, at the Stone Stairs pier next to the Tower of London and close to where the Navy Office was based off Crutched Friars. The kedge anchor was returned to *Aldborough* as Cook closed the ship down:

27 JUNE. Employed putting everything below and securing the hatches.

Cook's log for his time on *Triton* has evidence that suggests he did not write up his entries straight away every day. His entry for 14 June was originally entered in the box for the 13th, then crossed out and put in the box for the correct day, while his entries for the last three days in London all have the wrong date.

Cook makes no mention of it in his log, but it is possible that during his time in London he visited the Bell alehouse and friends in Wapping, which was only a few hundred yards away to the east. By the end of the month, *Triton* was shipshape and closed down. Cook was able to send the rest of the crew back to Plymouth and followed them the next day.

29 JUNE. Sent all the people away to Plymouth in order to return to their own ships.

30 JUNE. Set out myself to follow after the people.

Cook's log gives no details of how he travelled from London to Plymouth but, according to the log, he was back on board *Eagle* at the Hamoaze on 8 July after successfully completing his mission. On his arrival back in Plymouth, Cook found *Eagle* and its crew in poor condition. The extra ships that were now being used in the Western Squadron allowed for some rotation, and ships that were in a poor state could return to port for repairs. *Eagle* was such a ship and needed an overhaul; the patrols had also taken their toll on the men. Hugh Palliser, *Eagle's* captain, wrote to John Clevland, the Admiralty secretary, on 15 June 1756. In that letter, he stated that: 'His Surgeon is dead and both the Surgeon's Mates are ill and asks for replacements. Mr Head was appointed who is already at Portsmouth and will appoint some Surgeon's Mates after the next examination of Mates at Surgeons Hall next Thursday.'[2]

Cook rejoined a ship busy refitting and restocking in readiness for returning to sea. His log for July details the tasks and routines undertaken: working on the rigging, cleaning and painting the ship, taking on food, water and crew. On 20 July a new contingent of thirty marines was received on board. Five days later, *Eagle* came to sail and moved from the Hamoaze down into Plymouth Sound, where she anchored off Drake's Island.

The crew were paid two months' advance wages on 27 July. At the end of the month, thirty-six more seamen came on board and Cook was involved with finding berths for them all. These men were probably brought to *Eagle* close to the time of sailing and when the ship was in deeper water in the Sound in order to prevent desertions.

On 4 August *Eagle* came to sail and left Plymouth Sound, heading east up the English Channel. Two days later the ship joined Rear Admiral Henry Harrison's squadron at Spithead. The Royal Navy had a shortage of younger experienced admirals at the time and Harrison was typical in that he was close to seventy years of age. His squadron was charged with escorting a fleet of merchant ships into the Atlantic to avoid their capture by French shipping. Accordingly, eight men-of-war and twenty-four merchantmen left Spithead on 7 August.

The fleet sailed without incident down the English Channel, though on 12 August a signal was made for the men-of-war to sail line abreast with two miles separation between each ship. Having safely escorted the merchant ships out into the Atlantic, Harrison's squadron joined Admiral Boscawen's fleet once again, blockading the French port of Brest. That they were on a war footing is shown by a line of battle for men-of-war issued by Boscawen and copied in his log by Cook.

Boscawen divided the squadron into three parts: he remained off Brest with seven ships; Holburne patrolled off Cape Finisterre with five ships and Harrison patrolled between with four ships. *Eagle,* part of Harrison's command, remained at sea for the next three months. Cook recorded the ship's position at noon each day as they sailed back and forth in the Western Approaches to the English Channel and the northern Bay of Biscay. Apart from two sorties south towards the Spanish coast, the ship remained about a hundred kilometres west of the Brittany peninsula. The work was long and boring, with *Eagle* not being involved in any engagements. Cook's log also detailed the sightings of sails and how various frigates were dispatched to investigate, only to find

LA COMPAGNIE DES INDES (FRENCH INDIES COMPANY)

James Cook had at least two encounters with ships operated by the Compagnie des Indes during his service on HMS *Eagle* from 1755 to 1757. He was involved in the capture of two ships and was ordered to sail one of them back to port in Britain.

The French began sailing to India and the East Indies in 1603 with de Gonneville's voyage and, in 1604, King Henri IV authorised the first Compagnie des Indes Orientales (French East India Company), giving it a fifteen-year monopoly of the Indies trade. Few ships sailed east, though, over the next sixty years, and it was not until 1664 that the Compagnie des Indes Orientales was actually founded, to compete with the flourishing British and Dutch equivalents. This company was planned by Jean Baptiste Colbert and was chartered by King Louis XIV.

The Port of Port-Louis on the Brittany coast attracted the merchants who were trading with India and they established warehouses across the bay. This new site was named L'Orient (French: the East), later becoming Lorient and the home port for the Compagnie. Eventually shipyards were established there.

This company was granted a fifty-year monopoly of French trade in the Indian and Pacific Oceans. However, the Compagnie struggled; it lost its monopoly in 1682, but managed to survive until 1719, when it was formally dissolved. John Law had founded the Compagnie d'Occident in 1717 with a monopoly for French North America (Louisiana and Canada), but it and other French trading companies operating in St Domingue, Guinée and Sénégal were all weak individually. In 1719 all the small trading companies were combined to form the Compagnie Perpétuelle des Indes, which resumed its independence in 1723. Over the next twenty years the Compagnie flourished, bringing wealth to the home port of Lorient.

The Seven Years' War affected the Compagnie badly, resulting in severe losses of both territory and ships. The Compagnie was suspended in 1769 and transferred all its properties, assets and rights to the French state in 1770. A new Compagnie des Indes was formed by Louis XVI in 1785 and it prospered until 1790, when the National Assembly restricted its operations. It continued to trade, at much a reduced level, until it was dissolved in 1794.

often that the sail in question was another member of their own fleet. *Eagle* fared better structurally during this patrol than it had done the previous year and there is no mention of emergency repairs having to be carried out. Conditions, though, were poor and, around the time *Eagle* returned to port, the log contains several instances of seamen and marines dying.

In early November 1756, Boscawen ordered the fleet to make for Plymouth, and *Eagle* was back in Plymouth Sound on 11 November, moving up to the Hamoaze the next day. The sick were quickly sent ashore and the rest of the crew began stripping the ship. On the 22nd, *Eagle* was tied up alongside a sheer hulk before, on 24 November, going into the dock for inspection of the hull. Out of the dock the next day, the crew began the tasks of rigging and restocking the ship.

The ship was ready by mid-December, when a pilot was taken on to guide it down to the Hamoaze. However, weather conditions were not suitable and *Eagle* stayed put. Prize money was paid out on 17 December and outstanding wages were paid on the 28th. The pilot rejoined the ship on 29 December and they proceeded down to Plymouth Sound, leaving the next day as part of Vice Admiral John Knowles's squadron, with Knowles on *Essex*.

Cook's log for 31 December 1756 gives their position as being off Portland. It is, however, the last entry in his log, apart from some doodles and sailing directions for entering the Thames. Further information about Cook's time on *Eagle* is taken from Hugh Palliser's captain's log and other sources. On 4 January 1757, the ships were caught in a gale off the Isle of Wight and had to take shelter at Spithead before sailing back to Plymouth.

The Duke of Newcastle's government resigned in November 1756 and with it went Lord Anson as first lord of the Admiralty. The new government was led by the Duke of Devonshire with William Pitt as Secretary of State for the Southern Department. Pitt's brother-in-law, Richard Grenville, Earl Temple, became the new first lord at the Admiralty. Unlike Anson, however, Temple had not been a naval officer. One of the first actions of the new Admiralty board in January was to send out a squadron under Admiral West to replace that of Knowles.

On 30 January, *Eagle* left Plymouth once more, this time as part of West's fleet to patrol in the Bay of Biscay. After two and a half more months at sea, during which time Admiral Brodrick had assumed command, *Eagle* was back in Plymouth on 15 April. In those months, the British had missed the departure of three sets of French ships: Admiral Kersaint slipped out with six vessels for the West Indies, followed by Bauffremont with five; finally Dubois de la Motte escaped with a squadron. Many of the ships ended up at Louisbourg, where they frustrated British plans to capture that port later in the year.

In April, Captain Palliser had fourteen days' leave, during which he went to London on unspecified business. When he rejoined his ship, they accompanied HMS *Medway* out of Plymouth on 25 May to join Admiral Boscawen, who had resumed command of the squadron. *Medway* was a fourth rate of sixty guns built at Deptford in February 1755. In command was Charles Proby, who had made commander in 1745 and was appointed post-captain on 17 September 1746. This gave him two months' seniority over Palliser, who made captain on 25 November 1746.

On 30 May, the two ships encountered and captured *Duc d'Aquitaine*, a ship belonging to the Compagnie des Indes. According to Captain Hugh Palliser, the action took place at 48°N and 2° west of the Lizard. At 1am a sail was seen to north-west and the two navy ships gave chase. *Eagle* cleared for action but *Medway*, in the lead, failed to do so. *Medway* was forced, therefore, to bring to, which allowed *Eagle* to take the lead and make the attack. Their target was a French East Indiaman, *Duc d'Aquitaine*, which, carrying 259 men, was under Captain Jean-Baptiste de Lesquelen, when she encountered *Eagle* and *Medway*.

Palliser describes the action in his log:

LINE OF BATTLE (DATED 20 AUGUST 1756)

The *Eagle* to lead upon the starboard tack and the *Harwich* upon the larboard.

Name of ship	Captain	Men	Guns	Admiral
Eagle	Hugh Palliser	400	60	Boscawen
Royal Sovereign	William Boys	850	100	Boscawen
Royal George	John Campbell (with Vice Admiral Boscawen on board)	850	100	Boscawen
Devonshire	John Moore	520	64	Boscawen
Vanguard	John Byron	520	70	Boscawen
Invincible	Matthew Buckle	720	74	Boscawen
Essex	Robert Harland	520	64	Boscawen
Chichester	William Saltern Willett	520	64	Harrison
Monmouth	Alexander Innes (with Rear Admiral Harrison on board)	490	60	Harrison
Newark	John Barker	620	60	Harrison
Harwich	Joshua Rowley	350	50	Harrison

The frigates *Lyme*, *Kennington* and *Firebrand* were in attendance.

At ¼ before 4 came alongside the [chase] and engaged at about two ships lengths from her. The fire was very brisk on both sides for near an hour. She then struck to us. She proved to be the *Duc D'Aquitaine* last from Lisbon, mounting 50 guns, all 18 pounders, 493 men. We had 7 men killed in the action and 32 wounded. Our sails & rigging [were] cut almost to pieces. Soon after she struck her main and mizzen masts went by the board. Employed the boats fetching the prisoners and carrying men on board the prize. Employed knotting and splicing the rigging. Our cutter was lost alongside the prize by the going away of her main mast.

The foremast of the prize also went. Five men on *Eagle* died later of their wounds and eighty men were wounded. The French lost fifty men and had thirty men wounded. All three ships headed for Plymouth. *Eagle* was itself badly damaged, leaving *Medway* to tow the prize.

Another account from Lieutenant Walter Griffith recorded:

30 MAY. Saw a sail to the Northward. Ditto gave chase as did the Medway. ½ past 3am the chase hoisted French colours. The chase about two miles ahead. The Medway about ½ gun shot from the chase. We continued ditto and gave her a broadside which she returned. We engaged ¾ of an hour. She struck being the Duc de Aquitain of 50

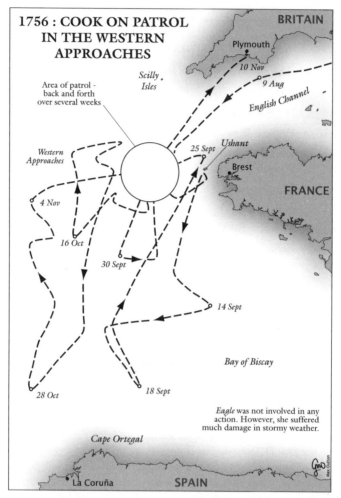

1756 : COOK ON PATROL IN THE WESTERN APPROACHES

BRITAIN

Plymouth
10 Nov
9 Aug

Scilly Isles

English Channel

Area of patrol - back and forth over several weeks

Western Approaches

Ushant
25 Sept

Brest

FRANCE

4 Nov

16 Oct

30 Sept

14 Sept

Bay of Biscay

28 Oct   18 Sept

Eagle was not involved in any action. However, she suffered much damage in stormy weather.

Cape Ortegal

La Coruña   SPAIN

guns all 18 pounds and 497 men of which 50 was killed and 32 wounded. We had 10 men killed and 30 wounded. Employed securing our masts and rigging being much wounded and getting on board prisoners.

31 MAY. At 1pm the prize's mainmast fell by the board. Employed securing our masts and rigging. At 6 the prize's foremast fell by the board. Prize and Medway in company.

After the capture of the *Duc d'Aquitaine,* John Clevland, the Admiralty secretary, wrote a report on 5 September 1757 in which he put:

The French ship the Duc d'Acquitaine, lately taken and brought into Plymouth by the Eagle and Medway, is to be fitted for sea to serve as a ship of 64-guns and to be registered as a third rate by the name of the Duc d'Acquitaine. The agents for the captors have attended us and have agreed with them for the purchase for £12,310.[3]

Cook and the other men were pleased to receive a small share of that prize money later on. A 1707 statute, the Act for the Better Securing the Trade of this Kingdom by Cruisers and Convoys,[4] established the rights by which seamen could capture foreign ships during times of war. A subsequent document set down the terms and conditions by which prize money was calculated and distributed. The High Court of Admiralty evaluated all prizes and assessed claims relating to them. If the prize, as in the case of the *Duc d'Aquitaine*, was an enemy merchantman, the prize money came from the sale of both ship and cargo. All ships in sight of a capture shared in the prize money, so *Eagle* and *Medway* shared the spoils of their fight and capture. Once the total had been determined, the prize money was distributed according to a precise formula, with allocation by eighths.

Method for Allocation of Prize Money

Share	Beneficiaries	No. of men	Individual's share
⅛ 12.5%	Admiral or commander-in-chief	1	12.5%
¼ 25%	Captain	1	25%
⅛ 12.5%	Wardroom officers, including the lieutenants and master	4	2.5%
⅛ 12.5%	Senior warrant officers	8	1.56%
⅛ 12.5%	Junior warrant and petty officers and midshipmen	50	0.25%
¼ 25%	Seamen and marines	340	0.074%

(In this table the numbers of men in each category are estimates based on averages for fourth-rate ships of the time.)

Cook, as one of the junior warrant officers, stood to gain approximately 0.25% of £6,155 (*Medway*'s crew would have received the other half), or approximately £15. Given that his annual wage as a master's mate on a fourth-rate ship was only £28 14s, even this small fraction of the prize money would have been very welcome.

According to Andrew Kippis, Cook's first biographer, who apparently received the information from Hugh Palliser, William Osbaldstone had written to Palliser at about this time on behalf of John Walker, Cook's previous employer in the North Sea coal trade. The letter from Osbaldstone, the MP for Scarborough, had suggested that Cook should be considered for commissioning as an officer and had asked how they could assist such a move. However, a Royal Navy midshipman or master's mate (as Cook was by this time) could only sit his lieutenant's examination after completing six years aboard a navy ship. Cook's time in the North Sea did not count towards this, so he was four years short. And, while a very few men might receive preferment if they were well connected or known by a personage of high rank and/or influence, Cook was not in that position. Neither Osbaldstone nor Palliser carried sufficient status or influence to help his cause.

However, Palliser pointed out that Cook was ready and able to sit his master's examination. He could support him in this and assist Cook gaining the highest non-

TRITON AND DUC D'AQUITAINE
— SHIPS OF THE THE COMPAGNIE DES INDES

Over the years, the Compagnie operated five ships called *Triton*. Their fourth vessel with that name was 350 tons, carried fourteen guns and was built at Havana. It was bought at St Malo by the Compagnie and it made its first voyage for them in 1747 from St Malo to the Île de France (Mauritius), captained by Jean-Bernard Michelot du Tertre. He remained in command until its last recorded voyage, when it sailed from Lorient on 14 September 1750 to St Domingue in the Caribbean.

Her recorded four voyages were:

4 January 1747 from St Malo to Île de France.
5 November 1748 from Lorient to Île de France.
10 April 1749 from Lorient to Guinée.
14 September 1750 from Lorient to St Domingue.

In May 1756, a *Triton* was captured by *Eagle* as it was sailing from St Domingue under a captain named Savage and carrying a cargo of coffee and sugar. As we have seen, James Cook was given the task of sailing the prize back to Plymouth and on to London. It is most probable that this was same ship that Tertre had taken to St Domingue. The Standing Interrogatories, as recorded in the High Court of the Admiralty, give the prize's tonnage as between 300 and 380 tons.[5]

A year later, on 30 May 1757, Cook encountered the *Duc d'Aquitaine*, a French East Indiaman of 1,200 tons (French), which carried fifty guns. It was built at Lorient and launched on 22 July 1754. The *Duc d'Aquitaine* sailed from Lorient on 24 February 1755 bound for Pondicherry, a French port in India. The ship, carrying 259 men, was captained by Théophile-Guillaume Dujonc de Boisquesnay, but he died during the voyage. It made its way to the Île de France and left there on 26 July 1756, now under the command of Charles Aulnet de Vaultenet. The ship discharged most of its cargo at Lisbon. After leaving Lisbon and now under a third captain, Jean-Baptiste de Lesquelen, the French East Indiaman met *Eagle* (with James Cook aboard) and *Medway*.

After a short sea battle, the two Royal Navy ships captured the French vessel and it was towed to Britain. After its capture, the *Duc d'Aquitaine* was entered into the Royal Navy as a third rate of sixty-four guns and 1,358 tons burthen, retaining its name. It sank in the Bay of Bengal in January 1761.

commissioned rank in the navy, that of master. Kippis's version of this story has some glaring errors, and so it remains uncertain how much credence may be placed on it. It is interesting to speculate, though, that one of the reasons for Palliser's visit to London in April of that year could have been to smooth the way for Cook in respect of becoming a master.

In late June 1757, Cook travelled up to London and on the 29th sat his master's examination at Trinity House in Water Lane, just west of the Tower of London. He was successful and the next day was discharged from *Eagle* by preferment and appointed to *Solebay*. Cook had been with *Eagle* for just over two years and was now beginning to realise his potential. Importantly, that potential and his ability had come to the attention of the ship's captain, Hugh Palliser, who would become one of Cook's benefactors and a lifelong friend. Palliser remained on *Eagle* until 25 February 1758, when he was replaced by James Hobbs. Palliser then joined HMS *Shrewsbury* and was present at the sieges of Louisbourg and Quebec, where he crossed Cook's path once more.

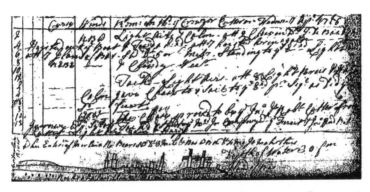

Part of a page from Cook's Eagle *log from his time in April 1756 on* Cruizer, *showing his first coast view of the coast of Brittany (Alexander Turnbull Library qMS-0537)*

❄ 4 ❄

HMS *Solebay*, 1757

On 29 June 1757, James Cook passed his master's examination; the Trinity House minute books record the event: 'Mr James Cook being examined by Captain Joseph Carteret and Captain Nathaniel Kerfoot and found qualify to take charge as Master of any of His Majesty's ships of the six rate from the Downs through the Channel to the Westward to Lisbon was certified accordingly.'[1]

Neither of Cook's examiners, Carteret and Kerfoot were Royal Navy officers, which probably should be no surprise. The master's examination involved testing a man's ability to sail a ship, and many naval officers of the period left such hands-on tasks to their senior warrant officers. Captains or masters of merchant ships had no such luxury and would have much better first-hand knowledge of what was required. Joseph Carteret was elected an Elder Brother of Trinity House on 15 October 1748. He died in November 1765 and was buried at St Paul's, Shadwell. Nathaniel Kerfoot was elected an Elder Brother of Trinity House on 2 December 1749; he died in October 1764.

In the mid-eighteenth century, the ship's master was the senior warrant officer, and he was in charge of the day-to-day running of the ship. He answered to the captain and lieutenants on important matters but all the other warrant officers, such as boatswain, carpenter and gunner – and through them, all the seamen – were the master's responsibility. The *Oxford English Dictionary* defines a master as 'a naval officer ranking next below a lieutenant, responsible for the navigation of a warship during naval operations'.

Masters were usually found on the quarterdeck (that part of the upper deck of a ship behind the main mast traditionally reserved for the use of superior officers), directing the navigation of the ship. They were also expected, if necessary, to supervise a watch (a period of time during which part of the ship's company remained on deck to work the vessel; watch also described that part of the crew). They had specific responsibility for navigation and for writing the daily entries in the ship's log, recording its progress, the weather, noteworthy events and the ship's position (see Appendix 2, p. 194).

For men to achieve the rank of master they had to be experienced and proven sailors and to pass the exam at Trinity House. The Corporation of Trinity House, which was incorporated by royal charter in 1514, may have had its roots in the Guild of the Holy Trinity from the thirteenth century. When the charter was granted, Trinity House was based in Deptford close to the naval dockyard. Initially, it was concerned with the 'pilotage of ships in the King's streams'.

Trinity House later assumed responsibility for lighthouses and was invested by charter with other powers, including the examination of masters of His Majesty's ships. The Corporation bought a property in Water Lane in the City of London in 1660 near the

Navy Board. The Water Lane premises burnt down and were rebuilt twice, in 1666 and 1714. Trinity House then bought land at Tower Hill and built the present Trinity House in the 1790s.

Until 1792, the Royal Navy was content to leave examination of would-be masters to members of Trinity House. It then attempted to introduce one of its own officers to the interview panel. Their nominee was Captain Isaac Smith, the second cousin of Elizabeth Cook, James Cook's wife, but Trinity House rejected this move.

Cook had learned the rudiments of seamanship and navigation from the masters that he worked under on colliers in the North Sea coal trade. Men such as John Jefferson (*Freelove* and *Three Brothers*), Robert Watson (*Three Brothers*), Richard Ellerton (*Friendship*) and John Swainston (*Friendship*) had captained the small ships sailing between the river Tyne and London on which Cook had served his apprenticeship. These ships all operated with only about fifteen crew, which meant that the master had direct supervision of all aspects of running his ship and would be expected to pitch in and help on occasions. In the same way, sailors were able to learn all the skills of seamanship and navigation.

Masters in the Royal Navy were very different from those in the merchant service. Unlike the colliers, where the master was in total command, the master on Royal Navy ships came under a captain and several lieutenants. The scale of operations was also very different, with *Eagle*, Cook's first ship, carrying over four hundred men. The Royal Navy master directed and delegated subordinates to run the various activities that combined to ensure that everything ran properly.

For his first two years in the Royal Navy, Cook had served on *Eagle* as one of the master's mates, working for Thomas Bisset, the ship's master. Bisset would have shown Cook everything that was expected of a master and appears to have groomed Cook for eventual promotion, as Cook succeeded Bisset on *Pembroke*. Bisset remains perhaps the least known and most neglected of the group of men who shaped Cook's future.

As a master, Cook enjoyed new status. He now worked alongside and communicated regularly with the ship's captain and lieutenants. His rank also allowed him a servant. Cook's elevation represented a marked rise in salary, too. He had started as an able seaman in 1755 at the salary of £1 4s per twenty-eight-day month. When he became a master's mate his salary doubled to £2 7s 10d. Masters' pay was more again, but depended on the rating of the ship on which the master served. Cook's first ship as master, *Solebay*, was a sixth rate, and his salary rose to £4. This increased again to £5 12s when Cook transferred to *Pembroke*, a fourth rate, in October 1757. At this time he was earning the same as the lieutenants on the ship. However, when Cook moved to *Northumberland*, a third rate, in 1759 he overtook the lieutenants, receiving £6 6s per twenty-eight-day month.

In late July 1757, James Cook joined HMS *Solebay* at Leith, the port for Edinburgh. Cook travelled north to join the vessel as master, his first appointment in that rank. Although he had been appointed to the ship on 30 June 1767, he did not join the ship until a month later on 30 July. Several factors caused this delay: he may have been allowed to retrieve possessions from *Eagle* and to sign off from that ship; he would also have needed to purchase equipment and a new uniform appropriate to his new rank and duties. It is probable that Cook was then granted a short period of leave so that he could visit his family on the way north to Scotland.

Solebay was the third vessel to carry that name, which commemorated the battle of Solebay that had taken place on 28 May 1672 in Sole Bay, located on the Suffolk coast between Aldeburgh and Southwold. The battle marked the opening of the Third Anglo-Dutch War (1672–4). Cook's *Solebay* had been captured by the French in 1744 and recaptured from them in 1746.

In 1757, *Solebay* was being used for general coastal duties and reconnaissance in Scottish waters, including the prevention of smuggling and the capture of French privateers. It was only twelve years since the 1745 Jacobite Rebellion in which the French had played a considerable role, supporting Prince Charles Stuart, the Young Pretender. Many Scots still had Jacobite sympathies and *Solebay* was one of several ships charged with preventing contact between the sympathisers and any French who might offer them support.

When Cook joined *Solebay* the ship was under the command of Captain Robert Craig (see section below). *Solebay* was entitled to one lieutenant and this position was occupied by Rawlin Champernowne. Champernowne (1725–74) was from an old Devon family who owned Dartington Hall near Totnes. After *Solebay*, he did not pursue a naval career

ROBERT CRAIG (1715?–1769?)

Robert Craig was captain of HMS *Solebay*, which James Cook joined at Leith. Little is known about Craig. According to his lieutenant's passing certificate, he was born around 1715. He joined the Royal Navy and served on *Kent*, *William and Mary* yacht, *Charlotte* yacht and *Deptford* storeship. On 27 February 1741 he became a lieutenant and then saw service on HMS *Tiger* in 1741 under Captain Edward Herbert. This was followed by time on *Chichester* in 1744, captained by William Dilke. In 1747, Craig was on *Lark* with Captain John Crookshanks in North American waters.

Near the end of the War of Austrian Succession, Craig was promoted to commander on 23 June 1748 and two months later, on 21 September 1748, was given command of the sloop *Vulture*. This command lasted until 16 June 1749. During the next war, the Seven Years' War, Craig was promoted to captain on 4 January 1757 and was given command of *Solebay* a month later, on 1 February 1757. *Solebay* captured *Chevalier Bart*, a French privateer on 24 April 1757; the French crew were landed at Leith and were held at Edinburgh Castle as prisoners.

Craig had, therefore, only been on the ship a few months when Cook arrived at Leith in July. Craig remained in command after Cook's departure in early September and it was Craig who was wounded in the throat by a musket ball during *Solebay*'s engagement with *Maréchal de Belle-Isle* in May 1758. This accident possibly caused his retirement from the service and may have led to his eventual death. No further actions are known for him. Craig relinquished command of *Solebay* on 25 January 1759 and it is believed that he died in 1769 in England.

and succeeded to the family estate in 1766. He married Agnes Trist in 1770 and they had a daughter, Margaret. His will also acknowledges two illegitimate children by two other women.

Champernowne's log records that *Solebay* had just returned to Leith, having undertaken a patrol to the north of Scotland – including Cape Wrath – that had begun on 8 June 1757. The ship returned on Saturday 30 July to Leith, where James Cook was waiting to join. Cook was entered as #285 on the muster the same day. Cook's new servant, Charles Connolly, was entered in the muster (#286) immediately after Cook.

A few days later, on 2 August 1757, *Solebay* left Leith on another patrol. The ship made its way up the east coast, passing Stonehaven (Cook used old versions of many of the Scottish names such as Stonehive) and Peterhead (Buchan Ness) before heading to the small islet of Copinsay (Copinsha) on the eastern edge of Orkney. They continued further north via Fair Isle to be at Lerwick in Shetland on 9 August. This was the northern limit of the patrol and *Solebay* then returned south to spend some days off the Aberdeen coast. *Solebay* sighted Morven (the Paps of Caithness) on 18 August before heading up via Copinsay to anchor in Cairston Roads by Stromness in Orkney on 19 August. After three days, *Solebay* left to the west of Hoy and passed through the Pentland Firth. By the 27th, the ship was off Girdle Ness (Aberdeen) and entered the Firth of Forth the next day. After stops in Largo Bay and off Inch Keith Island, *Solebay* anchored in Leith Roads on 30 August 1757.

Solebay only reported sighting a few ships during the month's patrol. None proved to be enemy vessels and no action resulted. Two ships that were stopped proved to be en route from Greenland and were probably whalers. In Leith, Cook began supervising the cleaning and restocking of the ship, but he had been ordered to Portsmouth and his log finishes on 7 September, the day he and his servant Connolly were both discharged from the ship. Cook made his way south to assume his next position. The six weeks between Cook leaving *Solebay* and joining his new ship remain unaccounted for. It is possible that he called in to see his family in Cleveland again during his journey south.

There is a sense that Cook's appointment to *Solebay* was only meant to be a temporary one, allowing him to gain experience and giving him an opportunity to demonstrate his capabilities in a practical way, while the ship that he was really intended for was completed. That ship, HMS *Pembroke*, was launched at Plymouth in early June 1757 and was still being fitted out when Cook was passing his master's examination. Cook's old master on *Eagle*, Thomas Bisset, had overseen the preparations on *Pembroke*, but on 18 October Cook received his next warrant requiring him to join *Pembroke* at Portsmouth, which he did on 27 October 1757, replacing Bisset.

The time Cook spent on *Solebay* in 1757 was the only time he was in Scotland and there is no evidence to suggest he ever visited Ednam near Kelso in south-eastern Scotland, where his father had been born. Seventeen years later, Cook named an island in the Pacific, New Caledonia, because it reminded him of Scotland (Caledonia being an ancient name for part of Scotland). He had just named another group of Pacific islands the New Hebrides but there is no evidence that Cook ever visited the Hebrides off the north-west Scottish coast.

The year after Cook left, *Solebay*, still commanded by Robert Craig, encountered François Thurot (see section 'François Thurot') in *Maréchal de Belle-Isle* on 26 May 1758 near the mouth of the Firth of Forth. Thurot attacked the British ships and Craig was severely wounded in the action.

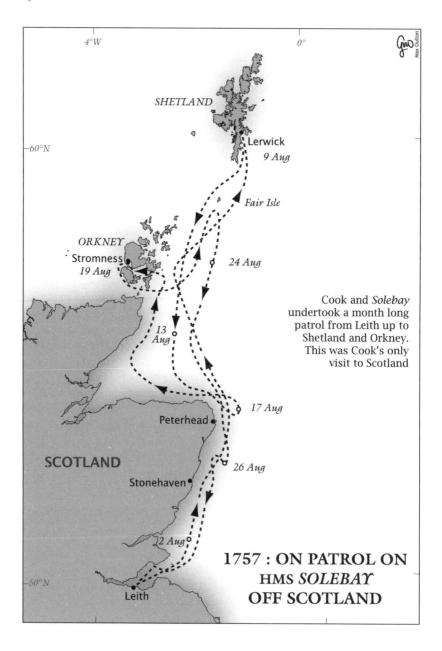

4°W   *0°*

SHETLAND

—*60°N*   Lerwick
                                      9 Aug

                                  Fair Isle

ORKNEY
Stromness   *24 Aug*
19 Aug

                   13
                   Aug

Cook and *Solebay*
undertook a month long
patrol from Leith up to
Shetland and Orkney.
This was Cook's only
visit to Scotland

                                 17 Aug
Peterhead

SCOTLAND   *26 Aug*

Stonehaven

                   2 Aug

—*50°N*   **1757 : ON PATROL ON**
                         HMS *SOLEBAY*
Leith   **OFF SCOTLAND**

FRANÇOIS THUROT (1727–60) – FRENCH NAVAL OFFICER

While the waters around Britain were nominally safe through the superior strength and presence of the Royal Navy, they were not entirely safe, because a few French naval ships and privateers did operate in the North and Irish Seas, attacking vulnerable ships. The most successful of these French sailors was François Thurot, born in 1727 at Nuits in Burgundy. Thurot sailed in *Maréchal de Belle-Isle* and had been given free rein to inflict as much damage as possible on British shipping. About the same time as Cook was being appointed to *Solebay*, Thurot was placed in command of a squadron consisting of two frigates and two corvettes, which sailed from St Malo on the 12 July 1757. During the next few months, Thurot captured numerous prizes but the squadron suffered so much from bad weather that he was forced to put into Gothenburg in Sweden to refit.

Thurot left Sweden early in 1758 and cruised off the eastern and northern coasts of Scotland, where he captured more ships. On 26 May 1758, near the mouth of the Firth of Forth, Thurot attacked four vessels that he thought were merchant ships, only to find they included two British frigates, one of which was *Solebay*, whose captain, Robert Craig, was seriously wounded in the action. Thurot survived but his ships were badly damaged and in need of more repairs so he sailed for Norway. The Royal Navy began an active campaign to capture or kill Thurot, who was eventually killed during a naval battle off the Isle of Man in February 1760. He was buried in Wigtownshire in south-west Scotland.

5

HMS *Pembroke*, 1757–1758

After his discharge from *Solebay*, Cook travelled south, from Leith to Portsmouth to join HMS *Pembroke*, which was under the command of Captain John Simcoe, assisted by lieutenants George Allen, James Norman and Edward Columbine. *Pembroke* was a new ship that Simcoe had commissioned earlier that year (commissioning involved preparing for and commencing the active service of a new vessel). Simcoe had taken it on its maiden voyage from Plymouth to Lisbon and back to Portsmouth

James Cook (#458 on the ship's muster) joined the ship as master on 27 October 1757 (per warrant of 18 October). Accompanying him was a new servant, William Wyatt (#459), inherited from Cook's mentor, Thomas Bisset, whom he was replacing as master. Thomas

---

HMS *PEMBROKE*'S OFFICERS AND MASTERS, 1757–9

Captains
John Simcoe to 14 May 1759, when he died
John Wheelock (#600) from 15 May 1759

First lieutenants
George Allen (#19) from 18 April 1757 to 26 March 1759, when he died in Halifax
James Norman (#51) from 28 March 1759 until 6 October 1759 (he then transferred to HMS *Sutherland*)

Second lieutenants
James Norman (#51) from 03 May 1757 to 28 March 1759
John Robson (#561) from 29 March 1759

Third lieutenants
Edward Columbine from 2 April 1757 until 22 August 1758, when discharged sick by order of Admiral Boscawen
John Robson (#561) from 23 August 1758 until 29 March 1759
Benjamin Bechinoe (#588) from 29 March 1759

Masters
Thomas Bisset from April 1757 to 26 October 1757
James Cook from 27 October 1757 to 23 September 1759
John Cleader from 24 September 1759

John Simcoe (1710–59)

John Simcoe was born on 28 November 1710 in Staindrop in County Durham. His parents were William and Mary (née Hutchinson) Simcoe, who had married earlier that year on 3 January 1710 in Staindrop. William Simcoe was a clergyman. John Simcoe joined the Royal Navy and became a close friend of Samuel Graves, who was rising through the ranks at the same time. Graves was born in 1713, became a lieutenant in 1740 and a captain in 1744. Simcoe himself became a lieutenant on 7 August 1739 and received his first command on 19 December 1743, that of a bomb vessel, *Thunder*. On 28 December 1743 Simcoe was made a captain and appointed to HMS *Kent*, where he remained until 18 February 1744.

Simcoe then transferred to be captain of HMS *Seahorse*, part of the Royal Navy squadron based at Jamaica. In 1745 he was still in Jamaica, this time in command of HMS *Falmouth*, having been moved to that ship on 29 January 1745. Simcoe left *Falmouth* on 24 October 1746 but it was several months before he joined a new ship, *Prince Edward*, on 14 March 1747.

While still captain of *Prince Edward*, John Simcoe married Catherine Stamford in Bath Abbey on 8 August 1747. The War of Austrian Succession ended and Simcoe left *Prince Edward* on 12 September 1748, allowing the Simcoes to settle at Cotterstock in Northamptonshire, where they had four sons. The two eldest, Paulet William (possibly named after Charles Paulet – sometimes Powlett – another captain in West Indies waters) and John William, both died in infancy, and the youngest, Percy, drowned in the river Exe in 1764. Only the third boy, John Graves, survived to adulthood.

When the Seven Years' War began, Simcoe was appointed as captain of *St George* on 3 July 1756, and in his position there had the unenviable task of hosting the court martial of Admiral John Byng in early 1757. On 5 April 1757 he was given command of the new ship, HMS *Pembroke*. In 1758, Simcoe took *Pembroke* across the Atlantic to take part in the siege of the French fort of Louisbourg on Cape Breton Island.

After the siege of Louisbourg James Cook encountered Samuel Holland, an army engineer, surveying on the beach at Kennington Cove; Simcoe encouraged Cook and gave him the opportunity to learn from Holland how to survey. In 1759 Simcoe and *Pembroke* sailed from Halifax as part of the British fleet heading for Quebec, but Simcoe died from pneumonia on 14 May 1759 off Anticosti Island at the mouth of the St Lawrence River in Canada.

Simcoe's widow, Catherine, and her two surviving sons moved from Northamptonshire to Exeter, where she had friends. She died in 1767, leaving John Graves Simcoe as the only surviving member of the family.

John Graves Simcoe became a colonel in the army and on 30 December 1782 married Elizabeth Posthuma Gwillim, the neice of Samuel Graves, at Buckerell in Devon. In 1791, John Graves Simcoe was appointed lieutenant governor of the new province of Upper Canada and he sailed for Quebec in September 1791. He remained in Canada for five years and left the colony in July 1796. By 1806 he was in poor health and he died on 26 October in Exeter.

The survey group from on board *Pembroke* was remembered when a lake in northern Ontario was named Lake Simcoe after John Simcoe. A river flowing into it is called the Holland River after Samuel Holland, while the place where it enters Lake Simcoe is Cook Bay after the explorer.

Bisset (#45) had been master from April to October during the ship's commissioning but had now been transferred to *Stirling Castle*. The purser on *Pembroke* was Richard Wise, and he and Cook would become close friends. Wise was later one of the executors of Cook's will.

The day that Cook joined *Pembroke* the ship was taken into the dock at Portsmouth for an overhaul. It left the next day and Cook supervised the stowing of stores and ballast as well as rigging the ship. On 6 November *Pembroke* left Portsmouth Harbour and sailed out to anchor at Spithead, where the crew prepared the ship over the next month and waited.

On 8 December, the ship came to sail and set off as part of a small squadron to patrol in the Bay of Biscay and beyond. Hawke had been out with the Western Squadron since October but they had missed Dubois de la Motte returning with the French fleet to Brest on 3 November. This was probably lucky as the French ships were riddled with disease and thousands would die in the port. Unlike Cook's experience on *Eagle*, *Pembroke* operated further out in the Atlantic, more to the west and south than before. On 16 January the ship was west of Cape Finisterre. Ships were sighted and chased but no significant action took place and after two long, cold months *Pembroke* returned to anchor in Plymouth Sound on 9 February 1758.

Only a short stay in port was possible as Simcoe was given notice that *Pembroke* would be sailing to North America as part of Admiral Boscawen's fleet. The time was spent provisioning the ship. On 21 February Boscawen arrived from Portsmouth in Plymouth in HMS *Namur*. On the 24th, Cook and *Pembroke* sailed from Plymouth as part of the fleet, with seventeen ships in company.

Admiral Edward Boscawen, who had been promoted Admiral of the Blue on 5 February 1758, was in command of the expedition whose aim was the conquest of the fortress of Louisbourg. Assisting him were Sir Charles Hardy, lately made Rear Admiral of the White, and Commodore Philip Durell, both of whom had already sailed for North America, the former in January, the latter in February.

Sir Charles Hardy, who had been promoted rear admiral in 1756, took part in an aborted attack on Louisbourg in May 1757. He had been Governor of New York from 1755 but resigned on 3 June 1757 and returned to Britain. In 1758 he sailed on HMS *Captain* and then HMS *Royal William*. After the siege of Louisbourg, Hardy transported three regiments under James Wolfe to the Baie de Gaspé.

Philip Durell hoisted his commodore's broad pendant in the frigate *Diana* on 15 January 1758. He arrived at New York on 7 March and organised the transportation of troops to Halifax. He left New York on 4 May and arrived at Halifax on the 17th. He moved to *Princess Amelia* and sailed for Louisbourg on 28 May with the fleet. Durell was promoted Rear Admiral of the Blue in July 1758 and remained in North American waters as commander-in-chief for the winter months.

The crossing of the Atlantic was very slow and largely uneventful. It was decided to make a long sweep to the south to use the trade winds so the fleet headed for the Tropic of Cancer, passing to the south-east of Madeira:

8 MARCH. 9.00am The body of Madeira NW by N 12 or 13 leagues.

They sailed between Tenerife and Gran Canaria and took sightings of Pico Tenerife, after which *Pembroke* set a new base longitude:

13 MARCH. 6.00am Saw Pico Tenerife WSW 10 or 12 leagues.

13 MARCH. 11.00am The body of Grand Canary S by E distance 10 leagues.

Six days later Cook reported:

19 MARCH. 6.00am Crossed the Tropic of Cancer to the south.

HALIFAX

Britain gained possession of Nova Scotia from the French in 1713 under the Treaty of Utrecht but made little or no attempt to settle the peninsula. In 1745, during the War of Austrian Succession, forces from New England captured the French fortress of Louisbourg on Île Royale, but the 1748 Treaty of Aix-la-Chapelle restored Louisbourg to France; the war showed the need for a British naval port in Nova Scotia to counter Louisbourg.

Chebucto Bay, with its magnificent natural harbour and its strategic location on Nova Scotia's south-east coast, was selected to be this port. In early March 1749, Lord Halifax, the new president of the Board of Trade and Plantations, submitted a report recommending the establishment of a port in Chebucto Bay. Colonel Edward Cornwallis was made captain general and governor of Nova Scotia and given command of the enterprise. In May 1749 Cornwallis and 2,576 settlers in thirteen transports and the sloop *Sphinx* sailed for Nova Scotia, arriving in Chebucto Bay in late June.

Cornwallis selected a site for the town on the west side of the harbour, which commanded the whole peninsula and was sheltered from the north-west winds. There was a convenient landing for the boats along the beach and good anchorage within gunshot of the shore for the largest ships.

A letter in the *London Magazine* in 1749 reported: '. . . pleasant town . . . which is to be called *Halifax*, in honour of that great and able lord, to whom this settlement owes its beginning'. Therefore, when Cook arrived in 1758, Halifax was not yet ten years old.[1]

After that the fleet began sailing westwards and, from early April, north-west. Bermuda was passed to the eastward:

> 22 APRIL. 2.00pm Saw the island of Bermuda bearing W by N 7 or 8 leagues. It appeared like the hulk of a ship.

Nova Scotia was finally sighted on 8 May. *Pembroke* anchored in Halifax Harbour on the 10th. It had been a long crossing of two months, and it had taken its toll on those on board. That night:

> 10 MAY. In the night between 12 and 1 Frederick Jacob, Simon Middleton, Samuel Divers, Daniel Gardner, Joseph Whaler and Henry Tullung, seamen, run away with the yawl.

James Cunningham, General Abercromby's aide-de-camp, who had sailed to Halifax from New York, wrote a letter to Lord George Sackville, describing events in the harbour from March through to May, including the arrival of Boscawen's fleet: 'The whole Fleet immediately on their arrival begun to take in Water and clean the ships all healthy, except the Pembroke and Devonshire.'[2] Cook's log described the death of twenty-four men during the crossing, in which one man fell overboard and was lost and another died when he fell to the deck. The other twenty-two 'departed this life', presumably from scurvy and other illnesses. After their arrival, some men were sent to the hospital in Halifax but Cook made no mention of general illness on his ship.

6

Louisbourg, 1758

Pembroke did not leave Halifax with Boscawen when most of the fleet sailed on 28 May because the crew had not yet recovered their health. James Cunningham reported: 'The Pembroke having: 200 Men sick, the Devonshire sickly ... were left at Halifax with orders to join the Fleet when in a proper condition.'[1] Instead, *Pembroke* was ordered to bring straggling transports and other vessels to Louisbourg when they were ready. Indeed, when *Pembroke* left Halifax on 7 June it was in company with five ships and a convoy of transports. They arrived in Gabarus Bay, near Louisbourg, on 10 June, minus two of the transports that had been lost en route, to find the assault had commenced two days earlier.

The British navy had maintained a presence off Louisbourg since March 1758. Sir Charles Hardy had arrived at Halifax on 19 March with eight ships of the line and two frigates. On 26 March Hardy headed off to blockade Louisbourg. On 2 June he was joined by Boscawen, who had waited in vain in Halifax for the arrival of the commander of the British army, General Jeffery Amherst. Amherst had not yet arrived when Boscawen finally left Halifax on 28 May with 19 ships and 135 transport vessels, but he met the general just outside the harbour. Amherst had sailed for America on 16 March 1758, on what had proved to be a slow voyage. He had sailed in *Dublin*, captained by George Rodney but Rodney was busy securing prizes during the crossing, causing delays. The British fleet and transports anchored in Gabarus Bay, south-west of Louisbourg.

The capture of Louisbourg was important for the British as the fortress and port controlled the waters leading to the St Lawrence River and, hence, Quebec and Montreal. It was also strategically placed close to the rich fishing grounds of the Grand Banks.

Amherst divided his army into three units under Brigade Commanders James Wolfe, Charles Lawrence – then the Governor of Nova Scotia – and Edward Whitmore. On 4 June, Amherst, with his brigadier commanders, went off in a longboat to reconnoitre the shore of Gabarus Bay to identify possible landing locations. An earlier plan had involved landing troops at Mira Bay to attack the fortress from the north-east but Amherst instead decided to land in Gabarus Bay and attack from the west. This would be the same mode of attack as the successful New Englanders had employed in 1745.

Amherst's own first plan to land at three different places in Gabarus Bay was modified in favour of a single landing at Anse de la Cormorandière (Freshwater Bay), the western-most of the small bays, while other units made feints to attack elsewhere. Unknown to the British, the Governor of Louisbourg, Augustin de Boschenry de Drucour, had antici-pated these moves. He had ordered trenches to be dug and batteries to be erected along the bay, especially at Anse de la Cormorandière, the likeliest spot for an assault.

LOUISBOURG HISTORY

After the Treaty of Utrecht in 1713 – which ended the War of Spanish Succession – had ceded Newfoundland and Acadia to Britain, France was only left with the Île Royale (Cape Breton Island) and the Île St Jean (Prince Edward Island) in Maritime Canada. Île Royale was important for its proximity to the rich fishing resources of the nearby Grand Banks off Newfoundland. The island also occupied a strategic position close to the mouth of the St Lawrence River, the conduit to the French possessions around Quebec and Montreal. Another result of the 1713 treaty was that France had to evacuate its settlement at Placentia in Newfoundland and its inhabitants were evacuated to form the nucleus of future Louisbourg.

Small French fishing and fur trading posts had existed along Île Royale's east coast since the mid-seventeenth century. In 1719 the French began to construct a fort at a protected harbour, which was named Havre Louisbourg. The settlement soon became a thriving community, attracting French settlers expelled by the British from other areas, such as Acadia. A lighthouse was constructed in 1734 on the south-eastern headland opposite the town.

British colonists in New England saw Louisbourg as a threat to their access to the cod fishery, and the declaration of war between France and Britain in 1740 (as the start of the War of Austrian Succession, 1740–8) was an opportunity for them to rid themselves of a problem. This anti-French sentiment among the British colonists was further increased when a French force from Louisbourg attacked Canso in 1744.

In 1745, William Shirley, the Governor of Massachusetts, called for an expedition to attack Louisbourg. A force was put together, paid for by and largely made up of New Englanders. Under the command of William Pepperrell, the expedition set sail from Boston in March 1745. By the end of the month the naval forces were blockading Louisbourg and at the end of April, Pepperrell's forces landed west of Louisbourg at Freshwater Cove. A siege of forty-six days ensued before the French forces surrendered on 16 June.

Three years later, in October 1748, Louisbourg was returned to France under the terms of the Treaty of Aix-la-Chapelle, much to the disgust of the people of New England. To counter the French presence at Louisbourg, Britain decided in 1749 to build its own fortified port on the Nova Scotia coast. A site was chosen on Chebucto Bay, which they named Halifax. It soon became a thriving naval port and provided the base in 1758 from which the final attack on Louisbourg was launched.

The three brigades were assigned code colours, with the Red Brigade under Wolfe given the task of the main attack at Anse de la Cormorandière. The Blue Brigade, under Lawrence, was to feint landing at Flat Point and the White Brigade, under Whitmore, was to feint landing at White Point. Bad weather, fog and rain from 5 to 7 June delayed the attack but conditions improved, and at 4am on 8 June the British attack began.

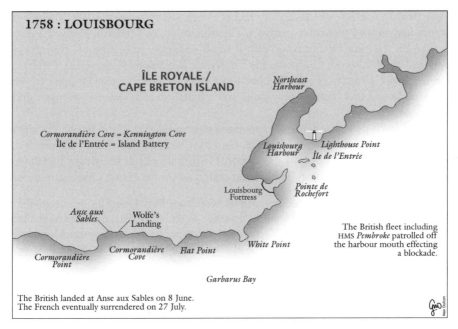

1758 : LOUISBOURG

ÎLE ROYALE /
CAPE BRETON ISLAND

Northeast Harbour

Cormorandière Cove = Kennington Cove
Île de l'Entrée = Island Battery

Louisbourg Harbour

Lighthouse Point
Île de l'Entrée

Louisbourg Fortress

Pointe de Rochefort

Anse aux Sables

Wolfe's Landing

The British fleet including HMS *Pembroke* patrolled off the harbour mouth effecting a blockade.

Cormorandière Cove   *Flat Point*

White Point

Cormorandière Point

Garbarus Bay

The British landed at Anse aux Sables on 8 June.
The French eventually surrendered on 27 July.

Initially, landing was impossible as the sea was extremely rough and the British came under heavy enemy fire from a thousand French troops under Lieutenant Colonel Saint-Julien. Two British ships, *Halifax* and *Kennington* (after which the cove was later renamed) maintained a bombardment to cover the assault. Wolfe and his men attempted to land but the advance was stopped by the French. Wolfe made a signal to retreat, which was misinterpreted by some junior officers, who found themselves sheltered from fire by a ridge at Anse aux Sables. They managed to get ashore and Wolfe, seeing this, diverted more men to this spot. The British had a most fortunate foothold and successfully stormed the French defences.

The French abandoned their position and retreated towards Louisbourg. Lawrence's and Whitmore's brigades followed Wolfe so that the initial British thrust quickly got ashore with relatively little loss. However, poor weather and heavy surf along the bay delayed the landing of the remainder of the troops. It also held up the siege operations by preventing the landing of artillery and stores to support the troops. Many transports were lost in the subsequent landing operations.

Louisbourg was commanded in 1758 by Augustin de Boschenry de Drucour, the Chevalier de Drucour. He was a fifty-five-year-old naval officer and Governor of Île Royale. He and his wife, Marie-Anne Aubert de Courserac, had arrived in Louisbourg on 15 August 1754. Throughout the siege Madame Drucour played a prominent role by rallying the French troops and the inhabitants of the town. She went onto the ramparts each day and personally fired three guns. After the siege the Drucours sailed from Louisbourg on 15 August 1758 for France. Drucour retired to Le Havre and died on 28 August 1762. Madame Drucour died two months later.

The British blockade of Louisbourg had not been totally successful. The Marquis des Gouttes had slipped through to arrive at Louisbourg on 24 March in *Prudent*. He was followed on the 28th by Beaussier with a small squadron consisting of: *Entreprenant* (captained by Beaussier), *Capricieux* (de Tourville), *Bienfaisant* (Courserac), *Célèbre* (de Marolle) and *Comhe* (Lorgeril). The last three were en flute, that is, stripped to serve as transports and had brought provisions and a battalion of *volontaires étrangers* under d'Anthonay.

On 30 March de la Houlière was appointed to command the land forces. He arrived in Louisbourg by *Bizarre* on 30 May 1758. On 1 June news arrived that du Chaffault had come to Port Dauphin (north of Louisbourg) with four vessels carrying a battalion of *cambis* to reinforce the garrison. They would march across the island. Drucour reported:

> At about 8 this evening, 2 officers arrived here from Port Dauphin, one from the marines and the other from the Cambis Battalion, to report the arrival of the vessels the Dragon, the Sphinx, the Hardi, le Zéphire and a Compagnie des Indes vessel. Monsieur Duchassault signalled to me that he had sent the Cambis battalion at the Baie de l'Espagnole to come here overland.[2]

On board one of the French ships that arrived at Port Dauphin was the future Pacific explorer La Pérouse. He had joined *Zéphire* under the command of Charles-Henri-Louis d'Arsac de Ternay, his friend and protector. They were part of Louis Charles du Chaffault's squadron escorting troop transports across the Atlantic. The squadron left Brest and sailed down the coast to Rochefort before heading across to Île Royale with troops and supplies. When they reached Île Royale in early June they found British ships blockading Louisbourg and a siege of the fort beginning. They decided to land the troops at Port Dauphin instead.

Du Chaffault needed to go on to Quebec to land troops there and dispatched Ternay and *Zéphire* back to France to report on the situation at Louisbourg. Ternay managed to slip out of the harbour past the British ships. He then sailed north through the Gulf of St Lawrence and on through the Strait of Belle-Isle between Newfoundland and Labrador. As they approached Ouessant the French encountered British ships blockading Brest but managed to evade them and sailed into port. La Pérouse was discharged from *Zéphire* on 21 July 1758.

Cook and *Pembroke* had missed the first assault but there was still much to do and they could play a significant role. Cook recorded in his log when *Pembroke* arrived to join the remainder of the fleet in Gabarus Bay:

> 9 JUNE. 10am Anchored in Gabarus Bay in 25 fathoms with the best bower.

Having reported his arrival, Simcoe took *Pembroke* to wait off Louisbourg Harbour:

> 11 JUNE. At 10 weighed and came to sail. Lost a hand lead line.

> 12 JUNE. At 1 pm anchored before the harbour of Louisbourg with the best bower in 36 fathoms ... could see laying in the harbour 12 sail of ships, 7 or 8 of which we took to be large.

On 12 June James Wolfe led a force of twelve hundred men round to the north of Louisbourg to attack Lighthouse Point, a strategic location from which to bombard the town, the ships in the harbour and the battery on the island in the harbour mouth. They reached the lighthouse to find it already abandoned. Over the next few days, the British set up gun positions on the headland. The bad weather had delayed the army getting its guns and stores ashore, and Cook reported:

17 JUNE. Longboat and cutter assisting to land the artillery.

Echo, one of the French frigates in the harbour, made an attempt to escape and sail for France on the evening of 13 June. HMS *Juno* was signalled by the admiral to chase, followed by several other British ships including *Pembroke*. *Pembroke* was back in position off Louisbourg two days later and *Juno* and *Scarborough* paraded the captured *Echo* on the 18th:

18 JUNE at 8 His Majesty's ships Juno and Scarborough brought in the Echo French frigate of 32 guns.

Wars were still conducted with civility during the eighteenth century and Drucour, the Louisbourg governor reported on 18 June that gifts were exchanged between the two sides. General Amherst sent Madame Drucour some pineapples: 'At 9 the Marquis des Gouttes sent a canoe under a flag of truce to the middle of the Bay with a basket of 50 bottles of wine in return for the general's noble gift of two pineapples to Madame de Drucour, with apologies for the anxiety that the circumstances were going to cause her.' This was, however, only a prelude to what was to follow. Wolfe had his guns ready and the bombardment of the island battery began on the 20th, as Cook recorded:

20 JUNE. At 10 pm General Wolfe opened his battery from the lighthouse against the shipping . . . at noon the firing on both sides.

Jean-Antoine Charry, Marquis des Gouttes and the other French naval officers on the ships in the harbour had wanted to leave when the British arrived and were unhappy about having to stay in port. Their ships had been positioned in the centre of the harbour and had contributed to the French defence but now the officers moved them so close in shore near the town as to be redundant. One officer, Vauquelin, in command of *Aréthuse*, a 36-gun frigate, disagreed with this move and wanted to take the fight to the British.

The island battery at the entrance to the harbour was silenced on 25 June and the French were now afraid that Boscawen would send some of his ships into the harbour for an attack. Accordingly, they planned to sink several of their smaller vessels in the entrance to prevent an incursion. On 27 June Drucour recorded: 'It was suggested that we sink the Apollon, the Fidèle, the Chèvre and a ship from St.-Malo in the harbour entrance, which I plan to carry out tomorrow at nightfall.' On the morning of the 29th, Cook recorded:

29 JUNE. Found in the morning that the besieged had sunk 4 ships in the entrance of the harbour.

In mid-July Vauquelin proposed to Drucour that he should attempt to escape in *Aréthuse* with dispatches for France. Des Gouttes, present at the interview, gave his opinion that Vauquelin might be of more use staying at Louisbourg. Vauquelin replied: 'Yes, by God, if you will give me one of your men-of-war of the line that are laid up doing nothing, you will see that I will do much more yet than I have done hitherto with the frigate.'[3] On 15 July *Aréthuse* managed to slip its moorings, make sail and head through the channel by the lighthouse battery and carried on, right out to sea. The British on Lighthouse Point made signals to the waiting British ships outside the harbour but they were too late and *Aréthuse* was able to get away, none of the British ships being able to catch up to her. Drucour wrote: 'At 9½ this evening l'Aréthuse frigate left for France. The lighthouse battery fired five times and sent up several rockets, no doubt as a signal ... it will arrive safely in Bayonne.'

Cook and *Pembroke* were still deployed outside the harbour and Cook recorded:

15 JULY. 11pm The signal was made at the lighthouse for discovering the enemy's ship in motion, which was repeated by the frigates in shore and the admiral ... Came to sail.

16 JULY. 4am 8 sail in sight. None of the enemy's ships in sight.

For two days *Pembroke* and other ships searched in vain for *Aréthuse* before returning once more to anchor off Louisbourg. The bombardment of the town continued unabated and even intensified. Early in the afternoon of 21 July a bomb fell on *Célèbre*, one of the French vessels in the harbour. The bomb set off some cartridges stored there and a fire resulted, which caught her mizzen mast. The men on board were unable to check the fire and the ship swung so that sparks from her caught aft on *Entreprenant*. She, in turn, set fire to *Capricieux*, unable to move. Drucour wrote: 'At ½ past 2pm, a bomb fell on the Célèbre and set fire to her; it was not possible to extinguish it and it spread to the Entreprenant and the Capricieux so that by 7pm they were almost consumed.' Cook wrote:

21 JULY. ½ past 3 pm One of the enemy's took fire, the flames communicated to 2 more which consumed them also.

The British bombardment now concentrated on the town. Bombs with combustibles were hurled into the town, and buildings caught alight. On 22 July fire spread to the King's Bastion and on the 23rd the wooden barracks of the Queen's Bastion caught fire. Once more Cook recorded:

22 JULY. At 6 am a large building in the city took fire which consumed the whole ... the besiegers keep a continual fire again the garrison.

24 JULY. At 12 at night the barracks in the garrison took fire which consumed the whole.

The British navy now contributed an action that proved a telling blow for the French. Boscawen ordered a foray into Louisbourg Harbour to capture the two remaining ships. These ships, *Bienfaisant* and *Prudent* were still anchored close to the town and only carried partial crews under the command of an ensign. Six hundred British sailors, under the command of Captains Laforey and Balfour, stole into the harbour during the night in barges and pinnaces and climbed on board the ships; both ships were captured easily. However, *Prudent* was aground and could not be moved so was set on fire. *Bienfaisant* was towed into the north-eastern corner of the harbour, away from the town. Admiral Boscawen gave his version of the exercise in his diary:

> The boats of the squadron were in two divisions, commanded by the Captains Laforey and Balfour, to endeavour either to take or burn the *Prudent*, of 74 guns, and the *Bienfaisant*, of 64, the only remaining ships in the harbour, in which they succeeded so well as to burn the former, she being aground, and to take the latter and tow her into the north-east harbour, notwithstanding they were exposed to the cannon and musketry of the Island Battery, Point Rochefort, and the town, being favoured with a dark night. Our loss was inconsiderable: seven men killed and nine wounded.[4]

While Cook noted:

> 26 JULY. In the night 50 boats manned and armed rowed into the harbour under the command of the Captains L. Foare [Laforey] and Balfour in order to cut away the 2 men of war and tow them into the N.E. harbour. One which they did, viz the Ben Fison [*Bienfaisant*] of 64 guns, the Pruden [*Prudent*] being aground she was set on fire.

On the morning of the 26th Drucour, the French governor, convened a council of war and sought the opinions of his senior officers. There was agreement that they should surrender and sue for peace. Drucour recorded:

> I convened the council of war consisting of Messieurs Prévost, Bonnaventure, la Houillère, Desgouttes, Saint-Julien, Marin et Dauthonnay.
> Result of the council of war convened by Monsieur le Chevalier de Drucour on the morning of 26 July 1758 on the approach to take regarding Louisbourg, besieged by the British:
> Given the opinions of the members of the council, I agree with them to send an officer to request a ceasfire in order to enter into negotiations with the British Commander.
> At Louisbourg on 26 July 1758, signed Chevalier de Drucour.

Cook wrote:

> 26 JULY. At 11 am the firing ceased on both sides.

Later that morning, a French officer, Louis Loppinot, was conducted to General Amherst's tent to tender Governor Drucour's terms of capitulation. These were rejected by Amherst, who demanded full surrender by the garrison. The French, who would all be prisoners of war, had only one hour to accept or reject the terms and there would be no negotiations. The French were horrified: they had expected a surrender with the honours of war, with rights to march out of the fortress with their drums beating and colours flying. Instead they were to be prisoners of war. Many were now for fighting on. The council resolved to resist the British, and Loppinot set out again with a letter to say the French would submit to assault rather than accept the terms offered. However, Commissaire Général de la Marine, Jacques Prévost, presented a memoir to the council

THE ROLE OF THE NAVY DURING THE SIEGE OF LOUISBOURG

Some commentators have sought to downplay the navy's role at Louisbourg, describing it as merely providing backup for a military operation, with responsibility for Britain's success being usually ascribed to the army. Amherst's overall management of the campaign and Wolfe's actions in carrying out the siege are the main factors mentioned. However, the victory owed much to the excellent working relationship between Amherst and Boscawen and the massive contribution of the navy. The navy transported the troops to Gabarus Bay and then acted as support for the remainder of the campaign, effectively blockading the port and preventing any relief for the French. Wolfe acknowledged this when he wrote: 'The Admiral and the General have carried on public service with great harmony, industry and union. Mr Boscawen has given all and even more than we cou'd ask of him. He has furnish'd arms and ammunition, pioneers, sappers, miners, gunners, carpenters, boats, and, I must confess, is no bad fantassin [infantry man] himself, and an excellent back hand at a siege. Sir Charles Hardy, too, in particular, and all the officers of the Navy in general, have given us their utmost assistance, and with the greatest cheerfulness imaginable. I have often been in pain for Sir Charles's squadron at an anchor off the harbour's mouth. They rid out some very hard gales of wind rather than leave an opening for the French to escape . . .'[5]

Boscawen was consulted at all stages and contributed to the decision making. Gunners, carpenters and other men were deployed to support the infantry and to relieve the land forces from other duties, including digging trenches. Naval artillery was landed to be used in the bombardment.

at 3pm in which he pointed out the hardships that the people of the town would suffer if they persisted in their defence. His argument was accepted and another officer was dispatched to overtake Loppinot with powers to capitulate. Drucour wrote to Amherst and Boscawen:

> Gentlemen.
>
> The little time your excellencies grant me does not allow me to enter into the detail that the capitulation you insist upon deserves. I have requested lieutenant-colonel Monsieur Dauthonnay assisted by Monsieur le Chevalier Duvivier, aide-major général and Monsieur Loppinot, major, to determine from your excellencies the changes in favour of the townspeople and the conditions you demand.
>
> I have the honour to sign le Chevalier de Drucour.

To this the British replied:

> Sir
>
> We are honoured to send your excellency the signed terms of capitulation.

Lieutenant-colonel Danthonnay did not fail to speak for the townspeople, and it is in no way our intention to make them suffer, but to provide them with all the assistance we can. Your excellency will be kind enough to sign a copy of the terms of capitulation and send it here. It remains only to assure your excellency that we will be delighted to convince you of our consideration.

Signed Boscawen and Jeff. Amherst.[6]

Cook, who had been a distant observer of this activity, simply wrote:

27 JULY. At 10 the garrison capitulated.

The British army occupied the fortress and the navy began sailing into the harbour. However, bad weather and the sunken French vessels at the harbour mouth delayed the navy and it was 2 August before Cook and *Pembroke* anchored inside. The next day they moved to the north-east harbour.

29 JULY. At noon laying to off the harbour.

2 AUGUST. At 4pm anchored in Louisbourg with the best bower in 9 fathoms water.

3 AUGUST. am Employed transporting up into the NE Harbour. At noon came to with the best bower in 6 fathoms water.

The British had captured Louisbourg but the French took one substantial satisfaction from the encounter: they had occupied the British forces for so long that it was too late for them to proceed on to Quebec that year. Drucour wrote: 'Our main purpose was to resist and postpone our end as long as possible.' They had bought time for Quebec, and if the authorities in France could organise reinforcements and supplies to reach North America then all was not lost.

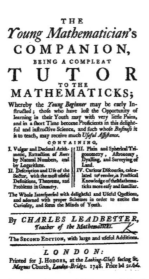

Title page to Charles Leadbetter's Young Mathematician's Companion

7

Surveyor, 1758

These days it would be most foolhardy to go to sea without up-to-date hydrographic charts and a global-positioning device. In the middle of the eighteenth century, however, sailors had no such 'luxuries' and left port often with only a vague notion of where they were going and whether they would reach their intended destination. For a large part of history, most European sailors rarely sailed a great distance from land, gauging their location by regular sightings of familiar features on the land they were passing. Gradually, Europeans began to be more ambitious, venturing out into the Atlantic Ocean, but their success rate in reaching their intended target at the first attempt was not high. The coordinate system of latitude and longitude had been developed, but most sailors still had great trouble determining what their coordinates were and, hence, their exact location.

Latitude, the distance that somewhere is north or south of the Equator, had become relatively easy to fix by the middle of the eighteenth century. A series of progressively more precise instruments, including astrolabes, backstaffs, quadrants and, finally, sextants (in the 1750s) had been produced that could measure the degree of latitude (up to 90° at the poles) quickly and correctly.

Longitude, the distance that one location was east or west of a base location was proving much more difficult to compute. The tragic loss of part of the British fleet on the rocks of the Scilly Isles in 1707 had occurred largely through their inability to calculate longitude, causing them to think they were further west than they really were. This persuaded the British government to set up the Board of Longitude in 1714 to administer the Longitude Prize to be awarded to anyone who could come up with a means of calculating longitude. People attempted this for much of the next seventy years, before John Harrison claimed most of the prize for his marine chronometers. An alternative method was devised by Tobias Mayer in 1755, in which tables allowed longitude to be calculated after sightings were taken of the moon relative to stars.

By the late 1750s, therefore, sailors with a sextant, a fair knowledge of the stars and basic mathematics (and clear weather) could take sightings and work out their position with a reasonable degree of accuracy. Cook was such a person and appears to have acquired his skills in astronomy over time through trial, experience and from textbooks. There is no evidence that any one person taught him the subject but it is typical of Cook that he became a more than averagely proficient astronomer and did not use astronomy just for navigational purposes. He was aware of astronomical phenomena and by 1766 was realising the value of observing a solar eclipse and forwarding the results to the Royal Society.

SAMUEL JOHANNES HOLLAND (1729–1801)

Samuel Holland, the engineer and surveyor, was baptised on 22 September 1729 in Deventer, the Netherlands, the son of Johann and Johanna Holland. He entered the Dutch artillery in 1745 and served in the War of the Austrian Succession, where he was promoted to lieutenant in 1747. He was married for the first time in 1749 in Nijmegen to Gertrude Hasse. In 1754, he left his wife and the Netherlands and moved to Britain where he joined the British army.

In 1756, Holland was sent to America, where he spent most of the rest of his career. He was soon employed in making a map of the province of New York before attending the siege of Louisbourg in 1758, when he served as one of Wolfe's engineers. He surveyed the area near the fortress, prepared plans, and gave engineering advice to Wolfe during the siege operations. Wolfe commended him for his bravery and technical competence. After the surrender of Louisbourg, while making a plan of the town and its environs, Holland met James Cook at Kennington Cove. Over the next few weeks he instructed Cook in the use of the plane table and other surveying techniques.

That winter he and Cook prepared a chart of the St Lawrence Gulf and river, based on charts captured from the French, for the attack on Quebec. In 1759 Holland accompanied Wolfe to Quebec and was promoted to the rank of captain. Wolfe presented him with a brace of duelling pistols and he was also present at Wolfe's death on the Plains of Abraham. Holland remained in Quebec with General Murray and was there when the French attacked in April 1760. In 1761 he began surveying the settled portions of the province of Quebec and in the following year carried his plans to England, where he remained until 1764. Holland reported that his belongings, including notebooks and plans from 1758 and 1759 were stolen during that time. Holland returned to Canada to map Prince Edward Island from 1764 until 1766. In 1766 he was appointed surveyor general of the province of Quebec and also of the Northern District of America. It was in this latter capacity that he surveyed and wrote his description of Cape Breton Island.

Holland completed surveys in the Gulf and the Lower St Lawrence and then in New Hampshire, New Jersey, New York and Massachusetts. In 1778 he was transferred to Quebec and in 1791 he drew the boundaries between Upper and Lower Canada. Holland married his second wife, Marie-Josephate (Josette) Rolette, on 3 September 1787 in Perth Amboy, New Jersey; they would have ten children together. Holland died at Quebec on 28 December 1801. A red rose and a river in Ontario are named after him.

Knowing your location was all very well, but it helped to also know what was supposed to be at that location. For this charts were required, but the state of marine charting at the time was appalling. The creation of the British Hydrographic Office – which would eventually oversee the production and maintenance of detailed and correct hydrographic charts – would not happen until 1795, still forty years in the future. Some naval officers had been proposing its creation since the 1740s but no action had been taken. The Royal Navy had no chart repository and no provision to issue them to ships leaving port. It fell to ships' officers to purchase their own charts before sailing, if suitable charts even existed. If they did, they could be error prone, long out of date and missing many features.

Many ships' officers were unable to draw their own charts and showed little inclination to learn this skill. Therefore, the tasks of surveying and drawing new charts had been incorporated in the regulations for the duties of the ship's master, the senior warrant officer. This was the position in which James Cook found himself in 1757, and nautical surveying and cartography would soon become the two tasks about which he cared most passionately and in which he became supremely proficient. He later wrote: 'The world will hardly admit of an excuse for a man leaving a coast unexplored he has once discovered.'[1]

Cook was lucky in that his captain on *Pembroke*, John Simcoe, was an educated man interested in the sciences and who had a library with him on the ship. Simcoe was also concerned for his crew and cared about them improving themselves so, when Cook met Samuel Holland (see section 'Samuel Johannes Holland') in July 1758, he was prepared to help Cook learn to be a surveyor. Simcoe also wanted to learn more for himself and invited Holland on board *Pembroke* so he could share in this new knowledge. We know something about the events surrounding Cook's first steps in becoming a surveyor from a letter in 1792 from Samuel Holland (by then the surveyor general of British North America, to John Graves Simcoe, by then the Lieutenant Governor of Upper Canada) in which Holland reminisced about Simcoe's father, John Simcoe.

Holland's letter (see section 'Letter from Samuel Holland to John Graves Simcoe') also described his first meeting with James Cook. For Cook, this was a momentous meeting as it changed his life, marking the beginning of his career as a surveyor and instilling in him the desire to draw charts. However, it is probable that Holland's memory was not quite correct in stating that the meeting took place the day after the siege finished. *Pembroke* was not then in Gabarus Bay but was positioned immediately outside Louisbourg, waiting to enter the harbour. She was still there on 29 July; it was only on 2 August that *Pembroke* managed to enter and anchor in the harbour. Cook, as master of *Pembroke*, would not have been away from the ship during any of this period. The wrecks in the harbour entrance would have made entering the harbour even more difficult than normal and Cook would not have trusted anyone else to perform the task. It is more probable that Cook met Holland some time in the following days.

The meeting took place on the beach at Anse de la Cormorandière, now called Kennington Cove, the site of Wolfe's first landing. Cook's initial interest was encouraged by Captain Simcoe and what followed is best described by Holland's letter.

So what were Cook's existing skills in July 1758 when he met Holland and how did he develop further? Apart from Holland's letter we have hardly any concrete evidence.

LETTER FROM SAMUEL HOLLAND TO JOHN GRAVES SIMCOE

Quebec, 11th January 1792.
Lt.-Governor Simcoe, York:
Sir, ——

    It is with the most sincere pleasure that I recall to memory the many happy and instructive hours I have had the honour of enjoying in your late most excellent father's company, and with more than ordinary satisfaction do I recollect the following circumstance which gave birth to our acquaintance. The day after the surrender of Louisbourg, being at Kennington Cove surveying and making a plan of the place, with its attack and encampments, I observed Capt. Cook (then Master of Capt. Simcoe's ship, the *Pembroke* man-of-war) particularly attentive to my operations; and as he expressed an ardent desire to be instructed in the use of the Plane Table (the instrument I was then using) I appointed the next day in order to make him acquainted with the whole process; he accordingly attended, with a particular message from Capt. Simcoe expressive of a wish to have been present at our proceedings; and his inability, owing to indisposition, of leaving his ship; at the same time requesting me to dine with him on board; and begging me to bring the Plane Table pieces along. I, with much pleasure, accepted the invitation, which gave rise to my acquaintance with a truly scientific gentleman, for the which I have ever held myself much indebted to Capt. Cook. I remained that night on board, in the morning landed to continue my survey at White Point, attended by Capt. Cook and two young gentlemen whom your father, ever attentive to the service, wished should be instructed in the business. From that period, I had the honour of a most intimate and friendly acquaintance with your worthy father, and during our stay at Halifax, whenever I could get a moment of time from my duty, I was on board the *Pembroke* where the great cabin, dedicated to scientific purposes and mostly taken up with a drawing table, furnished no room for idlers. Under Capt. Simcoe's eye, Mr. Cook and myself compiled materials for a chart of the Gulf and River Saint Lawrence, which plan at his decease was dedicated to Sir Charles Saunders; with no alterations than what Mr. Cook and I made coming up the River. Another chart of the River, including Chaleur and Gaspé Bays, mostly taken from plans in Admiral Durell's possession, was compiled and drawn under your father's inspection, and sent by him for immediate publication to Mr. Thos. Jeffrey, predecessor to Mr. Faden. These charts were of much use, as some copies came out prior to our sailing from Halifax for Quebec in 1759. By the drawing of these plans under so able an instructor, Mr. Cook could not fail to improve and thoroughly brought in his hand as well as in drawing as protracting etc., and by your father's finding the latitudes and longitudes along the Coast of America, principally Newfoundland and Gulf of Saint Lawrence, so erroneously heretofore laid down, he was convinced of the propriety of making surveys of these parts. In consequence, he told Capt. Cook that as he had mentioned to several of his friends in power, the necessity of having surveys of these parts and astronomical observations made as soon as peace was restored, he would recommend him to make himself competent to the business by learning Spherical Trigonometry, with the practical part of Astronomy, at the same time giving him Leadbitter's works, a great authority on astronomy, etc., at that period, of which Mr. Cook assisted by his explanations of difficult passages, made infinite use, and fulfilled the expectations entertained of him by your father, in his survey of Newfoundland: Mr. Cook frequently expressed to me the obligations he was under to Captain Simcoe and on my meeting him in London in the year 1776, after his several discoveries, he confessed most candidly that the several improvements and instructions he had received on board the Pembroke had been the sole foundation of the services he had been enabled to perform. I must now return to Louisbourg where, being General Wolfe's Engineer during the attack on that place, I was present at a conversation on the subject of sailing for Quebec that fall. The General and Captain Simcoe gave it as their joint opinion it might be reduced the same campaign, but this sage advice was overruled by the contrary opinions of the Admirals, who conceived the season too far advanced, so that only a few ships went with General Wolfe to Gaspe, etc., to make a diversion at the mouth of the River St. Lawrence. Again early in the spring following, had Captain Simcoe's proposition to Admiral Durrell been put into execution, of proceeding with his own ship, the Pembroke; the Sutherland, Captain Rous, and some frigates, via Gut of Canso, for the river St. Lawrence, in order to intercept the French supplies, there is not the least doubt but that Monsieur Cannon with his whole convoy must have been taken, as he only made the river six days before Admiral Durrell, as we learned from a French brig taken off Gaspe. At this place, being on board the Princess Amelia, I had the mortification of being present whilst the minute guns were firing on the melancholy occasion of Captain Simcoe's remains being committed to the deep. Had he lived to have got to Quebec, great matter of triumph would have been afforded him on account of his spirited opposition to many captains of the navy, who had given it as their opinion that ships of the line could not proceed up the river, whereas our whole fleet got up perfectly safe. Could I have recourse to my journals, which have unfortunately been lost, it would have been in my power to have recounted many circumstances with more minuteness than I am at present enabled to do.

I have the honour to remain, Sir,
   With great respect,
      Your most devoted and most obedient and humble servant,

Samuel Holland.

[On the back of the letter John Graves Simcoe added:]

Major Holland told me that my father was applied to know whether his body should be preserved to be buried on shore, he replied: 'Apply your pitch to its proper purpose; keep your lead to mend the shot holes, and commit me to the deep.'[2]

THE RELATIONSHIPS BETWEEN
JAMES COOK, JOHN SIMCOE, SAMUEL HOLLAND AND JAMES WOLFE

General James Wolfe arrived at Halifax on 30 May 1759 ahead of the campaign against Quebec. According to Ashley Bowen, one of the first things Wolfe did was to visit *Pembroke*. Bowen wrote:

> As soon as the Neptune had come to anchor, I walk[ing] the quarterdeck of the Pembroke, saw a barge steering for us. I said, 'This barge is coming for us!' and as the orders are 4 men for side, four men for side these were placed, and as the Setter [sic] came up he said, 'Is Captain Simcoe on board?' The answer was 'Yes.' He paid no compliment to officer, but crossed the quarterdeck and went past the sentry into the cabin. Abd when Mr. Norman, our First Lieutenant, saw the surprise he inquired of the coxswain which was coming up the gan[gway], 'Who is this gentleman that came so on board?'. 'General Wolfe!' ... General [Wolfe] I believe he stayed with Captain John Simcoe upwards of half an hour.[3]

Such a visit suggests that Wolfe and Simcoe were already friends and that Wolfe valued Simcoe's opinion.

The origins of that friendship may lie in the meeting of James Cook with Samuel Holland at Louisbourg the previous year. Holland, then a lieutenant, was attached to Wolfe's command as engineer and was engaged in making surveys and preparing plans during the siege of Louisbourg. Wolfe appears to have had a high regard for Holland, and the men became close friends – evidenced by him giving Holland a brace of inscribed duelling pistols (made by Barber and sold by John Richards, 85 Strand). Holland met Cook and he began to spend a great deal of time on *Pembroke* with Cook and Simcoe. It is probable that Wolfe's permission would have been required and it is possible that Wolfe also visited *Pembroke* to meet Holland's new friends. Wolfe found an ally in Simcoe, who was all for pressing on to attack Quebec in 1758, as Holland confirmed in his letter to Simcoe.[4]

Wolfe is supposed to have held a very poor opinion of Admiral Philip Durell, which may have originated from this meeting, where Durell was one of those urging caution. Durell's standing was not helped when Saunders and Wolfe found him still in port when they reached Halifax in 1759. Holland reported that Durell had declined Simcoe's proposal for *Pembroke* to lead a small flotilla to patrol in the Gulf of St Lawrence. No doubt Wolfe learned of this when he called on Simcoe.

Pembroke sailed from Halifax with Simcoe and Cook a few days later, but Simcoe died on 14 May. Holland was reunited with Wolfe at Quebec. As Wolfe's engineer, Holland was in a position to recommend Cook for the various operations he carried out and which brought him into personal contact with the general. Holland claimed to have joined Wolfe on the battlefield after Wolfe had been hit and to have been one of the people present when the general died.

Further evidence of the close relationship between Wolfe and Holland comes from a letter written on 14 May 1789 after Holland's salary had been cut appreciably. Holland wrote to William Pitt (the Younger), the prime minister, petitioning for restitution: 'Having had the honour and good fortune to be recommended to the Notice and Patronage of your Excellent father the Earl of Chatham, by my good friends General Wolfe, after the Campaign of 1758 and General Murray after that of 1759 who presented to him my Plans of the Gloriuos Attacks at Louisbourg and Quebec . . .'[5] A supporting letter was enclosed, which said:

> . . . That when General Amherst took the command of the Army his Lordship was pleased to continue your Memorialist as Acting Engineer, and at the landing at Louisburg his Lordship approved of General Wilfe's Proposal to have your Memorialist with him as an Engineer to carry on the attack from the Lighthouse to the West Gate. That after the surrender of Louisburg your Memorialist surveyed the said Town and its Environs and mad a Plan of the same, with a View of the whole Attack which General Wolfe was pleased (at his Return to England) to present to the late Lord Chatham. That at General Wolfe's arrival at Halifax in Nova Scotia in the Spring 1759 he was pleased to take your Memorialist with him as Engineer on the Expedition against Canada, and promoted him to a Captaincy, and that your Memorialist remained with General Wolfe to the moment of his death.[6]

Two possible benefactors were taken from Cook in 1759 with the deaths of Simcoe and Wolfe. He had also, however, been mixing with senior figures and showing his worth and ability.

We can, though, consider the state of marine surveying at the time, and the texts and the instruments available; we can also extrapolate back from the writings of Cook, Wales and Bayly in the 1760s and 1770s, which provide a few clues.

During his time on the North Sea and then in his initial period in the Royal Navy, Cook learned the fundamentals of navigation and how to pilot a ship from A to B. To this he would have added various skills involved in using factors such as winds, tides and currents. He would also have developed a rudimentary knowledge of astronomy sufficient to be able to take sightings of the sun, moon and stars so that he could determine location and set a course. His logbook for *Eagle* records latitude, longitude and other features, though we have no way of knowing whether Cook was already taking those sightings himself or simply recording the work of others. From what we know of Cook, it is more probable that he could take sightings himself and certainly, by the time he had become master on *Pembroke*, he was proficient in these areas. Cook, though, in 1758 was ready to advance himself further, as ERG Taylor wrote:

> Nothing less than the most efficient methods and procedures available would satisfy him, whether for marine surveying, charting or navigating. He was alive to all that was going

on around him, to all that was new in his profession. And he was willing, when already in adult life, to set himself to the daunting task of mastering the necessary preliminaries – to getting a grasp of elementary mathematics and astronomy, disciplining himself to handle instruments of precision, to make the tedious records of innumerable delicate observations.[7]

Cook's introduction to the world of marine surveying, navigation and astronomy was well timed. New developments were taking place as people worked on the scientific principles underlying these disciplines. The 1740s and 1750s saw many textbooks published dealing with surveying and navigation. Holland mentions that Leadbetter's two books were present in Simcoe's small library, available to Cook. It possibly carried some of the following selection of titles:

James Atkinson, *A Compleat System of Navigation: in Two Parts. I. Atkinson's Epitome. II. Navigation New Modell'd: or, the Whole Art Performed, Without Tables or Instruments*, Dublin: 1750.

Nathaniel Colson, *The Mariners New Kalendar. Containing the Principles of Arithmetic and Geometry*, London: 1749.

John Hammond, *The Practical Surveyor: Containing the Most Approved Methods for Surveying of Lands and Waters, by the Several Instruments now in use Particularly Exemplified with the Common and New Theodolites*, 3rd edn, London: 1750.

Charles Leadbetter, *Astronomy; or, The True System of the Planets Demonstrated. Wherein are Shewn by Instrument, their Anomalies, Heliocentrick and Geocentric Places both in Longitude and Latitude*, London: 1727.

Charles Leadbetter, *The Young Mathematician's Companion, Being a Compleat Tutor to the Mathematicks*, 2nd edn, London: 1748.

John Love, *Geodæsia: or, The Art of Surveying and Measuring of Land Made Easy*, 6th edn, London: 1753.

Archibald Patoun, *A Complete Treatise of Practical Navigation Demonstrated from its First Principles: Together with all the Necessary Tables to which are Added the Useful Theorems of Mensuration, Surveying, and Gauging with their Application to Practice*, 2nd edn, London: 1739.

John Robertson, *The Elements of Navigation; Containing the Theory and Practice. With all the Necessary Tables and Compendiums for Finding the Latitude and Longitude at Sea*, 2 vols, London: 1754.

Henry Wilson, *Navigation New Modelled: or, A Treatise of Geometrical, Trigonometrical, Arithmetical, Instrumental, and Practical Navigation*, London, 1750.

Henry Wilson, *Surveying Improved: or, The Whole Art, Both in Theory and Practice, Fully Demonstrated. In Four Parts*, 4th edn, with additions, London: 1755.

It was also an exciting time in respect of instrumentation and especially so for British sailors. British scientists and craftsmen were at the forefront of new developments in instrumentation and processes, which then were accessible to the Royal Navy. Telescopes, compasses, theodolites, sextants and chronometers made huge advances during this period, allowing sailors and surveyors to do their work more efficiently. The instrument-makers were mainly concentrated on or near the Strand and Fleet Street in London. George Adams, Jonathan Sissons, John Bird, Jesse Ramsden, John Short, Edward Nairne, Benjamin Cole and the Dollonds (father and son) were some of the foremost craftsmen working at the time and Cook used instruments by most of these men at some point.

But, as EGR Taylor wrote:

> It was, indeed, a task for mathematicians and astronomers, not for the sailors, to lay down new principles and new observations or calculations by which a ship's position could be found and her course directed at sea. And it was for the mathematical and optical instrument-makers to design and perfect the instruments by which such observations could be made. But in the last resort everything depended upon the ship's captains, the masters and the pilots.[8]

Although new instruments were becoming available, they were often costly and out of the price range of most seamen for them to own themselves. Cook as a master of *Pembroke* was earning £5 12s per month in 1758, when a plane table cost £5 15s 6d and a three-foot pocket telescope cost £1 5s, so that any instruments accessible to Cook would normally belong to senior officers or to the ship itself. By this time, though, Cook had probably invested in his own telescope and possibly had his own Hadley's octant, both instruments being important for ships' masters and their role in navigation.

Cook's introduction to surveying happened through an army engineer and it was army rather than naval influence that governed Cook's first few years as a surveyor. The instruments he became familiar with were obtained from the Office of Ordnance, which was based at the Tower of London and at Woolwich. The Ordnance purchased instruments and maintained a store for them at the Tower, and they were dispensed as required. Records show that drawing, optical and surveying instruments were supplied in January 1758 to engineers bound for Halifax and subsequently Louisbourg.[9] All the instruments involved were made by George Adams, who described himself as 'Mathematical Instrument Maker to his Majesty's Office of Ordnance'.

When Cook was appointed to survey Newfoundland in 1763 it was to the Office of Ordnance at the Tower that he went to obtain the services of a surveying draughtsman, as a drawing office was another department based there. In 1763, Cook submitted his first shopping list of tools for surveying and by the end of the year Governor Graves was requesting a theodolite for Cook to use.

Cook also asked for one each of a Knight's azimuth compass and a Knight's steering compass. Gowin Knight, a physician, had studied magnetism and developed geomagnetic instruments, many of which were made by Adams. Knight improved and introduced two maritime instruments: a steering compass, which showed a ship's course, and an azimuth compass, which measured the angle of variation (the angle at a particular place between geographical north and the direction in which a compass needle is pointing).

As mentioned above, Cook was already using a quadrant for navigational purposes. By the early 1760s he was using a sextant – the successor to the octant – and possessed his own instrument (made by Bird) when he sailed to the Pacific. The sextant was developed by John Campbell (who later introduced Cook at the Royal Society) and Bird by modifying a Hadley octant and extending its scale to 120 degrees. This was the first marine sextant and, used with Meyer's lunar tables, revolutionised navigation. John Bird was one of the finest makers of scientific instruments. He was employed in the workshop of Jonathan Sisson but in 1745 established in his own workshop on the Strand, making machine tools and small mathematical instruments. Bird gained a reputation for large astronomical instruments and he made the one-foot radius astronomical quadrant taken on *Endeavour* (it is possible that Cook had access to one in Newfoundland). Jonathan Sisson, Bird's teacher, made the original octants for John Hadley.

Sailors were already using simple telescopes and Cook possessed one made by Edward Nairne. At about this time, however, developments were taking place in telescopes to be used on land for astronomical purposes. John Dollond and his son, Peter Dollond, were makers of optical scientific instruments, specialising in telescopes and they had a shop, the Golden Spectacles and Sea Quadrant, on the Strand. John Dollond improved refracting telescopes and took out a patent on the achromatic telescope lens. James Short was another maker of optical instruments; many of his instruments were used during the transits of Venus in 1761 and 1769, even though he died in 1768. Cook carried Dollonds' and Short's instruments to the Pacific but in Newfoundland he had already used an instrument made by Francis Watkins: 'The Navy Board have been pleas'd to supply His Majestys Bark the Endeavour under my command with the Reflecting Telescope that was on board the Grenville Schooner for making Astronomical Observations at Newfoundland.'[10] Cook acknowledged the contribution of the instrument-makers during his second voyage to the Pacific: 'Much credit is also due to the Mathematical Instrument makers for the improvements and accuracy with which they make their instruments.'[11]

Before the 1750s most marine charting was done at sea using running traverse. A ship would sail along a coast taking regular intersecting cross-bearings of features on the land using compass and quadrant, all the while keeping a record of course and measuring distance sailed with the ship's log. Such charting was prone to errors, partly from the difficulty of fixing the ship's true position and partly from problems in sighting the land features. Murdoch Mackenzie, an Orkney sailor-surveyor, was one of the first to blend this traditional marine charting with land-based surveying practice. Mackenzie set down base lines on land and used a theodolite and triangulation to survey the land features along a coast before adding to them by taking observations inshore and at sea. In this fashion the underlying basis of the survey was more accurately established and the less precise marine components would not compromise the end result unduly. It is not known if Cook was aware of Mackenzie's work but he developed a similar strategy. Seeing Holland at work in Kennington Cove, Cook saw how he could add Holland's land-based techniques to his own and produce more accurate charts.

New, more careful surveyors such as Mackenzie and Cook might produce better charts, but that did not mean that their charts would be available for others to use. Commercial interests got in the way, especially as the navy did not itself publish charts or assist in their publication in any way, leaving it to the compiler of a new chart to find a printer to have it published. The printers of maps and charts were not always the most obliging or scrupulous. When it came to verifying data and keeping them up to date, they often copied from each other, perpetuating errors, and were more concerned with selling old stock than printing new corrected editions. Cook wrote several years later of 'the compilers and publishers who publish to the world the rude sketches of the navigator as accurate surveys'.[12]

The naval officer compiling a new chart needed permission from the Admiralty to publish it but the printing was at his own risk and cost. Copyright thus remained with the compiler unless signed away to the printer. Cook used Thomas Jefferys for his New-foundland charts and at first retained copyright. He appears to have sold the copyright to Jefferys before he left for the Pacific, as later versions belonged to the printer.

The Decision Not to Press on to Quebec

The siege of Louisbourg had started later in the year than planned and had taken longer than anticipated. Given that winter arrives in the St Lawrence River in October, it was felt by many that it was then too late in the year to press on to Quebec in order to attack the fortress there. While some officers, such as James Wolfe, were all for sailing to Quebec, Admiral Boscawen decided that it was too late and the attack would be made in 1759. About the same time, General Jeffery Amherst, in command of the British army, learned of the defeat of British troops under General James Abercromby at Fort Carillon (Ticonderoga). Amherst decided his priority was to send troops to assist Abercromby; leaving a garrison at Louisbourg under Whitmore, Amherst sailed for Boston.

Amherst also decided that they would make examples of other French settlements around the Gulf of St Lawrence by burning and destroying houses and fishing boats and removing inhabitants. Robert Monckton was sent to destroy the French settlements in the St John valley (now New Brunswick); Lord Rollo was sent to take possession of Île St Jean (Prince Edward Island); and James Wolfe, with three battalions convoyed by a naval squadron of twenty ships and transports under Sir Charles Hardy, was to lay waste to the settlements and fishery in the Gulf of St Lawrence.

Pembroke was part of Hardy's squadron, which left Louisbourg on 29 August having taken on soldiers:

23 AUGUST. Received on board 77 soldiers.

29 AUGUST. 4 pm Rear admiral Hardy made the signal to weigh. At 6 weighed and came to sail in company with Admiral Hardy in the Royal William, Bedford, Devonshire, Lancaster, Vanguard, Juno, Kennington, Etna fireship and 11 sail of transports.

After a slow passage across the Gulf of St Lawrence, the squadron anchored in Gaspé Bay on 6 September.

6 SEPTEMBER. At 2am anchored in Gaspe Bay in 19 fathoms of water. At 5 sent the long boat and cutter up to the transports to assist landing the troops.

Most inhabitants had already fled into the woods, but some were caught and taken prisoner. Wolfe sent separate forces to repeat the process around the region. One group was dispatched across the peninsula to attack Mont Louis on the St Lawrence while another was sent to the Baie des Chaleurs. Wolfe remained at Gaspé, where everything was burnt. Wolfe later wrote to Amherst that his task had been accomplished, and at the same time attempted to absolve himself from any blame for the actions: 'We have done a great deal of mischief, – spread the terror of His Majesty's arms through the whole gulf; but have added nothing to the reputation of them.'[13]

Cook, meanwhile, had found time to make a survey of Gaspé Bay and the inner harbour. Holland was not present in this expedition so it represents Cook's own work and the subsequent chart would be the first one he published.

Cook also wrote sailing directions for Gaspé and islands in the gulf. The National Library of Australia has manuscript pages that contain directions for Cape Gaspey and Cape Rosier, for Bird's Island and for Brion Island.[14] Cook reworked the information for his *Directions for Sailing from the Harbour of Louisbourgh to Quebec*, a manuscript written at Halifax in 1761 and now held at National Archives, Kew.[15]

While the army was chasing the French Canadians, reports were received about a French squadron leaving Quebec for France. Hardy took his ships back to sea to patrol for six days but after seeing no signs of the French they returned to Gaspé on 24 September to collect the army.

27 SEPTEMBER. At 9am weighed, came to sail per signal.

29 SEPTEMBER. At 7pm anchored before Louisbourg in 30 fathoms water with the small bower, the fleet in company.

It took three days before *Pembroke* could anchor in the harbour and discharge the sick and wounded to hospital. The crew then spent a month in Louisbourg with little to do and the only excitement occurred when 'One of the wrecks in the harbour's mouth broke away and drove across the harbour upon the north shore.' During this time Cook went in a schooner around the coast to obtain coal from 'Marquin Bay'. This was the Port Morien (Baie de Mordienne) coal mine, which was the first commercial coal mine in North America, having commenced production in 1720. In the 1760s Lieutenant Governor Michael Francklin tried to revive mining coal for export from Cape Breton but found that it had been banned eight years earlier by the Board of Trade. Francklin described the mine in 1766:

> There is at Cow Bay [Port Morien] a picketed fort 100 ft. square, with a blockhouse, barracks, and stores for lodging the workmen, tools, and provisions. Also, a wharf convenient for loading at the mine. That the mine is in good order and well-propped. That the vein appears to be good and large. That twenty men may be employed daily.[16]

Cook found the time to survey Louisbourg Harbour and wrote sailing directions (see section 'Sailing Directions for the Harbour of Louisbourg'), now held in the Houghton Library, Harvard University. Cook also included these directions in his *Directions for Sailing from the Harbour of Louisbourgh to Quebec*.

SAILING DIRECTIONS FOR THE HARBOUR OF LOUISBOURG

Author: James Cook.
Place and time when there: Harbour of Louisbourg in Cape Breton 1758
Descriptions for sailing in and out of Ports with soundings, Marks for particular rocks, shoals, etc, with the Lat., Long. Tides and Variations of the Compass.

In the mouth of this Harbour lies two small islands, the outermost is called Green Island and the innermost the Island Battery by reason of it being fortified. Between this last and Point Maurepas whereon is the town of Louisbourg, is a chain of rocks which shows themselves at low water. The passage into the Harbour is between the islands and the Light House which stands on the NE side of the entrance. It is near ½ mile broad and hath therein 10 and 11 fathom water and sets too on each side until you are within the light house for, from about ½ deg. D from the light house point to the point of the NE harbor on which lies the wreck of the Prudent is a ledge of rocks which runs off near two cables lengths. Upon this ledge is a rock which shows itself at half ebb. One third of the way from the Island Battery to Point Maurepas is a round rock which always shews itself called the Bearck rock. From this rock runs out a spit more than one cable length into the harbor. It lies in and out with the south part of Green Island and rock in one. It is very narrow and hath upon it near 3 fathoms at low water. Between the wreck of the Prudent and the Grand Battery on the opposite shore is a middle ground whereon is 14 feet water. Between it and the wreck is 7, 8 and 9 fathoms and between it and the flat ground which runs off from the Grand Battery is 3½ and 4 fathoms.

Being off the Harbor, bring the Light House to bear any way between the N and NW by W and steer for it until you bring the westernmost tower of the Grand Battery before the middle of a white stone quarry that is behind the battery. Keep in the direction until you are within the spit of the Breack Rock, then haul up for the town and anchor before Point Maurepas in 7 and 8 fathoms water. To sail in the NE Harbour keep the tower and quarry as above until the breack rock is brought in a line with a rock which lies between Green Island and Pt Maurepas, these two rocks in one leads you into the NE Harbour between the middle ground and the wreck of the Prudent, which last you may borrow pretty close to. After you are above this you may anchor any where along the SE shore in 8, 7 & 6 fathoms water very good holding ground. This is by far the best harbor as you are entirely sheltered from the sea and wind.

Latitude 46°N Longitude by computation.[17]

Finally, on 14 November, the fleet sailed from Louisbourg for Halifax, the latter being open all year while the former would regularly be iced in. *Pembroke* anchored at Halifax on the 18th.

18 NOVEMBER. ½ past 6 Anchored per signal with the best bower in 17 fathoms water just above Major's Beach. At 10 anchored in Halifax before the town.

Cook settled in for what would be the first of four winters based in Halifax. The crew began the routine of cleaning and repairing *Pembroke* with the cold and tedium only relieved by occasional events:

11 DECEMBER. ½ past 5 am The house in which the sailmakers lodged took fire by accident and in a short time consumed the whole, Andrew Lamb, seaman assistant to the sailmaker was burnt.

For Cook, though, it was a most important time. Samuel Holland was also in Halifax and spent much time working with Cook and Simcoe on *Pembroke*. While teaching Cook the rudiments of surveying and cartography, Holland also worked with him on the production of a chart of the St Lawrence River in readiness for the intended attack on Quebec in 1759. The British had previously only had very poor old charts of the river, which had caused earlier expeditions against the city to fail. However, Durell and his ships had captured French charts, and Holland and Cook used these to prepare better and more reliable ones for the British to use. Cook had begun combining the skills of four disciplines – navigation, astronomy, surveying and cartography – to become the consummate naval hydrographer.

❧ 8 ❧

Quebec, 1759

James Cook began 1759 in the cold port of Halifax, Nova Scotia. He was master of HMS *Pembroke*, a ship that had taken part in the successful attack on Louisbourg in 1758, but that action had taken longer than anticipated and the follow-up attack on Quebec had been postponed until 1759. After the siege of Louisbourg, Philip Durell had been promoted to Rear Admiral of the Blue and placed in command of a small squadron instructed to remain in Halifax over the winter. *Pembroke* was part of that squadron.

In late 1758 Cook had taken part in a raid on Gaspé in the Gulf of St Lawrence. He surveyed the bay and harbour and his resulting chart was forwarded to Britain, where it was published by Mount and Page of Tower Hill in early 1759. It was dedicated to the master and wardens of the Trinity House of Deptford 'by James Cook Master of his Majesty's Ship the Pembroke'. It is unclear how the manuscript chart reached London and who had it printed. It is unlikely that at that time Cook had his own naval agent to organise things for him in his absence from Britain so it is more probable that Captain John Simcoe arranged everything. It was still less than two years since Cook had been passed as a master by Trinity House and it was possibly as a sign of thanks whereby Cook dedicated the chart to that institution. Interestingly, the chart is drawn with SW at the top. There are also two accompanying coastal views, one of which is the coast outside the bay down to Bonaventura Island. Mount and Page have added elaborate cartouches to enclose the title and scale.

Durell spent the time in Halifax improving the facilities in the town, building storehouses and preparing a wharf. Realising that there was a shortage of seamen, Durell arranged for proclamations to be issued in New England inviting volunteers to enlist in the Royal Navy for the forthcoming expedition to Quebec:

> The ships here, and at Louisbourg, being short of their compliments of men, sometime ago I wrote to the Governors of the different Provinces desiring their assistance in raising such a number as would be sufficient to compleat them, and as an encouragement to such as would enter, I have offer'd them His Majesty's Royal bounty, and to discharge and send them to Boston, after the service of the ensuing September is over.[1]

Thomas Pownall issued a proclamation in Massachusetts on 29 March, which prompted a group of Marblehead (near Boston, Massachusetts) seamen to volunteer. Among them was Ashley Bowen (see section 'Ashley Bowen'), who would become a seaman on *Pembroke* and record incidents involving James Cook.

Admiral Boscawen had instructed Durell to prepare his squadron for sea as early as possible in the spring of 1759, ready to patrol the approaches to the St Lawrence River

ASHLEY BOWEN (1728–1813)

Ashley Bowen was born on 8 January 1728 in Marblehead, Massachusetts, and went to sea aged eleven. After the death of his mother, he was apprenticed in 1741 to a local sea captain, Peter Hall. With Hall, Bowen sailed to Europe and the Mediterranean but Hall was a cruel master and after four years Bowen fled when their ship was in the West Indies. Bowen relates that before then, during time on the island of Minorca in the Mediterranean, he was baptised and various Royal Navy captains were invited to attend the ceremony. One of those captains was John Simcoe, later captain of *Pembroke*. Bowen spent the next years crisscrossing the North Atlantic visiting Britain, the West Indies and Newfoundland as well as working on coastal vessels from North Carolina to New England. In 1758 he married the first of his three wives.

Early in 1759 Philip Durell, at that time in command of British ships at Halifax in Nova Scotia, sent word down to New England urging men to sign up and help in the forthcoming expedition to attack Quebec. Bowen was among a group of thirty-three seamen from Marblehead who were transported to Halifax on *Apollo* and were allocated to the ships *Pembroke* and *Squirrel*.

Bowen kept a journal during his time on *Pembroke*; he claimed to have acted as a midshipman but appeared on the muster as an able seaman. The journal provides another account of events on the ship, including the death of John Simcoe and the survey of the Traverse. Bowen often puts himself at the centre of many actions and credits himself with a greater role in some than is probable. As well as his writings, Bowen drew many sketches of the vessels he served on and depicted them in action. It is thanks to Bowen, therefore, that we have some of the only visual records of *Pembroke* at Halifax, on the way to Quebec, and at Quebec. Bowen was not a trained artist and some of his sketches have a naive quality but many are delightfully charming and represent a very important part of the Cook story.

In 1760 Bowen enlisted on a Boston ship, *Swallow*, which carried oxen to Quebec. There he met Cook once more and apparently drew *Northumberland* for Cook (sadly the drawing is lost). Bowen effectively retired from the sea in 1763 to be with his family in Marblehead. He worked as a rigger for the Marblehead fleet; his wife made flags. Life became difficult in 1776 as a result of his pro-British opinions and little work went his way. Somehow, he managed to survive and lived to be eighty-five. William Bentley, a Salem cleric, visited Bowen regularly in his last years and recorded that he invariably remembered with great pride and affection his time with his friend 'Cook the circumnavigator'. He remained a British loyalist through the War of American Independence and afterwards, but was also loyal to Marblehead and lived there until his death.

in order to stop French reinforcements and supplies reaching Quebec. However, Halifax experienced a bad winter and, in March 1759, Durell wrote to the Admiralty describing the conditions:

> This winter has proved the severest that has been known since the settling of this place – for these two months past I have not heard from Louisbourg – many vessels have attempted to go there, but have met with ice eighteen or twenty leagues from the land, so were obliged to return, after having had some of their people froze to death, and other frost bitten to that degree, as to lose legs and arms.[2]

Despite this, the ships were ready by 8 April 1759 but adverse conditions still prevented their departure and they were still in port when Saunders and the British fleet arrived in Halifax on 30 April. Unfortunately for Durell, a small French squadron carrying Bougainville and some relief managed to sail undetected through the pack ice in the Gulf of St Lawrence and on to Quebec. Durell would redeem himself somewhat in leading his squadron up the St Lawrence, preparing the way for the main fleet.

In the meantime, Cook and *Pembroke* had been stuck in Halifax, the ice and winter conditions at sea keeping the ships in port. The crew found ways of passing the time:

11 JANUARY. At 11 Fitzpatrick stabbed John Lamb under the short rib in a very dangerous manner. Put the former under confinement.

23 JANUARY. Confined the surgeon's mate for drunkeness and neglect of duty.

19 FEBRUARY. Court martial was held on board here, the trial of Edward Barton, surgeon's mate for drunkenness and neglect of duty – broke.

Sickness and death were common and not just restricted to the seamen. Officers also succumbed, leading to promotions and reorganisation:

27 MARCH. Departed this life Mr George Allen, first lieutenant.

29 MARCH. Mr Benjamin Bechinoe was appointed third lieutenant, Mr. Allen deceased.

The certificate of discharge by reason of death for George Allen, first lieutenant on HMS *Pembroke*, dated 12 May 1759, was offered for sale in 2008. The document, signed by Cook, had been in private hands; its present whereabouts are unknown.

Among the other ships in Halifax at the time was *Prince of Orange* and its purser was Richard Short. Short was also an artist and it is thanks to him that we have some images of Halifax and Quebec, drawn as events unfolded. Short later arranged for the marine artist, Dominic Serres, to develop his sketches into paintings. It is possible that *Pembroke* and *Northumberland*, Cook's ships, feature in these paintings, but actual identification is not possible.

Meanwhile in Britain, plans were being finalised and appointments made for the forthcoming campaign. Admiral Sir Charles Saunders (see section 'Sir Charles Saunders') was selected to command the fleet to be employed at Quebec. Saunders was another officer who would be impressed with Cook and who helped to promote Cook's career. He was

SIR CHARLES SAUNDERS (*c*1713–75)

Charles Saunders was baptised on 30 July 1713 in Holborn, the son of Ambrose and Ann Saunders. He entered the navy on HMS *Seahorse* on 17 October 1727 as captain's servant for his father. He then served in the Mediterranean before passing his lieutenant's examination in June 1734.

After several appointments, on 14 August 1739 he joined *Centurion* under Captain George Anson. Saunders sailed as third lieutenant on Anson's voyage to the Pacific in 1739, and returned to Britain in 1743 as a post captain. Anson remained a guiding and influential person throughout Saunders's career. Saunders then served successfully on several ships during the remaining years of the War of Austrian Succession, including securing a £30,000 share from capturing a Spanish vessel in 1746.

He became an MP for Plymouth in 1750 and married a banker's daughter in 1751. Saunders was commander-in-chief on the Newfoundland station in 1752 and in May 1754 he was returned through Lord Anson's influence as MP for Hedon in Yorkshire, a constituency he continued to represent until his death. In June 1756, Saunders was promoted rear admiral and served in the Mediterranean under Hawke after the loss of Minorca. Saunders assumed command for a few months in early 1757.

On 14 February 1759, Saunders was promoted Vice Admiral of the Blue, and appointed naval commander for the campaign to capture Quebec. Much of the success of the campaign was due to Saunders's management and his good relationship with Wolfe and his brigadiers. Saunders was received by the king on his return to London and applauded in the House of Commons. In April 1760 he was appointed commander-in-chief in the Mediterranean, where he successfully blockaded Cadiz. During his absence he was installed as a Knight of the Bath in 1761. Saunders served as a Lord Commissioner of the Admiralty and was briefly first lord from 1765 to 1766. He was promoted to admiral on 18 October 1770 but did not see active service again. He died at his home in London on 7 December 1775 and was buried in Westminster Abbey. He and his wife had no children.

Saunders arranged for Cook's chart of the St Lawrence to be published and Cook dedicated it to the admiral. Cook later named several features around the world after Saunders: headlands in New Zealand, Australia, South Georgia and the South Shetlands (later realised to be an island).

later described by Horace Walpole: 'The Admiral was a pattern of the most sturdy bravery, united with the most unaffected modesty. No man said less, or deserved more. Simplicity in his manners, generosity, and good-nature adorned his genuine love of his country.'[3]

James Wolfe (see section 'James Wolfe'), who had done so well at Louisbourg in 1758, returned to Britain late that year on *Namur* with Boscawen, but did so without permission and for this he was reproached by Pitt. It does not appear to have done him harm as, in

JAMES WOLFE (1727–1759)

James Wolfe was born in Westerham, Kent, on 2 January 1727. His father was Lieutenant General Edward Wolfe, one of a family of professional soldiers, and James was destined to follow in their footsteps. He was commissioned second lieutenant in his father's 1st Marines in November 1741. In April 1742 Wolfe, now with Duroure's 12th Foot, was ordered to Flanders but remained in quarters. He saw action for the first time in the battle of Dettingen on 27 June 1743; he came to the notice of the Duke of Cumberland and his subsequent career owed much to the duke's patronage. In 1745 Cumberland, now in command of the allied forces, signed Wolfe's commission as major of brigade in Flanders.

Wolfe returned to Britain, where he took part in countering the 1745 Jacobite Rebellion. In 1746 he became aide-de-camp to General Henry Hawley and took part in the battle of Culloden Moor in April. He was recalled to Flanders in November and in 1747, serving as major of brigade to Sir John Mordaunt, was badly wounded at the battle of Laffeldt on 21 June. Cumberland tried unsuccessfully to assist Wolfe's promotion in 1748, but a different attempt by the duke led to Wolfe becoming a major in Lord George Sackville's 20th Foot in 1749 and lieutenant colonel in 1750.

By this time Wolfe had met Elizabeth Lawson, a niece of Sir John Mordaunt, but his parents disapproved of the match and she rejected him, causing Wolfe great sadness. Wolfe was now no longer being championed by Cumberland and he failed to obtain the colonelcy of the 20th Foot, both in 1755 and 1756. Instead, he accepted the post of quartermaster general in Ireland in 1757. However, it did not gain him the rank of full colonel that he had hoped for and he was taken on to the staff of Sir John Mordaunt for the raid on Rochefort on the west coast of France. They sailed on 6 September but returned in failure at the end of the month. Wolfe, though, was not associated with blame for this defeat and he became a colonel in April 1758.

Pitt's military adviser, Sir John Ligonier, appointed Wolfe a brigadier general for the campaign to North America for attacks on Louisbourg and Quebec. He was to serve under Major General Jeffery Amherst in the expeditionary force. Wolfe led the landing on 8 June 1758 in Gabarus Bay and was most fortunate when some of his men misunderstood his order to withdraw and forced a landing. Wolfe quickly followed and secured the beachhead. After that Wolfe was the driving force of the siege and a major factor in the British success. Wolfe assumed that Amherst would move at once on Quebec. However, the siege had taken too long and Admiral Boscawen advised against attempting Quebec that year. Amherst also learned of Abercromby's loss at Ticonderoga and went to assist him. Wolfe led a force that raided French settlements around the Gulf of St Lawrence before sailing for Britain.

Wolfe wished to serve once more in Europe and petitioned Ligonier for a command in Germany. He was unsuccessful in this, but Ligonier offered him command of the British advance up the St Lawrence to attack Quebec. Before leaving for Canada, Wolfe proposed to and was accepted by Katherine Lowther. Wolfe sailed from Spithead with Admiral Charles Saunders, his naval equivalent, on

14 February 1759. They arrived at Halifax on 30 April, moved on to Louisburg and left for Quebec in early June. The fleet anchored off the Île d'Orléans near Quebec on 27 June. An eleven-week siege followed, with Wolfe becoming gradually depressed as his early plans came to nothing. Unsuccessful attacks were attempted at Beauport and Montmorency, while Montcalm, the French commander, remained in the city, refusing to be drawn out to fight a battle. Wolfe's health also suffered.

At the end of August he presented Saunders and his brigadiers with a series of options for a renewed attack on the Beauport lines, but they rejected them all and instead recommended a landing upriver of Quebec at Pointe aux Trembles for an attack from the west. Wolfe agreed but then, once again ignoring his brigadiers, modified the plan by deciding on a landing place nearer the city at L'Anse au Foulon. The attack was arranged for the night of 12 September; troops were transported by the navy during the night and they climbed the cliffs to appear at dawn on the Plains of Abraham and ready to fight the French.

Montcalm marched from Beauport and launched an attack. The French army was shot to pieces by Wolfe's battleline and utterly routed. However, Wolfe was fatally wounded during the brief battle. His body was taken back to Britain and buried at St Alfege, Greenwich. The victory, together with his death, caused Wolfe to be lionised and gained him a posthumous reputation. Only much later did people begin to question his achievements. His successes, Louisbourg and Quebec, were both achieved after pieces of great fortune: the landing at Gabarus Bay and finding the ascent at L'Anse au Foulon. However, he made the most of those opportunities, even if the second success cost him his life.

late December, Wolfe had an interview with Lord Ligonier, Pitt's military adviser, where he learned that Pitt was planning a three-pronged attack on the French in 1759. Jeffery Amherst would be in overall command but Wolfe would be promoted to major general and would have command of the river campaign up the St Lawrence River to attack Quebec. At thirty-two, Wolfe was young for such a role, but he had proved himself at Louisbourg while other officers, such as Abercromby, had failed in recent campaigns.

On 14 February, Admiral Charles Holmes and his squadron left Spithead for New York to collect troops for Quebec. Three days later Saunders on *Neptune* with Wolfe on board followed for Louisbourg. After a slow crossing, Saunders reached Louisbourg on 21 April 1759, only to be blocked by ice. He moved on to Halifax Harbour, which he entered on the 30th, only to be angry and amazed when he found Durell and his squadron still in port.

Durell was finally able to come to sail on *Princess Amelia*, but even then winds conspired to prevent the ships leaving the harbour. Cook's log recorded:

> 3 MAY. At 9am weighed per signal in company with the Princess Amelia, Rear admiral Durell. At 11 anchored with the small bower in 10 fathoms water a little above Major's Beach.
>
> 5 MAY. At 8 am weighed and came to sail. At noon Cape Sambro SW by S 4 miles.

The main body of the British force followed on 13 May transferring from Halifax to Louisbourg. Ice, which continued to block the harbour, delayed many troops joining them and delayed their departure for Quebec. Wolfe immediately had those troops who had arrived drilling and exercising. Much to Wolfe's disappointment no extra troops had been assigned to him from the West Indies so instead of an expected twelve thousand men he only had about seven and a half thousand. On 5 June the British were ready and embarked. Saunders led a fleet of 43 ships and 119 transports towards the Gulf of St Lawrence. The majority of the fleet reached the Île d'Orléans by 26 June.

Meanwhile Durrell's squadron had encountered a great quantity of loose ice at sea with attendant fog. Durell gave instructions that all ships would respond with small arms to his firing a gun every hour. By 12 May they had entered the Gulf of St Lawrence but tragedy struck on the 14th. Ashley Bowen recorded:

> 14 MAY. At 6am made a signal to speak the Admiral. Our cutter, sent her on board Admiral Durell and he made a signal for the Prince of Orange to bear down. Our captain brought on board the Captain of Marines of the Admiral and the Doctor of the Prince of Orange.

That night, at midnight, Captain John Simcoe died, probably from pneumonia. The ship was between Anticosti Island and the Gaspé Peninsula. Lieutenant John Robson wrote:

> 14 MAY. At 12 [midnight] Departed this life Captain John Simcoe.

There is confusion about what happened next. Cook wrote that Captain John Wheelock (see section 'John Wheelock') from HMS *Squirrel* went on board immediately to take the place of Simcoe. Others, including Robson and Bowen, state that a Lieutenant Collins took over temporarily. Bowen has:

> 15 MAY. At 6–7am Mr Norman went and acquainted Admiral Durell of Captain Simcoe's death. Came from the Admiral, Mr. Collins, the Second Lieutenant, to command this ship.
>
> 16 MAY. At 6pm read the funeral service over the corpse of Captain John Simcoe and threw him out at the Gun Room port where he sank immediately. We hoisted our ensign and pendent half-staff as did the Admiral and the rest of our fleet, and we fired 20 half-minute guns.

While Cook has:

> 14 MAY. 11am Captain Wheelock of the Squirrel came on board. Took upon himself the command of the ship in the room of Captain Simcoe, deceased. 6pm buried the corpse of Captain Simcoe. Fired 20 guns ½ minute between each.

Pembroke reached the Île du Bic on the 21st and was off the Île aux Lièvres (Hare Island) by the 26th. The next day Bowen stated that Wheelock joined the ship:

> 27 MAY. This evening came on board Captain J Wheelock to command this ship.

Cook reported their anchoring between the Île aux Coudres and the land on 31 May 1759. On 3 June Durell ordered Captain William Gordon of *Devonshire* to advance to the

Île d'Orléans, accompanied by *Centurion, Pembroke* and *Squirrel*. They were approaching the Traverse just downstream of the Île d'Orléans, which would require special attention. The ships' masters were to go out in small boats and survey this passage to find a route for the fleet to follow, allowing them to reach Quebec. On 4 June Saunders and Wolfe left Louisbourg with the main fleet and body of troops.

Gordon's ships were delayed for a few days by winds and only anchored near Cap Tourmente on the 8th. Cook and his colleagues began their survey in the very early hours of 9 June:

9 JUNE. At 4am a signal on board the Devonshire for all boats manned and armed in order to go and sound the Channel of the Traverse.

10 JUNE. At 3am all the boats went a sounding as before.

JOHN WHEELOCK (?–1779)

John Wheelock took over as captain of HMS *Pembroke* in May 1759 following the death of the previous captain, John Simcoe, while *Pembroke* was part of the British fleet advancing up the St Lawrence River to attack the French stronghold of Quebec.

Wheelock had been made a lieutenant on 26 June 1741 during the War of Austrian Succession. He served on *Duke*, a fireship, between 1746 and 1751, even taking charge in the absence of Captain Coleman for several months in 1746. Following several years of peace and near the beginning of the Seven Years' War, he was promoted to commander on 19 February 1756. He had command of the sloop *Fly* during 1756 and into 1757. Wheelock made captain on 21 December 1757 and was given command of HMS *Squirrel*.

Wheelock left *Squirrel* to take over on HMS *Pembroke* in 1759. He remained with the ship after the fall of Quebec when Cook moved to HMS *Northumberland*. *Pembroke* sailed to the West Indies and Wheelock was still in Jamaica and Cuba in 1763. In February 1764, they were back at Portsmouth.

In 1769 Wheelock had command of HMS *Achilles*, a guardship at Portsmouth. From there he moved in 1771 to HMS *Modeste*, and in 1778 Wheelock and HMS *Sultan*, his latest ship, were part of Admiral Byron's fleet that left Plymouth on 9 June bound to New York. In December the British sailed south to the West Indies, following d'Estaing and the French fleet.

Wheelock died in early 1779 and his will was proven in London on 20 March 1779. His brother, Anthony Wheelock of Yarmouth on the Isle of Wight, was executor and one beneficiary. The other beneficiary, in a codicil of the will, was Mary Davis from Alverstoke, near Gosport.

Anthony Wheelock died in London two years later. The brothers were perhaps the sons of Bryan Wheelock, who had worked at the Board of Trade in London. He was a clerk from 1700 to 1714 and then deputy secretary to the Board until his death in 1735.

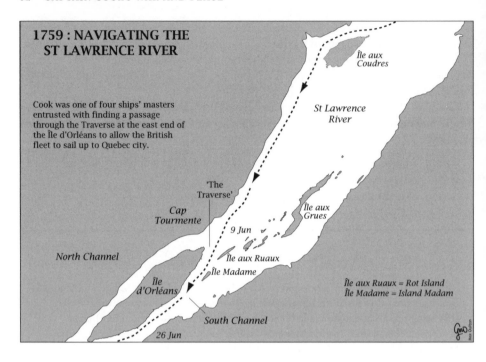

1759 : NAVIGATING THE ST LAWRENCE RIVER

Cook was one of four ships' masters entrusted with finding a passage through the Traverse at the east end of the Île d'Orléans to allow the British fleet to sail up to Quebec city.

Île aux Coudres

St Lawrence River

'The Traverse'

Cap Tourmente

9 Jun

Île aux Grues

North Channel

Île aux Ruaux

Île Madame

Île d'Orléans

South Channel

26 Jun

Île aux Ruaux = Rot Island
Île Madame = Island Madam

On 11 June Cook is reported to have 'returned satisfied with being acquainted with ye Channel', which had been marked by ships' boats and buoys. *Pembroke* and others sailed forward to wait off Île Madame.

> 13 JUNE. At 8 weighed and came to sail. At 10 anchored . . . between the Island Madam and Orleans.

Bowen added: 'Was sent a boat from our ship and one from the Devonshire and another one on the easternmost rocks of the Traverse and the other on the westernmost, one with a white flag and the other with a red, and, having a leading wind, we all came to sail and run through the Traverse.'

The French had naively assumed that the British would not be able to pass the Traverse and had, therefore, not set up any defensive positions. Only now did they send out troops and boats to fire on the British. *Squirrel* had advanced furthest and came under attack, so the other ships sent men to assist. Cook wrote:

> 14 JUNE. At 9pm every ship sent a boat manned and armed on board the Squirrel (she being the uppermost ship) to lay guard in order to prevent any surprise from the enemy.

> 16 JUNE. At 6pm a signal for all boats manned and armed to go and take a sloop which lay between the island Orleans and the north shore, which was attempted, but being attacked by a great number of boats and musketry from the shore, was obliged to return with the loss of the Squirrel's boat.

NEW FRANCE AND ITS LEADERS

French involvement with Canada began in 1534 when Jacques Cartier sailed into the Gulf of St Lawrence. He returned in 1535 and sailed up the St Lawrence as far as the future Montreal. Various unsuccessful attempts were made to establish settlements before Samuel de Champlain did so on the banks of the St Lawrence at a place called by the local Algonquin people Quebec (meaning the Narrows). The early years for the Quebec colony, or New France as it would be known, were hard, and the population grew slowly. The colony relied on France for supplies; the principal source of revenue was the fur trade. In 1642, Montreal was founded. A census by 1666 showed the population was 3,215.

New France was conscious of the expanding British colonies along the Atlantic seaboard and of the Hudson Bay Company's presence to the north, so the French sought to create a link with their colony of Louisiana by establishing a line of forts along the Mississippi and Ohio valleys. Their activity in the Ohio valley was a trigger for the war. British expeditions had already sailed up the St Lawrence on several occasions to try to conquer New France.

By 1750 the population of New France was still only fifty-five thousand. In comparison, the British colonies had twelve million people. As the Seven Years' War started, Pierre de Rigaud de Vaudreuil de Cavagnial, marquis de Vaudreuil, was appointed Governor General of New France. He had been born in Quebec in 1698 and was a proud French Canadian. He was appointed on 1 January 1755 and sailed for Quebec from Brest on 3 May 1755 in the squadron that was chased by Boscawen's ships.

Vaudreuil was affronted when the French government sent Montcalm in 1756 to command operations against the British; he felt that he was more than capable of performing the task. The new commander, Louis-Joseph de Montcalm, marquis de Montcalm, was a career soldier of no great reputation, who was born in 1712. In March 1756 he was appointed major general (maréchal de camp) and sailed from Brest. Louis-Antoine de Bougainville, the future explorer and his aide-de-camp, reported that relations were strained with the local people.

The lack of a bond between Canadians and the French army was an underlying factor in their eventual loss. Vaudreuil and Montcalm often worked against each other, rather than presenting a common front against the British. It did not help that France had lost interest in and commitment to North America, being far more concerned with the war in Europe. From 1754 onwards the French won a series of smaller confrontations (Oswego, Ticonderoga), but then lost the war in 1759 when they lost the major battle at Quebec, where Montcalm died. The British soon pressed home their advantage to force the French surrender at Montreal in 1760.

After Montreal, Vaudreuil sailed from Quebec on a British ship and landed at Brest in November 1760. He was detained in the Bastille on 30 March 1762 but was granted his provisional freedom on 18 May. A tribunal finally exonerated him on 10 December 1763, and he lived in quiet retirement in Paris until his death on 4 August 1778.

Pembroke and other ships now waited for Saunders and the fleet to arrive. As they approached, Cook reported:

> 25 JUNE. At 6am a signal for all boats manned and armed in order to and lay in the Traverse as buoys for the ships.

The fleet approached Île d'Orléans on the 26th. It had been shown that ships could pass through the Traverse, but Saunders was wary of taking his very large ships any further. He, therefore, switched his flag from *Neptune* (which remained below the Traverse for the duration of the siege) to the smaller *Stirling Castle*, captained by Michael Everitt. Thomas Bisset, Cook's old mentor, was master on *Stirling Castle* and he recorded in his log:

> 27 JUNE. At 10 Admiral Saunders hoisted his flag on board of us; ditto weighed and run above the transports and anchored with the best bower in 8 fathoms.[4]

The fleet next advanced past the Île d'Orléans to anchor off the west end of the island in sight of the city of Quebec. Troops were disembarked on to the island. Cook wrote:

> 27 JUNE. At 7 anchored in the Bason of Quebec in 16 fathoms water. At 10 weighed and dropped down the river in company as before. At ½ past noon anchored in St. Patrick's Hole; found riding here his majesty's ship Stirling Castle with Admiral Saunders. The most part of the troops were landed and encamped on the island of Orleans.

That night the ships experienced a gale with thunder and high winds that caused chaos, especially in the small transports, some of which were destroyed or blown ashore. Saunders recorded:

> A very hard gale of wind came on, by which many anchors and small boats were lost and much damage received among the transports by their driving on board each other. The ships that lost most anchors I supplied from the Men of War, as far as I was able, and in all other respects, gave them the best assistance in my power.[5]

Wolfe was shocked at the apparent unpreparedness of the navy and was very critical. Twenty-seven transports needed to be sent to Boston for repair. The French hoped to capitalise on the disarray in the British fleet by sending down fireships. This action was reproduced in a dramatic painting by Dominc Serres. Cook recorded:

> 28 JUNE. At midnight the enemy sent six fire ships down before the tide all in flames. The Sutherland, Centurion and Porcupine sloop got under sail and came down before them. Sent all the boats ahead to take them in tow. At 2am two of the fire ships drove on shore on the island Orleans and others was towed off clear of the ships.

Saunders urged the installation of a battery at Point de Lévis and Pointe aux Pères to protect ships in the Bason. He sent Wheelock to Wolfe with this recommendation on 29 June. The French had realised the importance of that part of the shoreline but had delayed sending their own forces to occupy it. Wolfe agreed to set up the battery, which would carry out a prolonged bombardment across the river to the city, and the British had no problem establishing themselves. *Pembroke*'s small boats helped move the guns

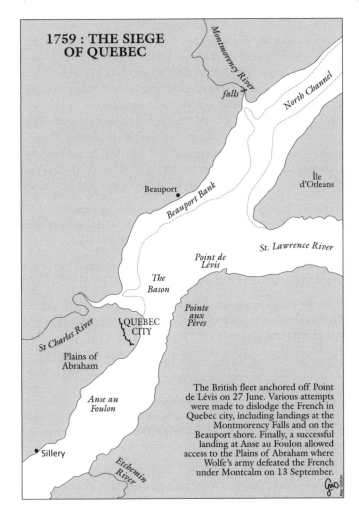

1759 : THE SIEGE OF QUEBEC

Montmorency River

falls

North Channel

Beauport

Beauport Bank

Île d'Orleans

St. Lawrence River

Point de Lévis

The Bason

Pointe aux Pères

St Charles River

QUEBEC CITY

Plains of Abraham

Anse au Foulon

The British fleet anchored off Point de Lévis on 27 June. Various attempts were made to dislodge the French in Quebec city, including landings at the Montmorency Falls and on the Beauport shore. Finally, a successful landing at Anse au Foulon allowed access to the Plains of Abraham where Wolfe's army defeated the French under Montcalm on 13 September.

Sillery

Etchemin River

Max Oulton

and troops ashore at Point de Lévis over the next few days. The ship's small boats also acted as guard patrols. Cook wrote:

> 29 JUNE. 10pm Sent the barge manned and armed on board the Hunter sloop to lay guard and kept the ship's company under arms all night.

> 2 JULY. Our long boat employed sending the artillery on Pt. Levi.

Wolfe had arrived at Quebec with no clear plan as to how to attack the city. An early plan involved landing somewhere upstream of Quebec and attacking from the west. This was quickly dropped and Wolfe centred his efforts for many weeks on Beauport on the north shore of the river to the east of the city and attacking from the north-east. Unfortunately, the French commander, Montcalm, concentrated his defences there.

Whatever was contemplated required the cooperation of the navy and, on 3 July, Wolfe and Saunders met to consider their options. Cook and Bisset had quickly surveyed the Beauport Bank, a wide expanse of shallows in front of the French position and had determined that it was impossible for the fleet to get close to shore to provide cover for possible landings. Cook was also involved in setting lines of buoys to mark channels and passages in the Bason, and to protect against more fireships.

The problem for Cook and others in the Bason, though, was coming from French gunboats that could operate in the shallows and fire on the British. Wolfe was dismayed at the inability of the navy to repulse them and that the British had been forced to anchor off the Île d'Orléans. The gunboats were organised by Jean Vauquelin, Commandant of the Road – the man who had escaped from Louisbourg the year before. Cook recorded:

> 7 JULY. The enemy came down with their armed boats in which they had 24 and 2 pounder and fired at the shipping on the North Shore which were returned by them and from a battery on Pt Levi which obliged them to retire back . . .

Bisset was nearly captured by one of these boats when out surveying (some writers have ascribed this story to Cook) and he recorded:

> 7 JULY. At 1pm the barge in sounding between Orleans and Falls was cut off by the French and Indians and taken; lost with dd [dead departed] one man, a leads and lines, a brass compass, sails, oars, etc . . .

Wolfe now proposed a landing on the north shore, east of the Montmorency Falls. The navy was called into action to provide transport and cover by bombarding the French emplacements. Cook noted:

> 8 JULY. At 11am his majesty's sloop Porcupine and Boscawen tender went down the North Channel of Orleans and anchored below the falls of Monmorenci in order to cover the landing of the troops.

Troops landed at midnight on the 8th and the two armies faced each other across the Montmorency River. Cook had sent long boat and pinnace to row guard and *Pembroke* was involved in the bombardment for the next few days. On the 12th Monckton's artillery began its heavy bombardment of Quebec from Pointe aux Pères and over the next month inflicted huge damage on the city and alarm among the inhabitants. The British fire muted the French response and allowed the British ships the opportunity to slip past the city.

Admiral Saunders directed a small group of ships to sail up river past Quebec to establish a presence there. On 18 July *Sutherland* and *Squirrel* made it through the narrows but *Diana* grounded in the attempt; Cook was involved in trying to move *Diana*. The French bombarded the vessels while the rescue was taking place, but the rescue was eventually successful, as Cook recorded:

> 18 JULY. At ½ past 10 his majesty's ships Sutherland, Diana and Squirrel, 2 transport ships and 2 sloops got under sail and ran up past the town through the fire of all the

enemy cannon. They all got safely past except the Diana who got ashore between Priests Point and Point Levi. At daylight the enemy fired several shots from the town at the Diana but did her no damage.

19 JULY. At 2 pm . . . and run up the river in order to cover the Richmond and Diana which attacked by a number of the enemy row boats which rowed off as soon as we got up . . . sent the long boats and 30 men on board the Diana to assist in getting her guns out.

20 JULY. At 2am we and the Richmond hove her off the ground.

Hawkins, the master of *Diana* recorded:

20 JULY. The Admiral sent his majesty's ship Pembroke, who came near us and sent on board his stream cable and brought it to to his own capstan in order to heave us off, as did also the Richmond; we had anchors out both ahead and stern, the hawser brought to own capstan; hove overboard 12 more of our guns. At ½ past 1 hove off in deep water.

Admiral Holmes followed his ships on 21 July to take command of the small flotilla. Meanwhile, Wolfe determined to capture a French redoubt at Beauport and Cook was involved in surveying the north channel prior to the attack. Cook was asked by Wolfe (possibly at the suggestion of Samuel Holland, who was working closely with the general) how close it would be possible to bring vessels to the shore and Cook advised that it would be possible to land troops near the redoubt using shallow-draught transports. However, Cook had undertaken the survey while under fire from the French and had not been able to get close to the shore himself, so some guesswork was involved on his part. Wolfe wrote: 'The master of the Pembroke assures the Admiral that a cat can go within less than 100 yards of the redoubt – if so, it will be a short affair. The business will be to keep it.'[6]

The French next sent down another mass of fireships at midnight on 27 July. This time they had been better assembled and handled so offered more of a threat. The British, though, had received a warning and were able to avert the danger. Bisset reported that 'at midnight saw a sky rocket from the French camp which proved a signal for setting on fire a large raft of fire stages which they sent down upon us'. To celebrate, Bisset 'served the boatmen for the above service ½ pint of brandy each'. Cook reported:

27 JULY. At 11pm sent the flat boats to row guard and kept all the other boats in readiness upon having intelligence the enemy was preparing to burn the ships. At ½ past midnight the enemy set fire to one hundred stages in one raft, piled up with wood and other combustibles and sent them down before the tide burning with great violence. The boats took hold of them and towed them clear of the whole fleet.

Wolfe's attack on the Beauport redoubt took place on 31 July. Two transports, *Russell* and *Three Sisters* were run ashore to allow troops to land and attack. Shallows that Cook had not located prevented them from getting in close and men had to wade through the water. *Centurion* and *Porcupine* provided bombardment cover, together with *Richmond* and *Pembroke*. One thousand grenadiers landed, but the attack was poorly led and enemy fire and a sudden thunderstorm forced a retreat, with over two hundred men killed. Bisset recorded:

> 31 JULY. At 11 am the Three Sisters and Russel transports, who was armed and manned for the purpose, slipped, got under sail, and was run on shore abreast of the enemy's faschine batteries above the Falls and began to engage ditto; and likewise 5 bateaux whose men soon deserted them. The Centurion at the same came to in the channel and began to engage the above batteries, while the North Shore towards Beauport was lined with our frigates to prevent anything coming down to hinder our troops from landing under the cover of the transports. ½ past noon all the boats with the troops on board put off from Orleans and kept rowing up and down in the North Channel waiting a favourable opportunity for landing. There happened a very heavy squall of wind and rain which rendered the mounting a high and very steep hill to come at the enemy's lines impracticable, together with the troops being exposed to a terrible fire from the above lines, made our Generals think it necessary to embark the troops again, which was done at ½ 7.

Wolfe's frustration over the lack of progress in the siege led him to take desperate measures. He began a campaign against the people of the surrounding district, destroying property and boats. He had previously issued a proclamation on 28 June:

> The formidable sea and land armament, which the people of Canada, now behold in the heart of their country, is intended by the king, my master, to check the insolence of France, to revenge the insults offered to the British colonies, and totally to deprive the French of their most valuable settlement in North America. For these purposes is the formidable army under my command intended. The King of Great Britain wages no war with the industrious peasant, the sacred orders of religion, or the defenceless women and children. To these in their distressful circumstances, his Royal clemency offers protection. I expect the Canadians will take no part in the great contest between the two crowns. But if by vain obstinacy and misguided valour, Canadians presume to appear in arms, they must expect the most fatal consequences: their habitations destroyed, their sacred temples exposed to an exasperated soldiery, their harvest utterly ruined. Should you suffer yourselves to be deluded by any imaginary prospect of our want of success, should you refuse those terms and persist in opposition, then surely will the law of nations justify the waste of war and the miserable Canadians will perish by the most dismal want and famine. Britain stretches out her powerful yet merciful hand. Let the wisdom of the people of Canada show itself.[7]

Wolfe's patience had worn thin, as shown by two letters to Monckton in early August. On the 4th he wrote, 'I propose to destroy the habitations & settlement in the Bay of St. Paul; & will employ Goreham in that service with 200 or 220 men', and on the 6th he put, 'If any more fire attempts are made, I shall burn all the houses from the village of St. Joachim to the Montmorency River'.[8] Cook became involved in these events when the British burnt houses on the north shore between Montmorency and Cap Tourmente:

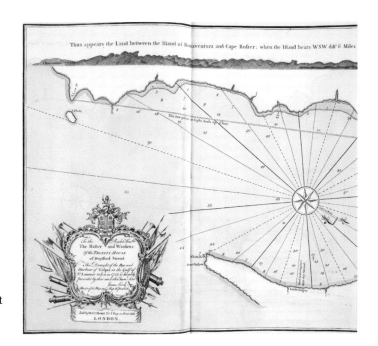

Part of *Draught of the Bay and Harbour of Gaspée*, 1758. Cook's first published map (*British Library*)

The manuscript version of a 'Plan of the Traverse or Passage from Cape Torment into the South Channel of Orleans', by James Cook. This is the chart Cook made in 1759 after surveying the channel, allowing the British fleet access to Quebec. A version of it was published the next year (*British Library*)

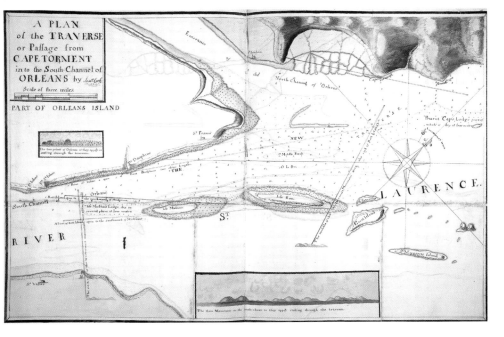

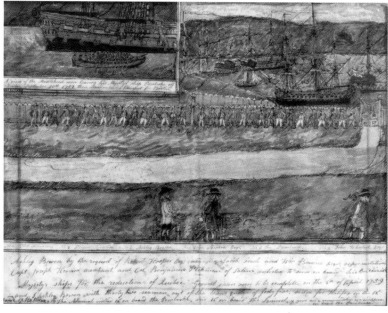

The Town and Harbour of Halifax in Nova Scotia, as they appear from the opposite shore, called Dartmouth, by Dominic Serres (after Richard Short). Cook spent three years in Halifax (*Art Gallery of Nova Scotia*)

Part of Cook's manuscript chart of Northern Newfoundland. The triangulation lines used by Cook to compile his survey can be seen (*UK Hydrographic Office*)

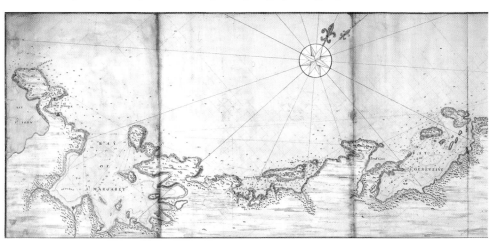

Facing page: (top) HMS *Pembroke* at Quebec, by Ashley Bowen(*Marblehead Museum*)
(bottom) Ashley Bowen meeting Captain John Simcoe at Halifax, by Ashley Bowen
(*Marblehead Museum*)

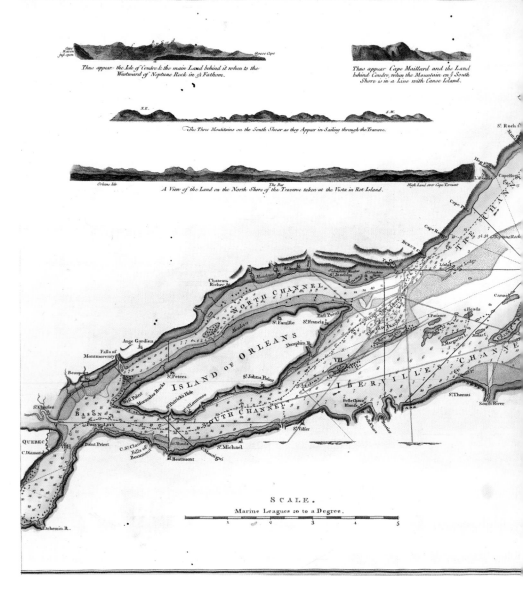

Part of Cook's *New Chart of the River St Lawrence* published in 1760 showing the Traverse. This was based on his earlier chart (*National Library of Australia*)

26 AUGUST. At 6am came on board our flat boats from Montmorenci having been assisting to burn all the houses on the North Shore between the camp at Montmorenci and Cape Torment.

In early August, both sides began activity upstream of Quebec. Brigadier General James Murray joined Holmes on 3 August and together they led an expedition further up the river from 8 to 25 August. Montcalm responded by increasing the army up there to a thousand men under Bougainville; the French were concerned that the British would cut their line of communications with Montreal. Their troops maintained an exhausting patrol along the north shore, watching the British and stopping any attacks. On the 8th Murray attacked Pointe aux Trembles but was repulsed with a heavy loss of men. A more successful attack took place on 18 August, when the British sacked Deschambault. Wolfe had other plans by the end of the month and called Murray back to Point de Lévis. He and Holmes were back on the 25th, but more ships were dispatched up the river on the 27th, including *Hunter* and *Lowestoffe*.

By the end of August Wolfe was a sick man and running out of ideas. He had distanced himself from his three brigadiers and was not involving them in decision making. He was still intent on attacking Beauport and sent a letter to his brigadiers, offering three options. The brigadiers met with Saunders on *Stirling Castle* to discuss a response; they all disagreed with Wolfe and recommended, instead, an attack on Quebec from the west, which Wolfe grudgingly accepted.

Cook and Bisset were still occupied in the Bason below Quebec. Cook recorded:

2 SEPTEMBER. At 10am the master of the Stirling Castle and ours lay several buoys close in shore between Beauport and Charles River.

Wolfe, having accepted his brigadiers' plan, now began to put it into action as his health recovered. He went upriver to join Admiral Holmes and together they inspected the north shore for places they could land for an attack. Alexander Wood, the master on *Hunter* under Captain William Adams, reported:

7 SEPTEMBER. pm Came on board the Generals Monckton and Murray; got a pilot on board, weighed, and went up the river. At 7 anchored; likewise came on board the Generals Wolfe and Townshend. At 9 weighed and dropt down to the fleet; anchored in 15 fathom water; the Generals left the ship.

Wolfe was modifying his brigadiers' plan and he needed an army west of Quebec for his purposes. Accordingly, troops marched along the southern shore or were transported up the river. At the same time, the British wanted to give the impression that an attack was still planned for below Quebec from the east, so Saunders and the navy continued to behave as if an attack there was imminent. On the 7th Cook reported:

7 SEPTEMBER. pm All the row boats in the fleet assembled at Pt. Levi in order to make a feint in the night at Beauport to favour the proceedings of General Wolfe above the town.

11 SEPTEMBER. At 10pm the master went in the barge and placed some buoys upon the shoals of Beauport. At noon the enemy attempted to cut away the buoys but was beat off by the fire of the Richmond.

By the 9th Wolfe had decided on L'Anse au Foulon as the place from which he would make his assault. Holmes and his officers worked out how to deliver the troops to the exact location at the exact time, with the least chance of being discovered by the French. The British were most fortuitous in that all the factors were at their most favourable on the night of 12 September, which was therefore ideal for their purposes.

They had to take into account the nature of the tide and the time when it changed from flood to ebb at St Nicholas, where the transports were waiting (12.08am on the night in question). The strength of the river current also varied, causing it to increase where the river narrowed near Le Sault. At 2am, when the transports cast off, the current was flowing at 2.4 knots and at about 3.15am when they passed Le Sault it had risen to a maximum 5.7 knots. Finally, the stage of the moon and its position in the sky would determine how much, if at all, the troops would be illuminated. That night the moon was in the south-east, which provided lighting from the side as the British floated ENE.

Holmes described the events of the night of 12 September:

A plan was immediately set on Foot, to attempt a landing about four Leagues above the Town; & it was ready to be put in Execution, when Genr'l Wolfe reconnoitered down the River, & fixed upon Foulon; a spot adjacent to the Citadel, which, tho' a very strong ground, being a steep Hill with abbatis laid across the accessable parts of it, & a Guard on the Summit, He nevertheless thought that a sudden brisk attack, a little before Day-break, would bring his army on the Plain, within two Miles of the Town. . . . The Care of landing the Troops & sustaining them by the Ships, fell to my share- The most hazardous & difficult Task I was ever engaged in- For the distance of the landing place; the impetuosity of the Tide; the darkness of the Night; & the great Chance of exactly hitting the very spot intended, without discovery or alarm, made the whole extremely difficult: And the failing in any part of my Disposition, as it might have overset the Generals Plan, would have brought upon me an imputation of being the Cause of the miscarriage of the attack, & all the Misfortune that might happen to the Troops in attempting it, which, you agree with me, had a most hazardous aspect. . . . About Midnight, 1800 Troops embarked from the Ships, in Boats: About half past two the Boats got underway, & proceeded for the landing Place: The armed sloops & those with Ordnance Stores & ammunition, followed next: After them, I got underway in the Lowestoff, and had with me the Sea Horse, Squirrel, & Hunter Sloop, and two Transports, all full of Troops: The Sutherland was left behind to keep an Eye on the Enemy's Motions, their floating Batteries, & Small Craft. The Boats were to go close in shore & land the Troops, The Sloops were to lie next them; The Men of War without the Sloops & as near the shore as possible; & the two Transports without the Men of War, ready to disembark the Troops when ordered. Every thing was conducted very happily, & the greatest good Fortune seconded our Wishes. Captain Chads conducted the Boats; they observed the most profound Silence; the night was moderate; & he landed the Troops undiscovered by the Enemy a little before Day; but not without

Cook's Progress Down the St Lawrence

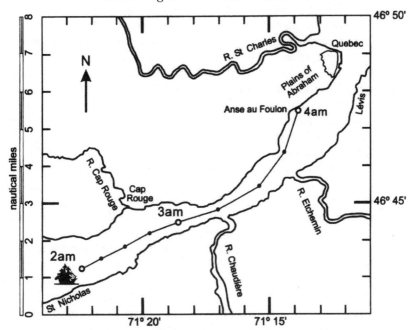

hazard of being drove by the Currant, below the Town- The Sloops drew close in; and the Men of War & Transports got to their Station at Day break. ... In this manner, the General had his Army on the Enemies Shore, within two Miles of the Town, before his arrival was well known at their Head Quarters: For Mr. Montcalm had taken all our latter Motions for so many Feints, & thought our grand Aim was still below Quebec & pointed towards Beauport; And he was confirmed in this, by the several well laid Feints & Motions of Mr. Saunders, who laid Buoys in the Night, close in shore, towards Beauport, as if he intended them for Moorings to the Ships, to come as near their Shore as possible, and land the Troops under Cover of their Fire.[9]

At the same time as the British were assembling at St Nicholas, the French were attempting to transport supplies to Quebec. The preferred method was to use boats down the river but this plan was cancelled on the 12th. However, the guardposts along the river were not informed of the change of plan and still expected French boats to appear.

Details of the events of the next twenty-four hours remain very muddled. For almost any incident there are several British versions and several French versions and it is virtually impossible to know which to believe. I have used Donald Graves's edited edition of CP Stacey's *Quebec, 1759: The Siege and the Battle* as being the volume that presents the facts most clearly while pointing out the errors and inconsistencies of earlier works. Anyone wishing to know more about all aspects of the Quebec campaign should consult this excellent book.

At midnight, a single lantern on *Sutherland* was the signal for the troops to embark in transports. At 2am, two lanterns in *Sutherland* was the signal for the thirty-five transports to start floating down stream from St Nicholas. They were followed by more transports with supplies and ammunition and, finally, the British ships carrying more troops. *Sutherland* alone remained upstream. Near L'Anse au Foulon they were seen by French sentries expecting the supplies convoy, but a Captain Fraser's answer of 'La France' when challenged let them proceed unopposed. Captain James Chads was on hand to supervise the landing and, at about 4am, the first boats landed at Foulon. However, the first boats, containing twenty-four members of the 'Forlorn Hope', led by Captain Delaune, overran the designated site. Colonel William Howe was in command of the ascent and quick deliberations led to them scrambling straight up the fifty-three-metre cliff. Others landed in the correct spot and began climbing up the steep, narrow path. A small French outpost under Vergour was stationed at the top, but the British quickly overcame them. One sentry did manage to get away to inform Quebec of the landing but he was not believed initially because the French did not think an army could be brought up the cliff. Slowly the French realised the truth of the report and began to mobilise.

As transports landed troops at the foot of the cliff they crossed to Point de Lévis and the Île d'Orléans to pick up more. The navy also dragged two 6-pounder guns up the path to assist the troops. By 8am, all the troops and guns were at top of the cliff. Wolfe himself was in one of the first transports and onto the field of battle early. He had the troops march east then assemble in battlelines on the Plains of Abraham (named after Abraham Martin, a seventeenth-century pilot who owned the land).

General Montcalm, commander of the French army, advanced his troops to meet the British. The two armies were approximately of equal strength (about four and a half thousand men), but the British were all regulars and the French contained many Canadian militia. At 10am on the morning of 13 September, the French moved forwards. Their line was erratic and began firing haphazardly. The British held fire until the French were about forty yards away. The effect was devastating and the French were immediately in disarray. At about this time, though, Wolfe was hit by at least two bullets and soon died. Samuel Holland, the engineer-surveyor, is supposed to have arrived at Wolfe's side as the general was dying. A famous painting of the death of Wolfe, by Nathaniel West, does not depict Holland, though, but introduces instead a host of people who were not present. Holland wrote: 'In the battle of September 13, I lost my protector while holding his wounded hand at the time he expired. For reasons best known to Mr. West, the painter, I was not included amongst the group represented. Others exhibited in that painting were never in the battle.'[10]

Monckton was also injured and carried to *Lowestoffe*, as was the body of Wolfe shortly after. Townshend assumed command of the British force.

Montcalm was also hit but managed to ride back to Quebec, severely injured. Bougainville arrived with the part of the French army under his command but was too late and withdrew his troops. The defeated French army retreated into the city and to Beauport. Vaudreuil convened a council to consider options and it was decided to take the army to Montreal. The army marched north and then west to avoid the British. De

Ramezay was left in command of Quebec, with orders to hold out as long as possible. Montcalm died in the early hours of 14 September.

Townshend brought the British troops forward to begin a siege of the city. De Ramezay realised the futility of his situation and decided to surrender, signing the capitulation on 18 September. The British artillery entered the Upper Town that day while Hugh Palliser landed with a squad of British sailors to take over the Lower Town. Brigadier François de Lévis had travelled down from Montreal to take over command of the French army but retreated when he heard of the city's surrender.

The British were amazingly fortunate. So many things could have gone wrong floating down the river and negotiating the cliffs to reach the battlefield, but everything had run like clockwork, largely due the work of the navy. Added to which, Montcalm handled his troops badly on the day, effectively handing victory to the British. Wolfe, though, just as he had been at Louisbourg the previous year, seized his opportunity and led by example in battle. He may have been totally indecisive over the previous three months but in action he was supremely positive and he was most unlucky to have lost his own life. The victory was Wolfe's. Unlike all the other battles fought on North American soil, Quebec was fought in the traditional European manner with opposing battlelines. The French Canadians and Indians were largely redundant in those conditions.

Bisset reported the final surrender:

18 SEPTEMBER. ½ past 10am Captain Palliser came on board and informed us that the town had capitulated the night before.

As the senior surviving officer, Admiral Saunders immediately dispatched a ship to Britain with the news of the victory, including a letter to the Admiralty:

I have the greatest pleasure in acquainting you, for their Lordships information, that the town & citadel of Quebec surrendered on the 18th instant; that the Army took possession of the gates on the land side the same evening and sent safeguards into the town to preserve order and to prevent any thing being destroyed and Capt. Palliser, with a body of seamen landed in the lower town & did the same. I have omitted in my last letter, to acquaint their Lordships with the death of Captain Simcoe, which happened on his passage from Halifax to the River St. Lawrence, & that I had appointed Capt. Wheelock of the Squirrel to succeed him, Capt. Cleland of the Scorpion to be captain of the Squirrel & my first lieutenant to succeed him as captain of the Scorpion. I have the pleasure also of acquainting their Lordships that during this tedious campaign, there has continued a perfect good understanding between the Army & Navy: I have received great assistance from Admirals Durell & Holmes, & from all the captains; indeed every body has exerted themselves in the execution of their duty.

Admiral Durell will sail for England with the great ships in two or three days, and I shall, myself follow, as soon as possible, leaving at Halifax, Lord Colvill in the Northumberland with four more ships of the line, & two or three frigates, with orders to come up here as early in the spring as possible. I propose to appoint a captain to the Northumberland under Lord Colvill & to direct his Lordship to hoist a broad pennant.[11]

Townshend, now the senior army officer, wrote an official dispatch to William Pitt in which he acknowledged the role and huge contribution of the navy:

> I should not do justice to the Admirals and the naval service if I neglected this occasion of acknowledging how much we are indebted, for our success, to the constant assistance and support received from them, and the perfect harmony and correspondence which has prevailed throughout all our operations, in uncommon difficulties which the nature of this country, in particular, presents to military operations of a great extent, and which no army itself can solely supply; the immense labour in artillery, stores and provisions; the long watchings and attendances in boats; the drawing up [of] our artillery by the seamen, even in the heat of action; it is my duty, short as my command has been, to acknowledge, for that time, how great a share the navy has had in this successful campaign.[12]

For James Cook, the Quebec campaign marked a turning point in his career. While not directly involved in the actions leading to the decisive battle on the 13 September, Cook played a prominent part in many of the actions leading up to it. He acquitted himself well throughout and had direct dealings with senior officers in both the army and navy, including Wolfe and Saunders. The death of Wolfe meant that the general could be of no assistance, but Saunders was soon helping Cook; Cook was rewarded for his actions by promotion to be master on a larger ship, *Northumberland*, a third rate. Wheelock, his captain on *Pembroke*, recorded:

> 23 SEPTEMBER. Mr. Cook, master, superseded and sent on board the Northumberland per order of Admiral Saunders.

❀ 9 ❀

HMS *Northumberland*, 1759–1761

The Royal Navy's success at Quebec in September 1759 led to many participants being rewarded for their contributions. Promotions and transfers were common throughout the fleet in late September before it sailed from the St Lawrence to avoid being trapped in the ice. Admiral Saunders was taking most of the fleet back to Britain but needed to leave a small squadron in North American waters as a precaution against French retaliation. This would be based at Halifax, which was the nearest ice-free port. The captain of *Northumberland*, Alexander, Lord Colvill (see section 'Alexander Colvill'), who had operated in these waters for several years, was promoted to commodore and placed in charge of the squadron. William Adams (see section 'William Adams'), who had performed well in command of the sloop *Hunter*, was promoted to be Colvill's flag captain and joined the ship on 22 September (muster #1228). Two days later, James Cook (#1269 on the muster) joined *Northumberland* as master, taking over from James Jones. Accompanying Cook was his servant, Joseph White (#1270).

Two of *Northumberland*'s lieutenants, Robert Haswell and James Ferguson, left the ship to take up more senior positions elsewhere in the fleet; Ferguson replaced Adams on *Hunter*. On 26 September John Boyd went on board *Northumberland* as the replacement first lieutenant in lieu of Haswell. The next morning Cook recorded the first of many punishments handed out to seaman Edward Lovely. Over the next two years Lovely featured in the log about eight times, for various misdemeanours.

Northumberland weighed at noon on 28 September and began a slow progress down the river. The large number of ships, the shallows, the tides, currents and winds made progress difficult and caused ships to foul each other. By 10 October, they had only reached the Île aux Coudres, where they anchored between the island and the land. Many ships reported losing anchors during this time, among them *Pembroke*, which, on the 14th, sent out distress signals. *Northumberland* was able to help and Cook recorded that:

17 OCTOBER. At 9am the Mary sloop came alongside & took in the spare anchor to carry on board the Pembroke.

The situation with regards anchors was serious enough for Colvill to write to the Admiralty on 16 October from Île aux Coudres: 'I pray the favour of their Lordships to order us a supply of anchors and cables as soon as possible; many of those articles having been lost in this river, where ground tackle is our only security.'[1]

At noon on 20 October, *Northumberland* passed the Île du Bic and headed for Halifax, where they anchored on the 28th. Cook would spend much of the next three years based in Halifax. His log became a listing of provisioning, cleaning and repairing, punishments,

ALEXANDER COLVILL, SEVENTH BARON COLVILL (1717–70)

Alexander Colvill was the son of John Colvill, sixth Baron Colvill, and his wife Elizabeth. He was born on 28 February 1717 in Dundee and joined the Royal Navy in 1733 on board HMS *Line*. He passed his lieutenant's examination in 1738 and is believed to have been made a lieutenant in 1739, serving in that capacity in the West Indies on *Alderney*. In 1742 he transferred to the Mediterranean fleet.

On 6 March 1744 he was promoted to captain and given command of *Dursley Gally*. He then took charge of HMS *Leopard* on 21 September 1744. He distinguished himself over the next few years and returned to Britain with *Leopard* in 1748, with £5,000 prize money. He left the ship on 19 December 1748.

For a month, from 11 March 1749, Colvill had command of *Shoreham*. He then transferred on 6 April to HMS *Success* and spent the next three years, until 1752, in New England. On 10 January 1753 he was given command of the 70-gun HMS *Northumberland*, on which he sailed for the next nine years. Colvill took part in the capture of Louisbourg in 1758 and was in the St Lawrence during the siege of Quebec in 1759. After the French surrender, Saunders appointed Colvill as commander-in-chief of the North America station on 16 October 1759. It was then that he met Cook, who was appointed master of *Northumberland*.

Colvill took his ships back to Halifax in Nova Scotia but returned to Quebec in 1760. The next year, and most of 1762 were spent at Halifax, where he was engaged in improving the dockyard facilities. News reached Colvill in July 1762 of the French capture of St John's in Newfoundland so he sailed to Newfoundland to take part in the recapture. Colvill took *Northumberland* back to Britain in late 1762 and his connection with Cook ended then, when both men left the ship. Colvill was made rear admiral on 21 October 1762.

Colvill was appointed port admiral at Plymouth in 1763 but later that year was persuaded to take on the North American command again, and he remained there until 1766. He was never employed again after his return to Britain. His marriage to Lady Elizabeth Erskine in 1768 produced no children, but he did have children with several women in North America. Colvill died on 21 May 1770 at Drumsheugh, near Edinburgh. He had given Cook the opportunity to prepare charts in Canada and Newfoundland and his commendations brought Cook to the attention of Thomas Graves, Governor of Newfoundland. Cook named a cape in New Zealand after Colvill.

the comings and goings other ships, and gun salutes for events such as the king's birthday. For example:

> 5 NOVEMBER. At 1pm fired 15 guns as did the Sutherland being Gunpowder treason day

WILLIAM ADAMS (1716?–63)

According to his lieutenant's passing certificate, William Adams was born in 1716. Before becoming a lieutenant on 26 March 1750, Adams served on *Gosport, Swallow, Lady Lucy, Deptford Prize* and *Lyme*. He served on HMS *Vigilant* in 1751, followed by time on *Yarmouth* in 1755 and *Royal George* in 1757. In 1758 Adams was on *Namur* with Boscawen, who promoted him commander on 2 August 1758 after the siege of Louisbourg and gave him command of the sloop *Hunter*. *Hunter* was one of the ships that sailed upstream of Quebec and ferried James Wolfe during one of his inspections.

In reward, Adams was promoted captain after the siege of Quebec on 22 September 1759. At the same time he was appointed captain of HMS *Northumberland*, the flagship of Alexander, Lord Colvill, who had just been appointed commodore of the North American squadron. Adams joined the ship the day before James Cook.

Northumberland spent the winter of 1759/60 at Halifax but returned to Quebec in 1760 as part of the force sent to prevent the French forces recapturing the city. One of Adams's servants as captain was Tomlin Adams, his son; Adams was carrying out a ploy common in the navy by placing his son's name on the books, even though that son was only three years old at the time. Adams transferred to HMS *Diana* on 21 September 1760 and was replaced as captain on *Northumberland* by Nathaniel Bateman.

William Adams and Martha Thrall were married at St Mary's Church, Portsea, on 31 October 1743. Adams died in late 1763; there is a will written on 10 September 1763 and proven on 3 January 1764. Three children are mentioned, but not his wife Martha, so she was presumably already dead. As well as the son, Tomlin, there are two daughters, Mary and Martha Maria. It may be that Martha Adams died in childbirth and the third child was named for her.

Captain George Hamilton of *Richmond* died on 30 March 1760, which meant that Colvill had to move officers. Captain John Elphinston of *Eurus* was promoted to *Richmond* and Nathaniel Bateman took over *Eurus*.

Meanwhile, back in Britain, on 22 April 1760 Admiral Charles Saunders sent a note to John Clevland, the secretary of the Admiralty: 'Having got materials ready for publishing a draught of the River St Lawrence, with the harbours, bays and islands in that river, I must beg you to acquaint their Lordships of it, that I may receive their directions thereon.'[2] The materials in question were the chart of and sailing directions for the St Lawrence Gulf and river, prepared by James Cook and Samuel Holland. At some point the drafts had been forwarded to Britain, but who forwarded them is unknown as Cook and Holland had been apart since September, when Holland had remained in Quebec with Murray. The admiral sought permission for the material to be published by Thomas Jefferys, whose premises were close to the Admiralty, at Charing Cross (Saunders may

OFFICERS AND MASTERS OF *NORTHUMBERLAND*, 1759–62

Captains
William Adams (#1228) from 22 September 1759 to 21 September 1760
Nathaniel Bateman (#1343) from 22 September 1760 to December 1762

First Lieutenants
John Boyd (#1271) from 24 September 1759 to 26 May 1760
James Harmood (#1) from 27 May 1760 to July 1760
Robert Dugdale (#1331) from 3 July 1760 to 1762

Second Lieutenants
James Harmood (#1) from 1 May 1758 to 27 May 1760
William Denne from May 1760 to December 1762

Third Lieutenants
William Denne from May 1759 to May 1760
John James (#1308) from 27 May 1760 to December 1762

Fourth Lieutenants
Samuel Ferrior (#1304) from 31 March 1760 to December 1762

Midshipman
Alexander Scott (#1019) from 1 March 1759 (AB from 25 November 1758 to 1 March 1759)

Masters
James Jones (#8) from 1 May 1758 to 23 September 1759
James Cook (#1269) from 24 September 1759 to 11 November 1762
John Major (#1501) from 12 November 1762 to 30 November 1762

have paid for the publication as his name appears on it, not those of Cook and Holland). The chart was entitled *A New Chart of the River St Laurence, from the Island of Anticosti to the Falls of Richelieu: with all the Islands, Rocks, Shoals, and Soundings. Also Particular Directions for Navigating the River with Safety. Taken by Order of Charles Saunders, Esq.r Vice-Admiral of the Blue, and Commander in Chief of His Majesty's Ships in the Expedition against Quebec in 1759.* It comprised twelve sheets and its overall dimensions were 35 × 90 in. The scale was 1 inch=2 leagues (approx. 1:380,000). The accompanying sailing directions were entitled *Directions for Navigating the Gulf and River of St Laurence* and comprised thirty-one pages.

With the death of Wolfe and the serious injury to Monckton, Townshend had assumed command of the British army and negotiated the surrender terms of Quebec with de Ramezay. Then, having sent Wolfe's body back to Britain and Monckton to New York, Townshend decided to leave for Britain himself. James Murray was instated as

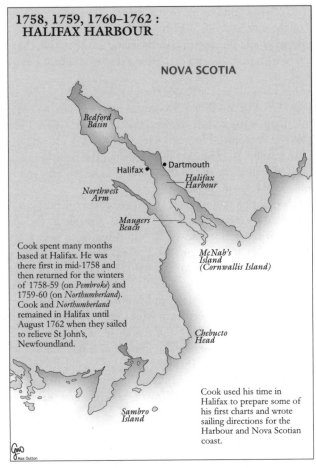

1758, 1759, 1760–1762 :
HALIFAX HARBOUR

NOVA SCOTIA

Bedford
Basin

Halifax • • Dartmouth

Halifax
Harbour

Northwest
Arm

Maugers
Beach

Cook spent many months
based at Halifax. He was
there first in mid-1758 and
then returned for the winters
of 1758-59 (on *Pembroke*) and
1759-60 (on *Northumberland*).
Cook and *Northumberland*
remained in Halifax until
August 1762 when they sailed
to relieve St John's,
Newfoundland.

McNab's
Island
(Cornwallis Island)

Chebucto
Head

Sambro
Island

Cook used his time in
Halifax to prepare some of
his first charts and wrote
sailing directions for the
Harbour and Nova Scotian
coast.

Max Oulton

Governor of Quebec with the unenviable prospect of spending a winter in the city. Most of the army remained with him.

Murray quickly realised that the grip on Quebec was precarious as the British only held the city and the immediate hinterland, leaving them vulnerable to a counterattack. He therefore stationed troops at strategic points on the approaches to the city. Recent British actions had done nothing to endear them to the Canadian population at large; Wolfe's policy of destroying villages and homes had alienated most of them. British troops could not move freely away from the city, except in large groups, for fear of being attacked. The British success had come on the back of its naval forces and Saunders had taken his fleet away at the first opportunity, leaving Murray and his garrison in a very lonely position. In October 1759 Murray had about seven thousand soldiers at his command but the number of sick grew at an alarming rate. The cold of winter took its toll, while the limited diet generated scurvy-type illnesses. By early 1760 Murray only had fewer than four thousand active troops ready to defend the city.

Townshend had offered good terms to the French, especially respecting the rights of the inhabitants of the city, and the British now had to demonstrate to the people that their good intentions would be carried out. By doing so, of course, they hoped that the Quebecois would remain peaceful and do nothing that would help Lévis and the French forces at Montreal.

In 1760 Brigadier François de Lévis, who had succeeded Montcalm, was in command of the French army. Lévis believed that Montcalm had been rash to engage with Wolfe's forces and should have waited until reinforcements arrived. Now Lévis was the man who had to make the decisions. He was aware that the British would probably attack Montreal from three fronts in 1760: as well as Quebec, the British were now established to the north of Lake Champlain and to the south of Lake Ontario and it was likely that these armies would converge on Montreal.

To pre-empt this situation and to open up lines of communication with France, Lévis realised that he needed to retake Quebec as early as possible in the spring, before the melting of ice in the St Lawrence allowed British shipping to pass. If word could reach France and reinforcements arrive before the British, then the French could offer better resistance to any attacks. The French government, however, was in financial straits and more interested in events in Europe, so Canada had to fend for itself. Meanwhile, during the winter, Lévis put together an army in Montreal of over seven thousand men. On 17 April 1760 the French army set off from Montreal to march to Quebec, with Lévis hoping to attract more soldiers during the march. A week later the French advance guard was on the outskirts of Quebec. The French also had a small squadron up the St Lawrence under Jean Vauquelin. This was the same Vauquelin who had audaciously slipped out of Louisbourg Harbour in *Aréthuse*, past waiting British ships in 1758. He was now in command of *Atalante* as well as *Pomone*, *Pie* and several transports. They sailed from Sorel on 20 April 1760 in support of Lévis's army. Vauquelin, in *Atalante*, reached L'Anse au Foulon on the 28th.

Governor Murray had been expecting such an attack and his pickets warned of French advances. There had been small skirmishes throughout the winter and Murray had previously sent troops to the south shore to chase away French soldiers and to fire on Pointe aux Trembles and St Augustin. When the British navy left Quebec in October 1759 they left two ships at the city to act as protection, the sloops *Racehorse* (Captain George Miller) and *Porcupine* (Captain John Macartney). In November, a French vessel, attempting to pass Quebec, went ashore on rocks opposite the city and was abandoned by her crew. Captain Miller, with most of his crew from *Racehorse*, went on board the vessel but, either by design or accident, she blew up, killing everyone. Captain Macartney assumed command of *Racehorse*, taking his crew with him from *Porcupine*.

Murray did not know if and when British reinforcements would arrive and he felt that his forces could not endure a long siege such as the French had experienced the previous year. Neither side was in prime condition: the British army was reduced in numbers after a long, cold winter in Quebec with scurvy and other diseases taking their toll; the French had endured a similar winter and had just marched from Montreal. Murray went out on 27 April to withdraw his pickets as the French army approached.

On 28 April Murray decided not to wait for the French to attack and marched his troops out of the city. He had his troops digging trenches, when he saw a chance to catch the French unprepared. Lévis's troops were still arriving and had not yet been deployed into battle formation. Using the element of surprise, Murray attacked near St Foy, just beyond where Wolfe and Montcalm had met the year before. He hoped to break through the left side of the French line and trap Lévis's army near the St Lawrence River.

Initially, superior British artillery gave Murray the advantage and they severely depleted the French troops, who were forced to retreat. Murray, believing that he had defeated the enemy, then advanced but in doing so crossed the line of fire of his own artillery, reducing their effectiveness. Hand-to-hand fighting ensued, involving bayonets and knives. The French began circling and the British flanks were pushed in upon their centre, forcing Murray to order the retreat into the city, leaving dead, wounded and artillery on the battlefield. The British had lost 1,180 men, dead, wounded or taken prisoner, whereas Lévis's losses totalled 833 dead and wounded.

Lévis's troops moved forward and entrenched six hundred metres from the city's fortifications. In less than a year, the positions had reversed and it was now the French who were besieging Quebec. For the moment, French vessels could move freely on the river above Quebec and supply material to support a siege for as long as was needed. Lévis installed batteries in order to force a breach in the wall, while the British reinforced the walls with cannons and fired on the French. The British were not about to leave the city and the French, who had not brought sufficient artillery and ammunition with them, were not strong enough to effect a quick result, so a long wait was in prospect.

Everyone now waited to see whose ships would arrive first, as that would determine the outcome of the siege. Both sides kept constant watch on the St Lawrence River; two separate British squadrons had set off to relieve the city and a small French flotilla, with reinforcements, was also on its way.

Colvill had instructions to return to Quebec as early in 1760 as conditions would allow, so in March he had his ships prepared to sail. On 3 April sailing orders were delivered to the ships in the squadron. Cook recorded:

> 3 APRIL. At ½ past noon delivered sailing orders to the following lieutenants, viz: Mr Fasson of the Eurus, Mr Boyd of the Trident, Mr J Robson of the Pembroke, Mr Dogget of the Richmond, Mr Bowey of the Alcide, Mr Dupine of the Prince of Orange, Mr Farriar of the Hunter, Captain Adams of the Northumberland.

This was followed a week later by the distribution of instructions for rendezvous. Finally, at 7am on 22 April the ships weighed, came to sail and left Halifax Harbour. Conditions out at sea, though, were terrible and the squadron could make no progress because of adverse winds and huge amounts of ice. Cook recorded:

> 23 APRIL. At 12 midnight the ship fast in the ice.

> 24 APRIL. 10am Could see nothing but ice from the masthead from the NW all round to the NE.

Over the next few days the ice relaxed its grip a fraction and the ships made some progress but still encountered large swathes of loose ice. Fog exacerbated the problem and it was necessary for the ships to fire guns to keep in touch. It was the morning of 6 May, two weeks after leaving Halifax, when the ships finally passed through the Cabot Strait between Newfoundland and Cape Breton Island. Conditions in the Gulf of St Lawrence were little better and they encountered strong gales:

9 MAY. 12 noon. . . . in hoisting ours, the ensign blew away from the staff.

It took until the 16th to reach the Île du Bic. Here, Colvill learned that Quebec was already under siege and that some British ships were ahead of him sailing up the St Lawrence.

It was Commodore Robert Swanton who was ahead of Colvill. Swanton, in *Vanguard*, had left Britain with a small squadron and had reached the Île du Bic on 11 May 1760, accompanied only by the frigate *Diana* (Captain Alexander Schomberg). Swanton had intended to wait for the rest of his squadron, which had been scattered during the crossing of the Atlantic, but when he learned of Quebec's plight he set off immediately to assist. Another of Swanton's ships was ahead of him and *Lowestoffe* (Captain Joseph Deane) was the first sail sighted at Quebec that year, on 9 May, much to the relief of the British and the despair of Lévis and his troops.

Aided by fresh north-easterly winds, Swanton reached Quebec on the evening of 15 May. Lévis had feared this outcome. He had written: 'I truly fear that France has abandoned us. . . . We have done and are doing what we can. It is my opinion that the colony will be lost without resources. If no help comes, all that we can do is prolong the time, in the hope that peace can be made during this interval.'[3] When he was certain that the three ships that had just arrived were all British, the demoralised Lévis ordered the end of the siege and a retreat once more towards Montreal. The inhabitants of Quebec awoke to find the plains deserted. Lévis also ordered the French ships anchored at L'Anse au Foulon to sail back up the St Lawrence as quickly as possible. Swanton realised the need to immobilise those same French ships and on 16 May he ordered *Lowestoffe* and *Diana* up the river to attack them. The two French frigates, *Atalante* and *Pomone* were both destroyed, but Vauquelin had put up stout resistance. After prolonging the fight, he nailed his flag to the mast and threw his sword into the St Lawrence before ordering his crew to leave the ship. He, himself, had been wounded and was taken prisoner but he was quickly released and returned to France. Once again, British sea power had been the telling difference between the two sides.

The British success came at a cost, however. *Lowestoffe* ran aground on unknown rocks in the middle of the river above Quebec and was lost. Colvill, who finally arrived at Quebec on 18 May, moved some of *Lowestoffe*'s crew onto *Porcupine* and distributed the rest among other ships.

Colvill and *Northumberland* left Île du Bic immediately on 16 May and made all speed up the St Lawrence. They anchored before the citadel at Quebec at 9.30am on the 18th and found several British ships at anchor there, including *Vanguard*, from whom Colvill learned that the siege of Quebec had finished and the French had retreated to Montreal. Colvill sent a letter to London:

... anchored with the Squadron at the Isle of Bic, after a most tedious and troublesome passage, being almost continually impeded, by running amongst great Quantities of loose Ice, and confused by thick fogs. Notwithstanding our greatest care all the Convoy lost company, more from their own bad conduct than on account of the Ice or Weather. At Bic I received a Letter from Governor Murray of Quebec, dated the 9 Instant. He acquainted me that the Enemy, having collected the whole Force of Canada, were then laying Siege to Quebec. Upon this Intelligence I sailed directly upwards with the Squadron, and on the 18, at 9 in the morning, we anchored at Quebec, where I found Captain Swanton in the *Vanguard*, being sent from England to reinforce me.

I have left the Pembroke at Coudre, as a guardship.

The Lowestoffe arrived a week before the Vanguard. This ship & the Diana have effectually destroyed the enemy's force above the town; but the Lowestoffe is irrecoverably lost on unknown rocks in the middle of the river about ten leagues above the town.

In November last one of the French vessels, in attempting to force her passage downward, got ashore upon rocks opposite the town, and was abandoned by her crew; soon after which Captain Miller of the Racehorse, with most of his people went on board her and were all blown up. Captain Macartney of the Porcupine carried his whole ship's company with him into the Racehorse, and sailed hence on the 2n instant for New York to carry the account of Quebec's being besieged to General Amherst ... I propose to reman the Porcupine with part of the Lowestoffe's people, and distribute the rest among the ships that are in want of men.

The Diana, the only frigate with me, has lost her bowsprit, and been much hurt in her masts above the town. The Porcupine is in all respects in so destitute a condition that she cannot be got ready for service for some time. I therefore think it proper to send Captain Ferguson in the Hunter, to England with the important news of the siege of Quebec being raised.

Captain Hamilton of the Richmond died last March at Halifax, upon which I moved Captain Elphinston of the Eurus into the Richmond, Captain Bateman of the Hunter into the Eurus , and Lieutenant Ferguson of the Northumberland, I appointed to command the Hunter. I beg leave to recommend this gentleman to their Lordships for confirmation. He has sailed with me more than fourteen years, in the stations of midshipman, mate and lieutenant.[4]

Northumberland was too large to proceed further up the river and take any part in the British advance to Montreal being led by Governor Murray. Colvill, Cook and the crew settled in for the summer, anchored in the Bason. Colvill, as senior British officer present, spent time ashore in an effort to consolidate the British hold on the city. Cook remained on board running the ship and noting the arrival of transports carrying provisions for the ships and the city.

One of the transports was *Swallow* from Boston, carrying a cargo of cattle. On board as mate and pilot was Ashley Bowen, who had sailed with Cook on *Pembroke* the previous year. *Swallow* encountered *Pembroke* at the Île aux Coudres, where that ship was acting as guardship. She arrived at Quebec on 28 June and discharged the cattle on the Île d'Orléans on the 30th. Bowen and Cook had several meetings and in his journal Bowen recorded:

> 13 JULY. This day laying off the town of Quebec. This day my friend Mr. James Cook came on board to see me, and I gave him a plan of the Traverse between Cape Torment and east end of Orleans.

> 19 JULY. This day laying at the wharf at Quebec . . . I engaged to draw the Northumberland for Mr. James Cook after he had given me her dimensions.

Unfortunately the drawing he mentions has not survived.

On 5 July, a court martial was called on *Vanguard* for three deserters from that ship. The three men were James Mike, Thomas Wilkinson and William McMillard. A week later Cook reported the outcome:

> 12 JULY. At 10 am the Vanguard made the signal for pinnaces manned and armed to attend the execution of the 3 criminals pursuant to the sentence of a court-martial but the Commodore having pardoned 2 they cast lots who should die. The man was executed accordingly.

Colvill had given the following order:

> You are to hoist a red pennant at the fore-top-gallant-mast-head, and fire a gun, as a signal for the boats of the squadron to attend; and when all things are ready for the execution of the three prisoners, above named, you are to cause them to throw dice, or draw lots, so that only one may suffer death, who is to be immediately executed, upon firing a gun as a signal for the same. The other two are to be reprieved until further orders.[5]

At 11am on 12 July the prisoners, attended by two members of the clergy, proceeded to the forecastle, where James Mike drew the short straw and was hanged. William Adams, *Northumberland*'s captain, wrote in his log that the three men absconded from the hospital at Point de Lévis without leave but were captured in a canoe a few days later. They were all condemned to death for desertion, but on account of their families 'whose subsistence must depend on their labour', two were pardoned. It has also been suggested that, as seamen were in short supply, hanging three men served little purpose.

British ships from the two squadrons had been posted to prevent any French ships getting through to the St Lawrence. French reinforcements (four hundred soldiers of the Compagnies Franches de la Marine) had embarked in France on transport ships and were escorted across the Atlantic by the frigate *Machault*. When they reached the Gulf of St Lawrence, they were sighted and pursued by British ships led by Captain John Byron in *Fame*, before taking refuge in Baie des Chaleurs. A battle ensued on 8 July 1760 at the mouth of the Restigouche River. *Machault*, *Bienfaisant* and *Marquis de Malauze* were all destroyed.

In 1760 the three British armies advanced on Montreal. General Jeffery Amherst, the victor at Louisbourg, approached down the St Lawrence River from Lake Ontario, and Brigadier William Haviland led an army down Lake Champlain and the Richelieu River from Albany. After Lévis retreated from Quebec, Murray followed up the St Lawrence with what was left of his army.

The French put up strong resistance and both Amherst and Haviland were held up in their advance in August; Amherst's army was thwarted at Fort Lévis, while Haviland encountered fierce fighting at Île aux Noix, where Bougainville was in command. Bougainville withdrew toward Montreal on 28 August, aware that his retreat could be blocked by Murray's force.

The British armies converged on Montreal in early September, Vaudreuil and Lévis having pulled back the French troops within the city walls. Amherst's army landed on 6 September at Lachine, while Murray arrived to the east of the city and Haviland reached the south shore of the St Lawrence, opposite the city. The British had seventeen thousand troops to the French two thousand, who had little choice but surrender. Much to the disgust of Lévis, Amherst insisted on strict terms and denied the French the honours of war. The British occupied Montreal on 9 September, thus ending the war in North America (apart from a skirmish in Newfoundland in 1762). News of a British victory at Montreal reached Quebec on 12 September. Cook wrote:

> 12 SEPTEMBER. At 5am Capt Deane of his Majesty's ship Diana came down from Montreal and informed us of the surrender of that city to his Majesty's troops on the 8th instant.

By late September the British were making preparations to leave Quebec. Colvill wrote to the Admiralty:

> Captain Wheelock of the Pembroke, who has been hitherto a guardship at Isle au Cudre, is gone down the river to cruise off Gaspey; and agreeable to their Lordship's order of 25 April, I have directed him to be at Newfoundland in time enough to convoy the Trade that must sail from thence to England in the end October.
>
> The joint request of Generals Amherst and Murray, concurring with my own inclinations to serve Captain Deane of the Diana, has induced me to send him to wait on their Lordships. He commanded all the vessels employed on the expedition from Quebec to Montreal ... he is very capable of giving an account ... with relation to this country.[6]

Alexander Schomberg, who had captained *Diana*, requested to be sent back to Britain on health grounds and Colvill assented. Twenty years later, Schomberg wrote 'An Ode to the Memory of Captain James Cook, of His Majesty's Navy', which was published in Dublin in 1780. Despite its title, Cook's name is not mentioned once in the ode. A reviewer in *The Gentleman's Magazine* described the poem: 'This Ode, we understand, is by Sir Alexander S------- to whom it can be no disparagement to say that we doubt not he is a better officer than a poet.'[7] A sample verse:

> No more he'll wing the flying Sail,
> The vast Abyss of Ocean to explore;
> Expecting Nations shall bewail
> The SON of SCIENCE, now no more!

Schomberg was replaced by Joseph Deane, who had lost his ship, *Lowestoffe*. However, Colvill later chose Deane as the officer to return to Britain entrusted with the dispatches and news of the final surrender by the French at Montreal. This created another vacancy, which Colvill filled by moving his flag captain on *Northumberland*, William Adams, across to *Diana* on 21 September. Nathaniel Bateman (see section 'Nathaniel Bateman') became the new captain on *Northumberland*. Bateman was temporarily without a command: he had been in charge of *Eurus*, which sank near Cape Chat on 26 June while passing down the river. The ship ran ashore about midnight in very thick fog and little wind, but everyone was saved when the weather cleared. Bateman was acquitted of all blame by a court martial held on *Northumberland* on 14 August. Bateman was mustered on 22 September but Cook reported his arrival on board only on 9 October (muster #1343). Bateman missed dining with General Jeffery Amherst, the victorious commander of the British army, who was entertained on *Northumberland* on 5 October.

The day after Bateman's arrival, *Northumberland* came to sail and was saluted by the garrison. Another slow descent of the river followed. Cape Gaspé was passed on the 18th and *Northumberland* anchored alongside the wharf in Halifax Harbour at 8pm on 24 October. Two days later Colvill wrote to the Admiralty with a list of the ships he had with him at Halifax. They were HMS *Northumberland, Sutherland, Falkland, Rochester, Penzance, Diana, Lizard, Repulse, Porcupine* and *Racehorse*. They were 'to winter at Halifax, except such of the frigates as may be required for convoys'.[8] Cook's log over the next few months recorded the comings and goings of these vessels.

James Cook and his companions settled in for another cold winter in Halifax on *Northumberland*. The war in North America might have finished but the Seven Years' War still continued in Europe and India. Britain was still at war with France so it was necessary to maintain a naval force in North America in case France attempted a new campaign there.

The end of the war had left British forces spread far and wide, and not everyone had been accounted for. Some soldiers had been stranded on nearby Sable Island, off Nova Scotia, unbeknown to anyone else:

9 JANUARY. pm Anchored here a schooner from Island Sable with some soldiers which had been cast away there some time since.

11 JANUARY. Employed fitting out a schooner to send to the Island Sable to fetch off the soldiers which remained there.

Cook's chartwork had been reaping rewards in terms of recognition. It now paid dividends in monetary terms, as Colvill gave instructions for him to be paid a special sum of £50 for his efforts.

19 JANUARY. ... directed the Storekeeper to Pay the Master of the Northumberland Fifty pounds in consideration of his indefatigable Industry in making himself Master of the Pilotage of the River Saint Lawrence, &c.

As Beaglehole points out, 'This can be regarded as a handsome bonus on the master's regular pay of six guineas a month.'[9] It represents recognition for Cook's abilities and shows that his skills were, by now, well known to senior officers. Otherwise life in Halifax continued as normal, with the routine occasionally interrupted by celebrations:

NATHANIEL BATEMAN

Nathaniel Bateman took over as captain of HMS *Northumberland* under Commodore Alexander Colvill in 1760. He remained with the ship, on which James Cook was the master, until it returned to Britain in November 1762. A biography of Admiral Rodney by Donald Macintyre records that: 'Nathaniel Bateman . . . had been raised from the lower deck as a reward for conspicuous gallantry – in his case during Mathews' ill-starred Battle of Toulon [in 1744].'[10] That promotion did not happen immediately, though; Bateman had been an AB on *Marlborough* during the battle of Toulon, and he served on several ships over the next ten years as midshipman, master's mate and AB. He was thirty-two years old, with thirteen years' service by the time his lieutenant's passing certificate was issued, in June 1755. Bateman became a lieutenant on 5 July 1756 and served on *St George*. He was on *Neptune*, Saunders's flagship during the Quebec campaign in 1759.

Bateman was promoted to commander on 22 September 1759, immediately after the siege of Quebec, and he was further promoted to captain on 31 March 1760. He was appointed to HMS *Eurus* and remained there until the ship sank in the St Lawrence on 26 June 1760. Shortly after, Bateman replaced Adams as captain of *Northumberland* in October 1760.

Bateman stayed with Colvill and Cook on *Northumberland*, based in Halifax until August 1762, when they all took part in the relief of St John's, Newfoundland. Bateman left the ship on 8 December 1762 after it had returned to Britain. On 24 February 1763 he moved to *Ludlow Castle* and remained there as captain until 18 July 1764. He may have commanded *Bellona*, a guardship at Plymouth from 1765 to 1767. On 20 February 1776 he took command of *Winchelsea* for two years. He was then appointed on 25 July 1778 to HMS *Yarmouth* which, in April 1780, formed part of the British fleet under Admiral Sir George Rodney in the West Indies. Rodney engaged the French, under Admiral de Guichen, off Martinique; the admiral sent out directions and signals that virtually all of his captains found difficult to understand and implement. As a result, the battle proved indecisive. Rodney blamed his captains for not delivering him a famous victory and was very critical of most of them, but Bateman was singled out for a court martial. At the court martial in New York he was found guilty and he apparently insulted the judges after being sentenced.[11] He was dismissed from the navy but, on 13 November 1780, his name appeared on the superannuated captain's list. Nothing further is known of him.

James Cook named Bateman's Bay on the south New South Wales coast. It has been suggested that that is was to honour Nathaniel Bateman, but another Bateman, John Bateman, who was one of the Lords Commissioners of the Admiralty in the mid-1750s is a more likely namesake.

11 FEBRUARY. Received advice of the death of his late Majesty King George the 2. This day was appointed to proclaim his present Majesty King George the 3, which was done accordingly.

The punishments of Edward Lovely continued:

30 MARCH. At 8am the Devonshire made the signal for all Captains to hold a court-martial on Edward Lovely, seaman, of this ship for several crimes and misdemeanouring.

1 APRIL. At 8am made the signal for boats manned and armed to attend the punishment of Edward Lovely with 13 lashes alongside each ship being part of the punishment inflicted upon him by the sentence of a court-martial.

The crew of *Northumberland* had to endure miserable and cold conditions but their commodore did not share the bleak circumstances on the ship as he lived ashore where he took part in the administration of the province. From the comfort of his billet ashore, Colvill wrote another letter to the Admiralty in April 1761 recalling the winters he had experienced in Halifax:

... I have now been three winters at Halifax, and have found by experience, that in general, this season is not so boisterous, as 'tis commonly thought. We have much less blowing weather than in England, and much more sunshine. 'Tis the frost that makes the coasting navigation so difficult, and most impracticable to ships. The running ropes freeze in the blocks; the sails are stiff like sheets of tin; and the men cannot expose their hands long enough to the cold, to do their duty aloft; so that topsails are not easily handled; however, sloops and schooners where the men stand on the deck and do all their work succeed well enough, and we have always been very well supplied with frozen beef from Boston, which keeps our seamen healthy while they continue in port; but the scurvy never fails to pull us down in great numbers, upon our going to sea in the spring.

PART OF COOK'S DESCRIPTION OF THE SEA COAST OF NOVA SCOTIA

Harbour of Halifax
In turning here you may make free with both sides until the length of the ledge of Point Pleasant. Then you must not stand to westward to shut Chebucto Head behind Point Sandwich until you are above the ledge, nor to the eastward as soon as you are the length of the NW point of Cornwallis Island to lose sight of the house on Maugers Beach until Mr. Gerrish's store house at Point Pleasant is brought in a line with the dwelling house. You will then be clear of all danger and may stand over to the eastern shore as near as you please, it being very bold too having 9 & 10 fathoms close to it. You must not make quite so free with the other side until above George's Island. You will then be clear of all danger whatsoever and may anchor any where before the

town in 12, 13 and 14 fathoms, excellent clear good holding ground and sheltered from all winds.

From George's Island to the Navy Yard is NNW ¾W 1½ miles. Ships that want to go there may run up and anchor before the place, or if convenient go along side of the Careening wharfs at once where there is sufficient water for almost any ship in the Navy with all her stores in.

Bedford Bason

From George's Island to the entrance into the Bason is NNW & NW by N 3 miles. In this passage is 12 and fathoms in the middle of the channel and on each side 7 & 8. The entrance is not quite a ¼ of a mile broad and 12 and 13 fathoms deep, bold too on both sides.

The Bason is between 4 and 5 miles in length, N by W & S by E, 2 miles in breadth, in many places between 30 and 40 fathoms deep and navigable up to the very head. It is frozen up the greatest part of the winter so that people travel over it to and from Fort Sackville.

The harbor of Halifax is without doubt one of the best in America sufficiently large to hold all the Navy of England with great safety. Both its in and outlet is very easy and open in the most severest frosts.

Latitude 44° 36'N per Observation

Longitude 63° 26'W from London by computation

Variation of the compass 12° 50' degrees per oberservation.

The tides flow in the harbor full and change half an hour after seven, about eight feet up and down but is greatly governed by the winds.

Marks for anchoring	Of wooding and watering	Of provisions and refreshment	Descriptions of fortifications and landing places
Ships generally anchor before the town being the most convenient. They may notwithstanding anchor in other places with equal safety it being everywhere good anchoring ground all over the whole harbour.	Wood and water may be got here in great plenty. There are two watering places with spouts, one in the yard and the other close by it, where you can fill the casks in the boats. It some time may happen in a very dry season that there may be a scarcity of water at those places. If so you may water at Dartmouth where there is never not want. There you will obliged to land your casks.	Fresh and sea provisions in general is pretty well supplied by the contractor and refreshments such as stock, vegetables, etc., may be got at most times of the year.	There are several batteries for the defence of this harbour all of which are pointed out in the plan. Ships may come near enough to silence some and entirely destroy others.

The ice which comes from the Gulph of St Lawrence and Gut of Canso in the spring, never reaches so far west as this place; but generally collects itself in compact bodies, to a great extent on the southern coast of the Island of Cape Breton; insomuch that last year when we ran amongst it in a dark night, it closed upon us and kept us fixed as in a dock for three days; but a swell arising, made a small opening thro' which we forced the ships. Luckily for us the weather was moderate.[12]

It would be interesting to know the opinions of Colvill's crew on some of these comments and whether they agreed. The men were not regularly issued with suitable clothing and what they had was often wet and cold. The hospital continued to do good business as seamen succumbed to the conditions.

At some time, probably while he was based in Halifax early in 1761, Cook drew up a new set of sailing directions covering Louisburg to Quebec. This document, now at the UK National Archives, was never published.[13] It is interesting for the personal tone of many entries with several 'in my opinion' and 'I believe' phrases. For example, when discussing Flat Island near Gaspé: 'You will have 28 and 30 fathoms water within ½ mile of the Island and I believe may approach it much nearer with safety.' And when describing tides: 'As the Tides here are but trifling and from other remarks I have made, I am of the opinion that there is a constant (but inconsiderable) southerly current in most part of the Gulf.'

Cook mentions some sources of information in these sailing directions, including French sources such as the surveyor, Chabert. In 1750 Joseph-Bernard de Chabert de Cogolin, an ensign in the French navy, was chosen to go to Île Royale to carry out a coastal survey. He also surveyed parts of the coast of Nova Scotia and the south coast of Newfoundland, returning to France in 1751, where he prepared his surveys for publication. The result appeared in 1753 as *Voyage fait par ordre du roi en 1750 et 1751, dans l'Amérique septentrionale*. Cook wrote: 'The Passage between Birds Islands and Brion Isle seems to be very good. Mr Charbert assures us that there is not less than a 11 fathom water in it.'

Cook was now an 'administrator' and required to keep various records, which were submitted to London on a regular basis. When based overseas, the records would be collected from all the ships and sent back by messenger:

11 APRIL. Put on board His Majesty's ship Fowey to be sent to the Navy Office the ships monthly books, pay lists, tickets & victualling accounts completed to the 31st of March.

Northumberland remained in port, as it was considered inadvisable to leave such an important naval port open to attack by the French. However, the other ships in the squadron were out on patrol. As well as keeping watch on the Gulf of St Lawrence, Colvill's ships regularly sailed down to New York and on to the Carolinas, where they could be used to accompany convoys of merchant ships across the Atlantic. Colvill had also to check that merchant ships operating in the region were not trading illegally. *Rochester* arrested a snow in the St Lawrence and, in early 1762, Cook reported that the vessel and cargo were confiscated:

2 SEPTEMBER. pm Anchored here a snow from the River St Lawrence taken by His Majestys ship Rochester carrying on an illicit trade.

Lying at anchor in Halifax Harbour did not prevent *Northumberland* from requiring an overhaul and in September 1761 the ship was taken into the careening wharf. While the ship was in there, Colvill shifted his pennant to *Rochester* in case he needed to go to sea. Cook noted:

17 SEPTEMBER. At 6am unmoored and hove short on the small bower. At 8 hove up the anchor and begun to warp up to the yard. At 6pm let go both the best anchors and hauled alongside the careening wharf.

19 September The Commodore shifted his pendant onboard the Rochester.

A broad pennant was a swallow-tailed tapering flag at the masthead of a man-of-war, designating that a commodore was on board (both pennant and pendant were terms used). Repairs took one month and *Northumberland* was ready on 17 October. No alarms and excursions had occurred and Colvill restored his pennant to the ship the next day.

17 OCTOBER. At 7am hauled off from the wharf and dropped down the harbour.

18 OCTOBER. The Commodore shifted his pennant from the Rochester to this ship.

Winter was approaching again, and Cook recorded:

10 DECEMBER. ... and made all snug for the winter.

St John's, Newfoundland, 1762

James Cook was still in Halifax, Nova Scotia, as 1762 began. He and his ship, HMS *Northumberland*, had been stationed at the port for fourteen months and had never once been out to sea during that time. Instead, Cook had endured the routines of repairing, cleaning and maintaining his ship and keeping the crew alert and healthy. He was failing in the last activity, as his log recorded. Throughout January the entry invariably read 'sent men to the hospital'. Halifax was a new port and did not yet have a hinterland capable of provisioning such a large body of men as were now stationed there. Meat and other stores were regularly shipped in from New England and from across the Atlantic. However, the lack of fruit and vegetables took their toll, exacerbated by the bitter cold. An infectious disease (possibly typhus but unspecified) may have also played a part, as Cook mentioned the need for a thorough cleaning of the ship.

The British ships at Halifax were part of a squadron under Alexander, Lord Colvill. Colvill's role was to monitor the waters off North America and he was aware that merchant ships operating in the region were not just supplying Halifax but were carrying out illegal trade with ports that had been part of French Quebec and other locations around the Gulf of St Lawrence. Colvill sent his ships out on patrols to prevent this trade and they regularly arrested ships and confiscated their cargo. One such arrest was reported by Colvill in January 1762:

> Captain Burnett of the *Rochester*, at the Isle of Bic, took possession of a Snow from Guernsey for Quebec, which he also brought to this Place ... tried in the Court of Admiralty; and I inclose Copies of their Condemnation.
>
> ... Snow [was called] the Two Brothers Nicholas Le Masurer Master and her Cargo seized in the Port of Halifax ... for clandestine and Illicit Trade; ... We do adjudge and decree the said Snow Two Brothers, together with all her Guns, Tackle, Ammunition, Apparel and Furniture, as allso all and Singular the Goods, Wares and Merchandize of the Growth, Produce or Manufacture of Europe: the Cargo thereof to be forfieted ... and we do further order that the said Snow Two Brothers together with her Guns, Tackle, Apparel, Ammunition and Furniture ... be sold by the Marshall of this Court or his Dupty at Publick Auction ...[1]

The master of *Two Brothers*, Nicholas Lemesurier was the father of William Lemesurier, who, thirty years later, sailed to the north-west coast of America with George Vancouver.

One of the ways to break the monotony for Cook and his men was to help recover merchant ships that had gone aground in Halifax Harbour. The log recorded:

30 JANUARY. At ½ past 9pm the Elizabeth merchant ship parted from her anchors and drove onshore on St George's Island.

31 JANUARY. am Sent our boats to her assistance.

13 FEBRUARY. At 6pm the Charming Nancy snow from London in turning into the harbour struck upon a rock a little above Point Pleasant where she bilged and sunk.

18 FEBRUARY. am The master and boatswain with 40 seamen and craft went to endeavour to weigh the snow, she having drove off the rock into 8 fathoms water.

Winters in Halifax could be harsh and the seamen were poorly equipped to deal with the cold conditions. An Act had been passed making it illegal for men to sell clothes to each other, presumably to protect the weaker men from being coerced into selling or to prevent men from selling them ashore for alcohol or other pleasures. Even so, the trade did take place and occasionally men were punished, as when:

24 FEBRUARY. am Punished Peter Campbell with 24 lashes for neglect of duty and selling his clothes.

The clothes problem was highlighted by a letter Colvill sent to Britain in May: 'I have expected some Marine Cloathing by every Storeship that has arrived at this place; but as none has been sent out, I am under the necessity of acquainting their Lordships, that 'tis almost three Years since the Marines on board the *Northumberland* were cloathed.'[2]

While the British in Halifax were waiting for winter to break, events were hatching in France that would have direct consequences for Colvill and his squadron. The French had surrendered North America to the British at Montreal in 1760, thereby relinquishing all rights to land on the American mainland. The war had continued in Europe but, by 1762, it was nearing its end and the French, keen to have some land with which to bargain at the impending treaty negotiations, saw an opportunity to attack Newfoundland. French fishermen had long fished the Grand Banks off the south-east coast of Newfoundland and maintained seasonal settlements on the island. The French government wanted to maintain a base from which their vessels could continue to operate.

The Duc du Choiseul, the French naval minister, arranged for a force to be assembled at Brest, to carry out an attack on Newfoundland, knowing that is was very poorly defended. On 8 May 1762, four French ships, under the command of Charles-Henri-Louis d'Arsac de Ternay, set off and managed to evade the British blockade of Brest. Ternay was aboard *Robuste* and also on board was the twenty-year-old Jean-François de Galaup de La Pérouse, who would later emulate Cook in exploring the Pacific.

The French ships carried six hundred troops under the command of Colonel d'Haussonville and Ternay was able to land them at Bay Bulls, south of St John's, Newfoundland, on 24 June. Three days later, after marching overland, they easily captured St John's, which had been defended by less than a hundred British soldiers. A British frigate, *Gramont* lying at anchor in the harbour, was also captured. The French quickly began destroying fishing vessels and equipment, both in St John's and in harbours around Conception Bay. News of the attack began to reach Halifax in early July; Cook recorded:

1 JULY. At 3am arrived here his Majesty's ship Syren from Newfoundland and brought intelligence of five sail of the enemy ships being seen off that place.

Colvill wanted to sail immediately for St John's to relieve the port but the local lieutenant governor and the people of Halifax prevented him from doing so as they feared it would leave them defenceless. Colvill directed Charles Douglas, captain of *Syren*, to return immediately to his station off Newfoundland to gather more information. Douglas had already reinforced the garrison at Aquaforte and had also dispatched a small vessel to look out for Captain Graves and *Antelope*, accompanying the fishing fleet across the Atlantic, to inform him of events. Colvill sent off dispatches to London and also passed on the news to General Amherst, in charge of British troops in North America. It was arranged that Placentia, on the western coast of the Avalon Peninsula in Newfoundland, would be the rendezvous for a British response.

It was fortunate that Colvill had been persuaded from venturing to Newfoundland straight away. *Northumberland* was the only ship available and a single ship would have been useless for such an attack; it would take some time anyway to prepare the ship for sailing. Over the next days, Halifax was a hive of activity. Ships came in carrying further news of happenings in Newfoundland and *Northumberland* was moved out to anchor off Mauger's Beach on McNabs Island. Steps were taken to improve Halifax's defences and the crew of *Northumberland* helped in this. Cook wrote:

15 JULY. Master [Cook] and some hands employed making a boom across the NW Arm.

Colvill maintained a steady flow of correspondence to keep the Admiralty informed. In a letter of 24 July he said:

I would have sailed for Newfoundland immediately on receiving this Intelligence but was again prevented by a second Remonstrance from the Governour and Council, intreating me in the strongest Terms to continue with them ... I have a Letter from Captain Mouat of the Gramont Sloop, dated the 26th of June in St John's Harbour. He says he got in there the Day before, with the Trade from Ireland, and with his People was to stay in the Place for its Defence. We are informed that the Gramont fell into the Hands of the Enemy. Most of her Convoy escaped by getting out in time. I sent the above Account to Sir Jeffery Amherst without loss of time, and desired him to communicate it to the Commander in Chief of the Fleet in the West Indies, as I did not know how to direct to him. I am doing every thing in my Power for the Security and Defence of this Place.[3]

Captain Mouat was Patrick Mouat, who would take *Tamar* to the Pacific as companion vessel to Byron in *Dolphin* in 1764. His son, Alexander Mouat, was a midshipman on *Discovery* during Cook's third voyage. A few days later he wrote: '[The French] their whole number of Troops does not exceed nine hundred: that they had mounted the Gramon's Guns onshore, and were very busy in throwing up Entrenchments, and making Lines of Picquets.'[4]

Colvill finally received naval reinforcements on 2 August, when Captain John Jervis (later Earl St Vincent) brought *Gosport* in from New York. Colvill realised that naval forces alone would not defeat the French and he began efforts to use local militia. Local commanders would only act, though, if so ordered by General Amherst in New York. By now, the true size and nature of the French force was known:

A Cartel Brigantine with one hundred and forty Prisoners sailed from St John's for England on the 18th, past; but finding themselves badly provided with Water and Provisions, bore away for Louisbourg to get a supply. By this means we learn that the Enemy's Squadron under the Chevalier de Ternay consisted of the Robuste of 74 Guns, L'Eveille 64. Le Garonne 28. L'Unicorne 26. And according to the best intelligence that could be got, there were about fifteen hundred Troops under the Command of the Count D'haussonville. We are likewise informed that the *Antelope* was spoke with on the 18th. past near Trepassy, and that Captain Graves had received Intelligence of the French being in possession of St John's.[5]

Colvill was determined to wait no longer and set sail with *Gosport* for Newfoundland in the hope of meeting *Antelope* and *Syren* at Placentia. The armed brig *King George* had brought dispatches from Amherst that a force of British soldiers would follow. The brig was co-opted into the expedition. Cook recorded:

10 AUGUST. At ½ past 6am weighed and came to sail as did the Gosport & King George. Standing out of Chebucto Bay. Noon Cape Sambro S by W 16 miles.

Meanwhile, Thomas Graves, the Governor of Newfoundland had made for Placentia and had been strengthening its defences. Colvill and his small fleet approached Placentia on the morning of 14 August. Cook recorded:

14 AUGUST. 6am standing into Placentia Bay. ½ past 9 anchored with the best bower in Placentia Road in 5 fathoms water ... found riding here his Majesty's ships Antelope & Syren.

Graves and Colvill met to plan their attack. Colvill's intention was to patrol off St John's while waiting for the army to arrive. Meanwhile, in New York, General Jeffery Amherst had appointed his brother, Colonel William Amherst, to command that British army contingent. On 15 August, it finally departed New York in a series of transports. Colvill, having left a small contingent of marines to reinforce the fort, sailed from Placentia on 22 August and headed for St John's on the east coast. Another letter from him carried this opinion: 'If I may venture to give my opinion, I should think the French will remain at St John's with all their Force, untill they know whether any Endeavour is to be made to retake the Place before Winter.'[6]

From the time Cook left Halifax he recorded sailing directions in his remarks book as well as keeping his log. While in Placentia he surveyed the harbour and drew a chart; he also included a plan of the fort overlooking the harbour. As they headed for St John's, the British stopped any ships they encountered for news or to check if they were French:

24 AUGUST. 6am Spoke with a cartel schooner from St John's bound to Halifax out of whom we took men.

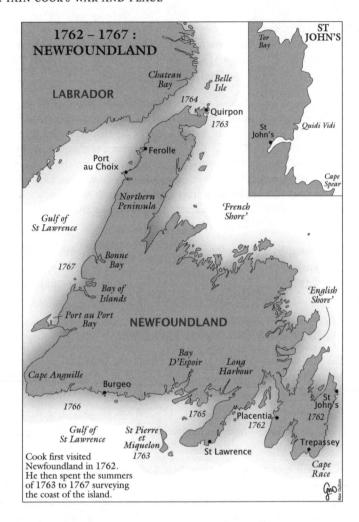

1762 – 1767 :
NEWFOUNDLAND

ST JOHN'S

LABRADOR

Chateau Bay

Belle Isle

1764

Quirpon
1763

Tor Bay

St John's

Quidi Vidi

Ferolle

Port au Choix

Cape Spear

Northern Peninsula

'French Shore'

Gulf of St Lawrence

Bonne Bay

1767

Bay of Islands

'English Shore'

Port au Port Bay

NEWFOUNDLAND

Bay D'Espoir

Long Harbour

Cape Anguille

Burgeo

St John's

1766

1765

Placentia
1762

1762

Gulf of St Lawrence

St Pierre et Miquelon
1763

St Lawrence

Trepassey

Cape Race

Cook first visited
Newfoundland in 1762.
He then spent the summers
of 1763 to 1767 surveying
the coast of the island.

25 AUGUST. At 4pm Spoke to a cartel sloop from St John's out of which we took 14 men. At ½ past 4 the Gosport brought to the chase which proved to be the Concord French armed schooner from St John's mounting 8 carriage guns & carrying 31 men. Took out the prisoners and sent a midshipman & 9 men on board.

The British put into Bay Bulls for water and Cook took the opportunity to survey the bay and produce a chart. He also wrote sailing directions and a description of the bay:

There is no kind of difficulty or danger whatever in going into this Bay it's a mile broad in the entrance and lies in NW by W and NW one league: with respect to the depth of water nature of the ground &c I refer you to the plan – Latitude 47° 26 N Pr Observation. Variation of the Compass 19 30 Wt

Marks for anchoring	Of wooding and watering	Of provisions and refreshment	Further descriptions in regard to trade, shipping, etc
The Best place to Anchor in this Bay, is from a little above Bread and Cheese point up to the head of the Bay close under the North Shore here the ground is very good and you are pretty well sheltered from the Sea winds.	Wood and Water may be got here, particularly the latter in great plenty and with little Trouble. Wood doth not abound in such great plenty or so convenient.	Some salt provisions may be got here sometimes but no fresh except fish. Some vegetables may be got here at the proper season of the year.	A Considerable fishing Trade is carried on in this Bay.

The British left again on 29 August and, after a cursory look into St John's Harbour, spent the next two weeks cruising off shore while they waited for the troops to arrive. Amherst had reached Halifax on 26 August and pressed Lieutenant JFW DesBarres on the expedition as assistant engineer and surveyor. As ever, Cook used the time positively and carried out a running survey of the coast from Cape Spear north to Cape St Francis. A chart of this coast represents Cook's work at this time.

Amherst reached Louisbourg on 5 September and collected more troops. On 11 September, the army finally made contact with the navy off St John's, as Cook recorded:

11 SEPTEMBER. am Off Cape Spear 1pm joined us 12 sail of transports with troops on board . . . came on board Colonel Amherst, commanding officer of the troops.

Amherst wrote: 'We discovered his Lordship's fleet about 10 o'clock and joined them about 2 off Petty Harbour. I immediately went on board Lord Colvill and we concerted measures together.'[7]

The troops were landed on the 13th at Torbay, twelve kilometres north of St John's, and immediately marched south to begin the assault. By the next day the British had secured Quidi Vidi and *Northumberland* was busy ferrying troops and lending support. On the 15th the British forces advanced to capture Signal Hill, overlooking St John's. Amherst recorded:

15 SEPTEMBER. Just at peep of day Captain McDonald had ascended Signal Hill, surprised the enemy and drove them from it.[8]

It was foggy on the evening of 15 September and the British ships were firing guns to keep in touch with each other. At about midnight, Ternay, realising all was lost, took advantage of an opportunity when winds and fog drove the British fleet offshore to escape from the harbour with all his four ships. He headed across the Atlantic but was unable to enter Brest and spent the next few months, until peace was signed, in the harbour at La Coruña in northern Spain. Colvill was highly indignant at this 'shamefull flight', probably as it denied him the chance for taking prizes:

In the afternoon I received a Note from Colonel Amherst, acquainting me that the French Fleet got out last Night. Thus, after being blocked up in St John's Harbour for three Weeks, by a Squadron of equal Number, but smaller Ships with fewer Guns and Men did Monsieur Ternay make his Escape in the Night by a shamefull Flight. I beg leave to observe, that not a Man in the Squadron, imagined the four sail, when we saw them, were the Enemy, and the Pilots were of opinion, that they must have had the Wind much stronger than with us, to overcome the easterly Swell in the Harbour's Mouth. ... Monsieur de Ternay seemed determined at all Events, to grasp an opportunity, which if once lost might never be regained, therefore, in the utmost Confusion, he left behind, his Grenadiers, Anchors, and turned his Boats a drift when they had towed him out. The Fog was so thick, that Lieutenant Colonel Tulliken, who was posted on an Eminence in the narrowest part of the Harbour's Mouth, could hear the Noise but could not discern any of their Ships.[9]

Cook recorded the events of Ternay's escape:

16 SEPTEMBER. 2am Saw a strange sail in the SE; ½ past 2 saw 4 sail in the SE which the Syren made the signal for seeing. ½ past 6 lost sight of the above 4 sail. At 3 pm came out the lieutenant with the pinnace and cutter and gave account that the French fleet sailed last night consisting of 5 sail.

On 18 September the French commander, d'Haussonville, surrendered to Amherst (Colvill was still out at sea). The news quickly reached *Northumberland*; it was carried by an interesting person as far as Cook was concerned – he had the same name:

18 SEPTEMBER. At 6pm came from the shore Lieutenant Cook of the Gosport with an account of the surrender of St John's.

This was probably the only occasion when these two James Cooks met (see section 'The Three James Cooks'). The British ships then entered St John's Harbour.

19 SEPTEMBER. 6am Made sail for St John's. am anchored in 6½ fathoms water.

Amherst and Colvill met to discuss the terms of capitulation, of which Colvill highly approved. On 20 September, a small squadron under Hugh Palliser (in HMS *Shrewsbury*) arrived from Britain to relieve the port. Palliser was Cook's former captain on *Eagle* and would be Governor of Newfoundland from 1764 until 1767. *Northumberland* remained in St John's Harbour for eighteen days. Cook, as had become his custom, set about surveying the harbour and produced a chart. On 25 September HMS *Enterprise* arrived from Havana with news that the British had captured that city from the Spanish.

Reports came in to St John's from surrounding districts about the damage that the French had done to harbours and shipping on the Avalon Peninsula and in Conception Bay. DesBarres, the army engineer who had come with Amherst, was sent in *Enterprise* to assess the damage. Cook accompanied DesBarres in order to survey the harbours of Harbour Grace and Carbonear, though he only spent one day on the survey.

The relief of St John's now successfully completed, Amherst sailed on 2 October: 'Having settled everything regarding the garrison and taken leave of Lord Colvill after the uninterrupted harmony that has subsisted between us, which he mentioned at our parting, I went on board the Enterprise and sailed out of the harbour in the afternoon.'[10] Colvill still had jobs to do such as arranging for about eight hundred French prisoners to be shipped back to France, but he was ready to sail for Britain on the 7th. *Northumberland* anchored at Spithead after an uneventful crossing on the 25th. Cook recorded:

25 OCTOBER. noon Saluted the Admiral at Spithead with 13 guns. Standing to Spithead. At 1pm anchored with the small bower in 10 fathoms.

Colvill immediately sent off reports to the Admiralty, highlighting, among other things, Cook's contributions:

. . . I have mentioned in another Letter that the Fortifications on the Island of Carbonera, were entirely destroyed by the Enemy. Colonel Amherst sent thither Mr. Desbarres an Engineer, who surveyed the Island and drew a Plan for fortifying it with new Works; when these are finished, the Enterprize's six Guns will be ready to mount on them. But I believe nothing will be under taken this Year, as the Season is so far advanced, and no kind of Materials on the spot for building Barracks or Sheds to cover the Men, should any be sent there. Mr. Cook, Master of the Northumberland, accompanied Mr. Desbarres. He has made a Draught of Harbour Grace, and the Bay of Carbonera; both which are in a great measure commanded by the Island, which lies off a Point of Land between them. Hitherto we have had a very imperfect Knowledge of these Places, but Mr. Cook who was particularly carefull in sounding them has discovered that Ships of any size may lay in safety both in Harbour Grace and the Bay of Carbonera.[11]

For his own part, Colvill received the good news of his promotion to Rear Admiral of the White. He hoisted his flag on the 27th and the fleet saluted him. He struck his flag three days later. On 3 December there was a declaration of cessation of hostilities and on the 8th the remainder of the ship's company of *Northumberland* was paid off. The master's log maintained by Cook finished on 11 November, when Cook was discharged and replaced by John Major. The last entry reads:

11 NOVEMBER. Clear'd out the Spirit room for takeing in the wine and Brandy, Shipwrights Still on Board. Ja⁵ Cook.

Cook was, no doubt, pleased to be home, having been away from Britain for four and a half years. He had a great deal to catch up on. Now relatively rich, having received pay of £291 19s 3d owing to him, Cook left Portsmouth and went up to London. It seems his main intent was finding a wife as, within weeks, the thirty-four-year-old Cook had proposed to and married the twenty-one-year-old Elizabeth Batts. He could have known or known of Elizabeth from the time she was a young girl as her parents ran the Bell alehouse in Wapping, which Cook probably frequented from his earliest days on colliers.

Samuel Batts, Elizabeth's father, had died in 1742 and Mary Batts had remarried, this time to John Blackburn, on 18 July 1745 at St Paul, Shadwell. Mary Blackburn had then arranged for Elizabeth to move away from the hustle and bustle of London and she had

THE THREE JAMES COOKS

By a very strange coincidence, three James Cooks were employed by the Royal Navy on the North America station in the early 1760s. All of the three were masters at some point and all carried out surveys and drew charts. Two of them, including the famous Cook, may have even met outside St John's Harbour, Newfoundland in September 1762.

James Cook #1 is the subject of this book. From 1759 until 1762, Cook #1 was master of HMS *Northumberland*, the flagship of Alexander, Lord Colvill, based in Halifax, Nova Scotia. During this time Cook surveyed Halifax Harbour and produced sailing instructions for the Nova Scotian coast near there. The French attacked Newfoundland in 1762 and Cook was part of the force that went to recapture the island. From then until 1767, Cook #1 was occupied in surveying Newfoundland.

James Cook #2 was commissioned as a lieutenant in 1760. He had been master of HMS *Mercury* but he was then posted to HMS *Gosport*, one of the other ships based in Halifax. Immediately after the fall of St John's, Captain John Jervis of the *Gosport* sent Cook #2 with the news to inform Colvill on *Northumberland* – of which Cook #1 was master. Cook #2 then moved to the West Indies, where he took part in actions to carry dispatches across the Yucatan Peninsula. This formed the basis of a small book (*Remarks on a Passage from the River Balise, in the Bay of Honduras, to Merida; the Capital of the Province of Jucatan in the Spanish West Indies*, London: 1769). In the 1770s he was back in Britain, where he produced a chart of Fowey Harbour in Cornwall, published in 1779. He disappeared from the navy lists in 1800.

James Cook #3 is known from three charts published in London in 1766 by Emmanuel Bowen. He arrived at Halifax in October 1762 as master of HMS *Mars*, just weeks after the other two Cooks had left the port. He was based there until April 1763 and used the time to survey Halifax Harbour. On his return to Britain, Cook #3 transferred to *Alarm* and sailed to Jamaica. In 1764 he was at Port Royal, South Carolina, which he also surveyed. However, in August 1765, he was court-martialled for disobedience (apparently spending too much effort and time on surveying) and he was dismissed in January 1766. Cook #3 returned to America, where he had acquired land. He became a land surveyor and several of his plans of the Carolinas and Florida remain. Cook #3, however, disappears from the record in 1776.

sent her to live with the Sheppard family in Barking. It was in Barking, therefore, that the couple were married. Cook obtained a marriage licence on 16 December from the vicar general's office and he and Elizabeth were married on 21 December at St Margaret's Church, Barking, by the Reverend George Downing before witnesses, John Richardson, Sarah Brown and William Everrest. The entry in the Parish register reads:

> 1762, DEC. 21. – James Cook of ye parish of St Paul, Shadwell, in ye county of Middlesex, batchelor, and Elizabeth Batts, of ye parish of Barking, in ye county of Essex, Spinster,

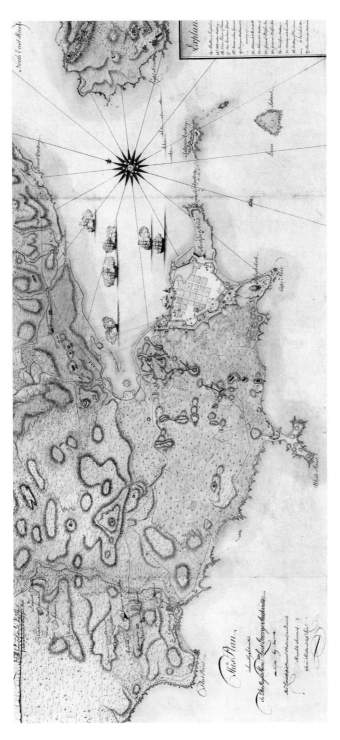

Plan of the siege of Louisbourg in 1758, by Samuel Holland (*National Archives of Canada*)

1759

May 16 Admirl Durell Buryed the Corps of Capt John Simco Esqr Cape Gaspy Lt NWN 48 Distance 8 Leuges Bunaventure WSW 7 League

(above) Ships off Anticosti marking Captain Simcoe's burial at sea, by Ashley Bowen (*Marblehead Museum*)
(right) 'West Shore of Richmond Isle, Near the Entrance of the Gut of Canso', from *Six Views of Cape Breton Island, etc*, by JFW DesBarres. The plate shows a surveyor with his crew at work in Nova Scotia at about the same time Cook was working in the region (*National Maritime Museum*)

Facing page (top) The coast at Kennington Cove and the rocks where General Wolfe landed prior to the siege of Louisbourg in 1758 (*Dave Fisher*)
(bottom) View of the present lighthouse of 1923 on Lighthouse Point (with the original of 1734 for comparison) and beyond to Battery Island at the entrance to Louisbourg Harbour (*Dave Fisher*)

A view of Halifax, in Nova Scotia, taken from Citadel-hill, looking down Prince Street, by Dominic Serres (after Richard Short). Cook's ship, HMS *Northumberland*, is probably one of the ships depicted (*Art Gallery of Nova Scotia*)

Plan of Cornwallis Island with ink detail of the town of Halifax with lettered explanation including north and south suburbs, fathoms marked, by James Cook (*British Library*)

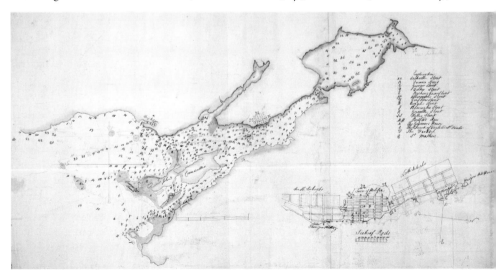

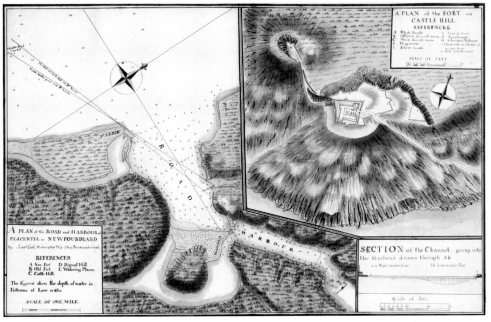

A Plan of the Road of the Harbour of Placentia in Newfoundland; with a Plan of the Fort on Castle Hill, by James Cook, 1762 (*UK Hydrographic Office*)

A Sketch of the Sea Coast of Newfoundland between Cape Spear and Cape St. Francis, by James Cook, 1762 (*U.K. Hydrographic Office*)

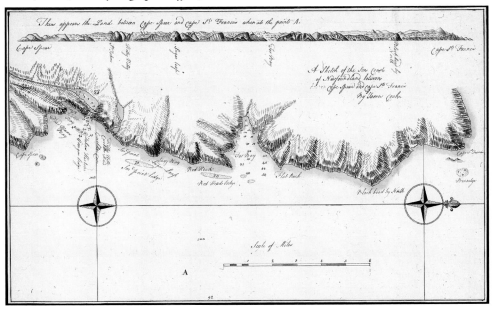

A Sketch of the Island of Newfoundland, by James Cook, 1763 (*National Archives of Canada*)

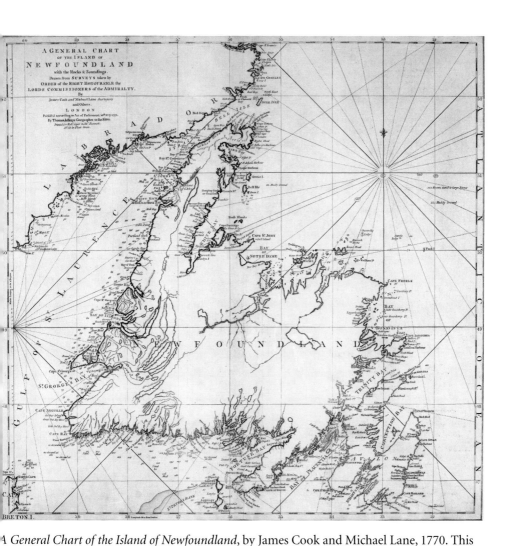

A *General Chart of the Island of Newfoundland*, by James Cook and Michael Lane, 1770. This map and the one opposite show clearly how Cook added to the knowledge of the coast of Newfoundland (*Memorial University of Newfoundland Library*)

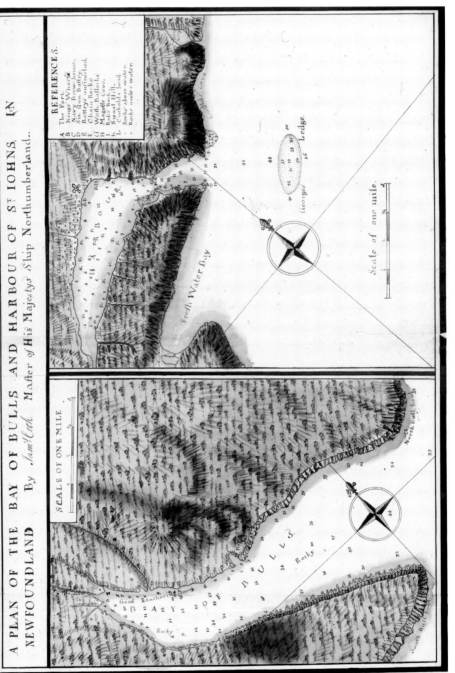

A Plan of the Bay of Bulls and Harbour of St. John's, Newfoundland, by James Cook, 1762 (UK Hydrographic Office)

were married by ye Archbishop of Canterbury's license, this twenty-first day of December, one thousand seven hundred and sixty-two, by George Downing, vicar of Little Wakering, Essex. This marriage was solemnized between us – Jams Cook, Elizabeth Cook, late Batts; in ye presence of John Richardson, Sarah Brown, William Everrest.[12]

William Everrest was the parish clerk, but it is not known who the other witnesses, John Richardson and Sarah Brown, were.

Colvill had not forgotten Cook after his return to Britain and he sent another letter to the Admiralty:

Mr Cook, late master of the Northumberland, acquaints me that he has laid before their Lordships all his draughts and observations relative to the river St Lawrence, part of the coast of Nova Scotia, and of Newfoundland.

On this occasion I beg leave to inform their Lordships that, from my experience of Mr Cook's genius and capacity, I think him well qualified for the work he has performed, and for greater undertakings of the same kind. These draughts being made under my own eye, I can venture to say they may be the means of directing many in the right way, but cannot mislead any.[13]

When Cook arrived back in Britain he discovered there had been a change of government and with it new leaders at the Admiralty. William Pitt had resigned and John Stuart, third Earl of Bute (1713–92), had succeeded as prime minister after the Duke of Newcastle's resignation as first lord of the Treasury on 26 May 1762. George Grenville (1712–70), William Pitt's brother-in-law, who had been instrumental in forcing the duke's resignation, was made the leader of the Commons. On 17 June 1762, George Montagu Dunk, second Earl of Halifax (1716–71), was appointed first lord of the Admiralty; he had no naval background and only remained in this post for four months.

Bute had accelerated the peace negotiations with France but there were sticking points, such as St Lucia, Martinique and Havana, where his Cabinet colleagues were not in agreement. Bute was not certain that Grenville would support the peace terms and push their acceptance in the Commons. Bute transferred Grenville to the Admiralty in place of Halifax on 18 October 1762 but, although Grenville remained in the Cabinet, he was excluded from the final phase of the peace negotiations.

Bute appointed the Duke of Bedford as special ambassador to Paris with instructions to finalise negotiations, and a preliminary treaty was signed at Fontainebleau on 3 November 1762. The terms of peace were vehemently attacked as inadequate by Pitt, who felt France should have been penalised more. Bute considered it was an honourable settlement, in which Britain was compensated and its new overseas possessions were confirmed, while France had lost heavily. It was felt that further humiliation of France would serve no purpose and would have worsened Britain's reputation, leading to her isolation. George III, who had wanted the war to end since his succession, called it 'a noble peace'.

There are several manuscript charts in the Admiralty Library, UK Hydrographic Office at Taunton from Cook's visit to Newfoundland in 1762. They are included in

Cook's remarks book.[14] None of these charts was ever published. The charts are entitled 'A Plan of the Road of the Harbour of Placentia in Newfoundland; with a Plan of the Fort on Castle Hill'; 'A Plan of the Bay of Bulls and Harbour of St John's, Newfoundland'; 'A Sketch of the Sea Coast of Newfoundland between Cape Spear and Cape St Francis'; and 'Plan of Carbonere Harbour and Harbour Grace in Conception Bay in Newfoundland, Surveyed by Order of the Right Honble. the Lord Colvill'. The text from Cook's remarks book was published as 'Capt. James Cook's Description of the Sea Coast of Nova Scotia, Cape Breton Island and Newfoundland', in the *Annual Report of the Trustees of the Public Archives of Nova Scotia for 1958.*

❦ II ❦

Captain Cook's Peace, 1763–1768

Cook's world changed completely at the end of 1762. He returned in November from North America, after being overseas for over four years, to a Britain ready for the peace that was agreed upon with the December truce. From then on Cook could pursue his career in the navy without the risk of being killed in battle. There were enough other ways of dying or suffering.

Cook had already quietly established a reputation for himself. The man who had joined the Royal Navy seven years earlier as an ordinary seaman had risen to be a ship's sailing master, the highest non-commissioned rank. Over the next five and a half years, he would build on that reputation, adding further skills to those he already possessed and ensuring that his name and ability were recognised by those in authority. That 'ordinary' seaman would become a regular visitor to the Admiralty in Whitehall and to the Navy Board in Crutched Friars. By the time the Royal Navy selected Cook to sail to the Pacific on *Endeavour* in 1768, he had advised first lords and the secretary to the Admiralty Board.

Cook had learned to survey and his aptitude for the work gained him his appointment in early 1763 to survey the island of Newfoundland off the east coast of Canada. The climate of Newfoundland dictated the modus operandi, with winters being too harsh to stay permanently on the island. Fishermen, who had used the island as a base to fish the Grand Banks for over a century, did so only during the summer. They crossed the Atlantic from Europe in about April or May, as soon as the ice cleared, and spent a hectic few months working. Then, in about October to November, they all headed back to winter in Europe. Cook adopted this procedure for his own work over the next five years.

Cook's new wife, Elizabeth, had grown up near the Thames among sailors and their families and would have expected that her husband would be away from her for long periods. She appears to have accepted her role as homemaker and that she would bring up their children largely by herself. The harsh Newfoundland winters proved a bonus for Elizabeth as they meant that James returned home for at least five months every year. Even then she had to share him with his work: Cook was expected to prepare charts, sailing directions and coastal views from the rough notes and versions he had made during the surveys and, as a perfectionist, Cook would have been meticulous and spent many hours on the work. He also had to make regular visits to Deptford to check on the state of his vessel, *Grenville*, especially in early 1765 when she was modified from a schooner to a brig.

By basing himself in London, Cook further distanced himself from his family in Cleveland. His mother died in 1765 but there is no record to say whether Cook went north at that time or any other during this period. Cook's father moved from Great Ayton to Redcar sometime shortly after his wife's death to live with one of his daughters,

Margaret Fleck. There was obviously some contact, though, as Frances Wardale, a cousin of Cook's through the Paces (she was a daughter of Deborah Pace, who was either a sister or niece of Cook's mother, Grace Cook), came to live in Mile End Old Town in order to help Elizabeth Cook with the children during Cook's absences.

The Cooks had three children born before Cook set off for the Pacific. James, the eldest, was born on 13 October 1763 and baptised at St Pauls, Shadwell. He joined the Royal Navy and was appointed commander of the sloop *Spitfire* in January 1794. He died on 25 January 1794 when he was lost in an open boat near Poole Harbour, his body being washed ashore on the Isle of Wight due to the strong westerly gale. He was later buried at St Andrew the Great, Cambridge. The second child was Nathaniel, born on 14 December 1764 and baptised at St Dunstan's, Stepney. He was on board *Thunderer* as a midshipman when she was lost with all hands at sea in a hurricane in the West Indies on 5 October 1780. Elizabeth was the Cooks' only daughter. She was baptised on 22 September 1766 at St Dunstan's but died on 9 April 1771, aged only four.

The Cooks' first home was 126 Upper Shadwell, about halfway between the junctions with Golds Hill and Love Lane. The north of the house backed on to one of the many rope walks in the district. It was owned by John Blackburn, the stepfather of Elizabeth Cook, who had moved to live in Starr Street behind Wapping Wall. Successive redevelopment of the area has left no trace of the house; Upper Shadwell is now The Highway.

The uncertainties caused by the Seven Years' War had slowed the building of new houses in Britain but, immediately the war ended, builders began again in earnest. Mile End Old Town lay to the north of Wapping and Shadwell, astride the main turnpike road leading out of London to Essex. In 1764, Ebenezer Mussell made land available for building on the south side of the main road, close to the junction with Stepney Green. Various builders, including John Sawyer, purchased plots and, over the next few years, built three-storey houses in a terrace. Wishing to be independent of the in-laws, James and Elizabeth Cook purchased a sixty-one-year lease on 7 Assembly Row (as the terrace was called). They bought it by an indenture of assignment on 24 February 1764 from John Sawyer. Derek Morris describes the house:

> The site was 139 feet deep and 15 feet wide, and the rack rent of £16 implied eight rooms, which is confirmed by the plan recorded in 1958 before the house was demolished. On 5th March 1764 he insured his brick house for £200 with the Sun Fire Office. On 23rd June 1768, just before sailing on his first voyage to the Pacific, he re-insured his house for £270 but now added his Household Goods for £200, the apparel for £50, the Plate for £25 and a timber shed behind the house for £10, all signs of his increasing prosperity.[1]

The Cooks' house was near the western end and one of the smaller houses in the terrace. Their neighbour to the east (no. 6) was David Witherspoon, a baker. To the west (no. 8), and separated from the Cooks by a passage, was William Honychurch, a watchmaker. James Cook only started paying land tax on the house in 1765; the delay may be accounted for by time taken to build the house and Cook's absence in Newfoundland. Added to which, Elizabeth was pregnant during 1764 with Nathaniel and it was his baptism on 8 January 1765 at St Dunstan's in Stepney that marked the Cooks' move to a new parish. Cook would have expected to move the family and belongings and not to leave it for Elizabeth to arrange while he was overseas. After Cook's death in 1779, Elizabeth Cook continued paying the land tax until 1787, when she vacated the house and moved to Clapham. The house was later renumbered as 88 Mile End Road and was demolished in 1958.

Richard Wise, who had been purser on HMS *Pembroke* when Cook sailed on her, had moved to Mile End Old Town and it may have been at his suggestion that the Cooks went there too. It was an astute move on Cook's part; the area was proving popular with the owners and captains of ships in the East India Company, as well as the senior members of Trinity House and officers in the Royal Navy. It brought Cook into close contact with people who could advance his career. When Cook was examined in 1768 for his lieutenant's certificate, one of the examiners was Captain Abraham North, a close neighbour of Cook's. The naval connection with Stepney was strengthened by St Dunstan's – where the Cooks worshipped – being the sailors' church and having the right to fly the red ensign, the flag of the merchant navy, from its tower.

If family life at Assembly Row was one major component in Cook's peace then his work in Newfoundland represented the other. The British had realised that their knowledge of the island's geography was dated and error strewn and that if they wished to govern it effectively they would need modern and correct charts. The choice of Cook to undertake the survey was a masterstroke as Cook spent the next five summers producing charts of such quality that they were still being used nearly a hundred years later. Admiral HW Bayfield, who resurveyed part of Newfoundland in the 1830s, wrote:

> The Chart of Red Bay and adjacent coast, soundings, etc., by the celebrated Captain Cook is extremely correct. If, in the style of drawing of his charts, the nature of the coast, cliffs, etc., had been shewn, the survey would have been perfect. He has, however, made up for this by numerous views of the land, and by remarks and directions for navigating the coast which he surveyed.[2]

Red Bay was in fact Lane's work. Captain JG Boulton, who edited Bayfield's writings, added: '. . . while assisting in the survey of the coast of Newfoundland, from 1871 to 1881, we had the same opinion of Cook's work.' Bayfield also wrote to the Hydrographic Office in 1849: 'I have not in the least exaggerated the defects of the old charts of the Gulf, Cape Breton and Nova Scotia. There are none that can with any degree of safety be trusted by the seamen, excepting those of Cook and Lane.'[3]

In retrospect, the five years in Newfoundland seem part of a plan to prepare Cook for some larger future project, allowing him to acquire experience and new skills. Cook was also fortunate in the men he worked closely with over this period. Hugh Palliser, appointed Governor of Newfoundland in 1764, was a rising star in the Royal Navy. He was later comptroller of the Navy and, having become a close friend, helped advance Cook's career. Another key player was Philip Stephens, the secretary to the Admiralty Board. Stephens was new to the position in 1763 and one of the first people he had to deal with was Cook. Again, the two men became friends and it was most probably Stephens who put Cook's name forward to lead the *Endeavour* expedition in 1768.

There was no real history of naval surveying for Graves (Palliser's predecessor) and Palliser to draw upon when writing instructions for Cook. Indeed, it would seem that Cook was writing his own instructions, and that they were content for him to do so, before he went off to carry them out. There is a sense that other captains on the Newfoundland station were a little envious of Cook's status and independence. Charles Douglas, captain of *Tweed* in 1763, was keen to point out that they could also prepare charts:

> And be moreover pleased to acquaint their Lordships, that agreeable to the commands of the Right Honourable Board of last April, between the beginning of September and the middle of October I took an incompleat one, of the whole Coast of Newfoundland, within the limits of the station prescribed me by their Lordships; viz: between the Capes Race and Ray. Which Sketch is (pursuant to the desire of the Captain Graves of the Antelope) now in the hands of M[r] James Cooke.[4]

Perhaps Cook was receiving special treatment, but he was earning it. He set off each year to survey new stretches of the coast and *Grenville's* log only carries occasional mentions that other ships were in contact. Extra responsibility was quickly thrust upon Cook's shoulders, as he now had the lives of twenty men and a vessel under his charge. Cook was on his own and he needed to find solutions if disaster befell them as, in 1766, when *Grenville* hit rocks in Long Harbour, Cook had to find ways to make repairs by himself as he could not sail back to St John's. Working this way in isolation was ideal preparation for taking a ship to the Pacific.

Cook was also developing interests in other things. The solar eclipse of 1766 was there for many to observe, but few were even aware of its happening and far fewer bothered to make observations. William Parker, Cook's assistant and later an admiral, did not mention the eclipse in the log and yet it would have been a spectacular event. Cook knew the eclipse was about to happen and made sure he was ashore so he could observe properly. John Bevis read a paper based on Cook's findings to the Royal Society, thereby bringing Cook to their attention.

There has been a suggestion that Cook was chosen for the Pacific because he was expendable. As he did not come from a well-to-do family with connections in 'society' he would not be missed should anything happen to the expedition and it failed to return to Britain. In fact, the opposite was probably the case. It was a time of peace and the navy had captains and lieutenants aplenty who were all on half-pay with nothing for them to do. There would have been many bored and ambitious men for whom leading such a voyage would have been a great opening. What the navy did not have in abundance was men who could undertake marine surveying. Cook was in a very small group with such skills and, in selecting Cook for this mission, the navy was potentially sacrificing one of its talents.

12

Newfoundland, 1763

Thomas Graves, a captain in the Royal Navy, was appointed Governor of Newfoundland in 1762. His term of office was marked by the capture of the island by the French and its subsequent recapture by the British in late 1762. The attack by the French on St John's had been one of the last acts of the Seven Years' War; the French had already lost their North American colony but had wanted a foothold in Newfoundland as a base from which to fish on the Grand Banks, south-east of Newfoundland.

Under the Treaty of Paris signed early in 1763, Britain gained control of Newfoundland (see section 'Newfoundland'), while France was granted the islands of St Pierre et Miquelon and also access to what was termed the 'French Shore' of Newfoundland. As a result, Newfoundland would not be straightforward to administer. The British complicated matters further by deciding to transfer Labrador, on the mainland, from the control of Quebec to that of Newfoundland, thus massively increasing the area under the governor's administration. The French Shore comprised the north-western and northern coast of the island from Point Riche round to Cape Bonavista, and French fishermen retained the right to dry their fishing catch there. Britain was expected to hand over St Pierre et Miquelon to the French but insisted on time to remove British subjects and the opportunity to survey the islands.

British knowledge of Newfoundland remained minimal. Existing charts were old and totally unreliable and those of the French were little better. The latest British survey had been carried out nearly a hundred years earlier, in 1677. Part of the duties of the governor was to accompany the fishing vessels back to the Iberian Peninsula at the end of the year with their catch. It was while he was at Lisbon with the fishing fleet in January 1763 that Graves wrote a letter to the Admiralty, expressing his concern at the poor knowledge that Britain had of the islands, which had hindered their response to the French invasion. High on his list of complaints was the near-total lack of charts of the coastal waters around the island. Graves strongly recommended that an immediate survey was made and a skilled surveyor should be appointed to carry it out: '. . . The Newfound Land station which I have been upon two years though only the last year as Governour, has been attended with many untoward and most perplexing accidents, which as they were totally unforeseen cou'd not embarras the more . . .'[1] The British government accepted Graves's suggestions and began the slow bureaucratic process of sanctioning a survey and the creation of a position of surveyor:

Mr Graves having represented to us that the imperfect Returns hitherto made by the Governors of Newfoundland have been chiefly owing to their want of a Secretary,

NEWFOUNDLAND

Newfoundland is an island in the North Atlantic off the eastern coast of North America. It is situated between 47°N and 52°N and 52°W and 47°W and covers an area of 405,720 square kilometres. Geologically, the island is the north-western extension of the Appalachian region. Its coastline, which contains many fjords and other inlets, is convoluted and stretches for over 13,500 kilometres. The Labrador Current affects the climate, which features fog, strong and variable winds, high rainfall and cold temperatures. Much of the island is covered in spruce and fir forests, though in the north the trees are stunted, forming impenetrable groundcover known as tuckamore. Life on the island is hard, shaped by a long winter and short growing season; poor soils and drainage compound the problem. There is also offshore pack ice and icebergs.

The original inhabitants of Newfoundland were the Beothuk, an Algonquian people who were hunter-gatherers. At the time of European contact there were only about a thousand of them and they became extinct about 1830. They had retreated to the interior and there is no evidence that Cook ever met them. The Beothuk painted their bodies with red ochre and it is possible that they were responsible for native North Americans being known as 'Red Indians'. The Strait of Belle Isle was the home for Inuit people. Though mainly based on the Labrador side, some communities existed on the Newfoundland coast. The Inuit are the descendants of the Thule people who migrated to Labrador from the Canadian arctic seven to eight hundred years ago. Another Algonquian people, the Mi'kmaq, was based in Nova Scotia. Bands had visited Newfoundland for some time but during the mid-eighteenth century some moved there on a permanent basis. The Mi'kmaq had sided with the French and some were looking to escape from the British, while others were looking for new fishing and hunting resources. Cook met Mi'kmaq in St George's Bay.

The first European presence occurred around AD 1000, when the Vikings founded a settlement at L'Anse aux Meadows on Newfoundland's Northern Peninsula. The settlement soon died out and its location was lost until its rediscovery in 1960. Fishermen and whalers from south-western Europe probably knew of Newfoundland but the first recognised visit was that of John Cabot from England in 1497. Others followed, from Spain, Portugal and France. Prominent among the first visitors were Basques, who formed many small temporary settlements, especially in the Strait of Belle Isle. Many modern placenames reflect a Basque origin. Sir Humphrey Gilbert formally claimed the island for England in 1583.

The huge cod fishery on the Grand Banks, to the south-east of the island, gave Newfoundland a strategic importance. Over the next two hundred years the British and French established bases on the island and disputed ownership. However, the severe climate and poor soils discouraged settlement; the fishery was more important than anything else the island could offer. The practice was established of fishermen basing themselves on the island during the summer months and returning each winter to Europe. Governments were content to allow this and did little to control matters or invest in the island's development. An unofficial law by 'fishing admirals' evolved.

The British concentrated at St John's and the Avalon Peninsula in the south-east, while the French settled Placentia on the south coast and around the Northern Peninsula. There were regular disputes between fishermen, and the many wars between France and Britain led to attacks on each other's Newfoundland settlements. The Peace of Utrecht, which ended Queen Anne's War in 1713, forced France to surrender its claims to Newfoundland. It was, however, allowed continued access to a long stretch of the north coast termed the 'French Shore'.

By 1728, misrule (or lack of any rule) had allowed a form of anarchy to prevail and Britain finally awoke to the need for proper control. The Royal Navy had already been providing some protection for British fishermen and now the head of the squadron was officially made the naval governor of Newfoundland. In 1729 Captain Henry Osborne was appointed the first governor but even then, he only spent the summer months on the island and deputed justices of the peace and constables to maintain peace during his absence.

In 1762, near the end of the Seven Years' War, France captured and held St John's for three months. The Treaty of Paris in 1763 granted France the islands of St Pierre et Miquelon off Newfoundland's south coast while affirming French access to the French Shore. Britain had taken control of Canada and now transferred control of Labrador from Quebec to Newfoundland. This was the situation when Cook arrived. He worked around the island's coast for five years and the experience gained helped shape his career.

Surveyor, or other Person, capable of collecting Information, keeping regular accounts and making Draughts of Coasts and Harbours, for which services there has never been any allowances, and that such assistance has now become still more necessary to the Governor of Newfoundland, by the enlargement of his Government, and his instructions to report as accurately as he can the conditions, fisherys, and other material particulars of a country at present little known. We beg leave to humbly submit to your Majesty, whether it may not be expedient that such an allowance should be made.[2]

Graves was well aware of the existence of James Cook and it is most probable that all along he had Cook in mind for the position of surveyor. Graves would have seen Cook's chart of the St Lawrence and would certainly have encountered Cook and his work during the recapture of St John's in September 1762.

Cook, meanwhile, was enjoying married life in Shadwell. It is possible that he had been warned that a position in Newfoundland was being organised for him. He had been discharged from *Northumberland* in November and there are no signs that he attempted to obtain any other position before Thomas Graves approached him.

In early April Graves was writing to Philip Stephens, the new secretary to the Admiralty, indicating that Cook was already informed of his new position:

I have this moment seen Mr Cook and acquainted him he was to get himself ready to depart the moment the board was pleased to order him, and that he was to have

10 shillings a day while employed on this service – He has been to enquire for a draughtsman at the Tower, but as this is a Holiday he found hardly anyone there – There are some who draw there at 1s 6d a day, and others who have two shillings a day – one of which last establishment he wants to have and is assured that the Board will contine any such Person who chuses to go on their establishment upon an application from your Office made for them. It is from this class/set they allways send draughtsmen with Engineers or Comanding Officers who go abroad – The additional Pay they require from your office Mr Cook will acquaint you of tomorrow as soon as he can see them & propose their going. If he does not find their conditions to come wth in their own office establishment. I have desired him to advertise for a draughtsman – acquaint you by letter with the terms he can bring them to, and wait your commands, as to the hireing any such, and as to the time of his setting out for the Ship.

There shou'd be a Theodilite and drawing instrumts which will cost about 12 or 15 £ and is a thing the ordnance always allow their People – The officers of the Yard shou'd be orderd to supply me with two or three spare Azimuth compasses & a number of Pendants of any colour to put as signals on different Points for takeing the Angls as the Survey goes on – I shall set out this afternoon for the ship and hope to be there by tomorrow.[3]

The above letter shows that Cook already had a good grasp of how a surveyor operated and what equipment he would need to perform his duties. A theodolite would be useless on a moving, swaying ship, so his intention to take readings ashore is clear. Surveying was still the preserve of the army engineers and Cook went to the Tower of London because that was the headquarters of the Office of Ordnance, where he might hope to engage a skilled draughtsman.

The Earl of Bute resigned early in 1763 after securing peace, but his successor was not obvious. Henry Fox declined the post of prime minister and, as neither the Duke of Newcastle nor William Pitt were agreeable to the king, George Grenville was unexpectedly offered the chance to form a government. He became first lord of the Treasury and Chancellor of the Exchequer on 6 April.

Grenville offered the position of first lord of the Admiralty to John Montagu, fourth Earl of Sandwich on 20 April 1763; Sandwich had previously occupied the position from February 1748 to June 1751. Three new members were introduced to the Board at the same time, and all these changes may perhaps explain the delays for decisions by the Admiralty, which caused Thomas Graves so much frustration over the next few weeks. Late April to early May was the preferred time for ships to return to Newfoundland as the winter would be over and the ports free of ice. Graves was keen to sail, but the Admiralty, Board of Trade and Navy Board were moving very slowly with regards to Cook. It was far too slow for Graves, whose impatience is shown in letters from him to the Admiralty:

Captain Graves Compliments wait upon Mr Stephens and beg to know what final answer he shall give to Mr Cook late master of the Northumberland who is very willing to go out to Survey the Harbour & Coasts of Labrador and the draughtsman he was to get from the Tower – as they both wait to know their Lordships resolution and the footing they are to be upon . . .[4]

He persisted three days later: 'You will excuse my takeing the liberty to ask if any change of resolution is taken about Mr Cook, the master and an assistant for him, and whither they are to go out with us.'[5]

The Admiralty was moving, albeit very slowly, and Stephens wrote to Cook on 13 April instructing him to purchase the instruments he required and to send him the bill for reimbursement. Graves was dogged, though, and a possible mutiny in his crew on *Antelope* did not help his mood. He now asked for the authority to purchase two small vessels, one of which the surveyor could use, thereby making him independent. 'The sending out Draughtsmen to Survey the Harbours, seems to Point out the necessity of their having a Small Vessel fit to use on that business . . . the one to send with Mr Cook upon the Survey of the Coasts and Harbours.'[6]

Another possible reason for delays and mix-ups at this time was the health of John Clevland, the secretary to the Admiralty Board. Clevland was dying and had petitioned the king in late 1762 for a pension for his wife. Clevland died in office on 19 June 1763 and was succeeded by Philip Stephens (see section 'Sir Philip Stephens'), who had been second secretary since 16 October 1759. Stephens would occupy the position for thirty-two years, serving ten first lords of the Admiralty. So in 1763 Stephens was taking over from Clevland and these early months would have been a transition period, during which wheels turned more slowly than usual. Stephens, no doubt, did not yet feel confident enough to make some decisions without reference to the Board.

Cook had given Graves a list of articles (which Graves forwarded) 'as necessary in the business of Surveying' that Cook 'apprehends may be supplied from the King's yard by order'. Graves, in the same letter, then added, 'If the Navy Board have not orders to supply these extra stores, no reason I can offer will have any weight.' Cook's list comprised:

12 Small Flags (which may be made from new Bunting or out of Old colours);
1 Knight's Azimuth Compass;
1 Knight's Steering Compass;
2 Deep Sea Leads;
1 Deep Sea Lines;
25 lbs Tallow;
2 Axes;
2 Pick Axes;
and 2 Common deal Tables to Draw upon.

Shortly after this, the Admiralty ordered the Navy Board to reimburse Cook the £68 11s 8d he had spent on surveying instruments.[7]

Finally, on 19 April, the Admiralty sent Cook confirmation of his appointment:

My Lords Commissioners of the Admiralty, having directed Captain Graves, of His Majesty's Ship, the Antelope, at Portsmouth, to receive you on board and carry you to Newfoundland in order to your taking a Survey of part of the Coast and Harbours of that Island. I am commanded by their Lordships to acquaint you therewith: that you must repair immediately on board the said ship, she being under sailing orders, that

SIR PHILIP STEPHENS (1725–1809)

Philip Stephens was secretary to the Lords Commissioners of the Admiralty from 1763 until 1795. As a result, much of the correspondence concerning Cook's voyages was written by Stephens or was addressed to him. Cook also worked and corresponded with Stephens during his time in Newfoundland; many business letters between the two men survive.

Stephens was born in 1725 in Alphamstone in Essex, the son of the rector. He was educated at the Free School in Harwich before becoming a clerk at the Victualling Board. Anson befriended him and made him his secretary. In 1759, Stephens became assistant secretary to the Admiralty, under John Clevland, and succeeded as secretary in 1763. While the title 'secretary' implies a junior role, the position actually carried much power and Stephens made many decisions without referring to the Lords Commissioners.

He was elected FRS in 1771, and from 1768 until 1806 he was MP for Sandwich. On his retirement he was knighted and made a Lords Commissioner himself. He died on 20 November 1809 and was buried in Fulham. He was unmarried but had one son, who predeceased him. He had property in St Faiths, Norfolk, and he has a short biography in the *Oxford Dictionary of National Biography*. Cook named several features after Stephens, including Stephens Island and Point Stephens near the northern tip of South Island, New Zealand, and Port Stephens on the New South Wales coast.

you are to follow such orders as you shall receive from Capt. Graves relative to the said service and that you will be allowed Ten shillings a day during the time you are employed therein.[8]

Instructions were sent to Graves, reflecting his earlier letters to the Board. The importance of charts had been recognised:

Whereas we have appointed His Majesty's Ship Antelope under your Command together with the Ships and Sloop named in the Margin for Convoy and Protection of the fishing Ships bound this Year to and from Newfoundland, You will receive herewith for your Information Copies of the Instructions We have give to the Commanders of the Pearl, Tweed, Terpsichore, Lark, and Tamer Sloop for proceeding immediately to different parts of that Island as mentioned against their Names, and for following your Orders upon your Arrival there.

Section 9 . . . and at the same time We have ordered them to make Charts of all the said Coasts, with Drafts of the Harbours, noting the Depths of Water, Conveniences for fishing and whatever Observations may occur worthy of our knowledge, which are to be transmitted by them to you, that they may be laid before us.

Section 13 By the end of October you are to take under your Convoy the Fishing Ships which may then be bound to Portugal and Spain, and seeing them off their respective Ports as far to the Southward as Cadiz, You are at liberty to tarry there ten days (but on no Account to exceed that time) and then put to Sea with any Trade that may be there, for which you are not to tarry at farthest above Eight days, and then make the best of your way with any Trade ready to proceed with you to the Downes where you are to remain for farther Order.[9]

Graves wrote instructions for Charles Douglas, captain of *Tweed*, who was to carry Cook to St Pierre et Miquelon and wait there until Cook had finished the survey of those islands. St Pierre et Miquelon are two small islands lying off the western end of the Burin Peninsula on the south coast of Newfoundland. The British had agreed to hand the islands over to the French to serve as a base for the French fishery. Their readiness to relinquish these strategically placed islands may have resulted from attitudes such as those displayed by Alexander Colvill, who wrote in 1763 that the islands were:

> ... barren and desart ..., destitute of all the Necessarys of Life, without Materials for building Houses, or Provisions to support them thro the Winter ... they trust to our Colonies for supplying all their Wants, and invites a Trade in very pathetic Terms, promising to pay for every thing in Molasses, French Goods, or Bills of Exchange.[10]

William Pitt, who had run the country through most of the war but had been dismissed in 1762 and was not involved in the peace negotiations, was outraged by the return of any part of North America to the French. His anger was matched by that of the British fishing community. A period of three months had been decreed for the British to finish their occupation of the islands, after which they would be handed over. Before leaving the islands, the British intended to survey them and this task was entrusted to James Cook. He had just a few weeks to chart the coastline and all the time he was delayed in Britain and on the Atlantic crossing meant less time for the survey and more pressure.

Cook made his way to Plymouth to join *Antelope*. His name was entered as a supernumerary on *Antelope*'s muster on 19 April, and he appeared on 4 May; his appointment was by Admiralty order of 19 April 1763. Edward Test, the draughtsman employed from the Tower, did not arrive, however:

> ... Mr Cook arrived here yesterday but without an Assistant, which defect I will endeavour to replace here if possible, under an expectation of the same encouragement their Lordships were to give Mr. Test. The first employment I shall give Mr Cook will be to Survey St. Pieres & Miquelon, before my getting there to surrender those Islands, to this end it would have been very convenient that one of the Sloops had been ready to sail with me who might have been detached to performe this Service, whilest I made some stay upon the Coast, to afford them the proper time before the surrender of those Islands to the French.[11]

James Cook arranged for two seamen from *Antelope*, James Biddon and Peter Flower, to act as his assistants. Flower would remain with Cook until the *Endeavour* voyage, when he died at Rio de Janeiro. *Antelope* arrived in Trepassey Bay at the south end of the Avalon Peninsula in south-eastern Newfoundland in early June, where it rendezvoused with *Tweed*. The Admiralty had recognised the need for a greater naval presence in Newfoundland waters and each ship had been given a specific area in which to operate. *Tweed*, a fifth rate of thirty-two guns, under Captain Charles Douglas, was to operate along the south coast, which included St Pierre et Miquelon, and was waiting for Graves in the bay. It fell to Douglas, therefore, to take charge of Cook and ferry him to the islands.

The other vessels in Graves's squadron were: *Pearl*, a fifth rate of thirty-two guns, captained by Charles Saxton, which was to cruise on the coast of Labrador between Belle Isle and the St John River and to the island of Anticosti; *Terpsichore*, a sixth rate of twenty-four guns, captained by John Ruthven, which was to cruise off the east coast between Cape Race and Quirpon; *Lark,* a fifth rate of thirty-two guns, under Samuel Thompson, which was to cruise on the west coast; and *Tamar*, a sloop of sixteen guns, under William Forster, which was to patrol on the Grand Bank.

On 13 June, *Tweed* embarked Cook, Biddon and Flower as 'Supernumerary born for Victuals only being an Engineer & his Retinue'.[12] Speed was now of the essence and Graves's instructions to Douglas stated:

> ... you are to proceed without a moment's loss of time ... to the Island of S[t] Peter[s], where you are to afford him (who you are to take with you) all the assistance in your power by boats or otherways in taking an accurate survey of the Island[s] of S[t] Peter and Miquelon with all the Expedition possible, that no Delay be thereby given to the Delivering these Islands up to the French.[13]

Unfortunately for Cook and Douglas, the handover date of 10 June had already passed and *Tweed* arrived at St Pierre to find the French already waiting, somewhat impatiently. The French governor-designate, François-Gabriel d'Angeac, arrived at the same time in *Garonne*, accompanied by soldiers, merchants and fishermen and their families.

François-Gabriel d'Angeac had been in charge of French troops sent to Canada in 1760 as reinforcements to assist in the recapture of Quebec. The presence of British naval vessels in the Gulf of St Lawrence had forced the French fleet, under François Chenard de La Giraudais, to seek refuge in the mouth of the Restigouche River. The British ships, commanded by John Byron, followed and routed the French. D'Angeac escaped and then led a French resistance in the region. As a reward, he was appointed governor of the new French colony of St Pierre et Miquelon in 1763. France was not allowed to construct any military buildings and only allowed fifty soldiers.

Douglas was immediately thrust into the role of diplomat as he persuaded d'Angeac to wait on his ship while Cook undertook the survey and Douglas oversaw the evacuation of British persons living on the islands. Douglas was determined that all his instructions were carried out in full before he would cede authority to the French. Gradually, Douglas managed to persuade and placate the French governor. He later wrote:

> I procured him all the time I could, by staying at S[t] Peter's under various pretences, untill towards the 17th, and then went to the Road of Miquelon – where we made shift to keep the Commandant in some sort of temper, untill the beginning of August;

when, thro' the unwearied assiduity of Mr Cooke, the survey of that Island too, was completed . . . I flatter myself Sir, that my Lords Comissioners will easily believe, that so delicate an affair, as keeping the French Governor so long on board; out of the exercise of his authority, the surveying of his Islands untill the beginning of August, due to France since the 10th of June; and to have thereby occasion'd no disturbance, must have caused an expensive intercourse on my side [and he thinks the Lords might be induced to] grant me some consideration for the extraordinary expences I was put to; without having incurred which the Islands in question wou'd have remained unsurvey'd . . . who was (you may believe with some difficulty) persuaded to remain onboard with his troops, untill the fourth day of July when (the survey of St Peter's being compleated) that Island was deliver'd to him in form: and our Surveyor began with the other; the weather still continuing foggy and unfavorable.[14]

The Admiralty was sympathetic to Douglas for his troubles and agreed to reimburse him for £50. In the meantime, d'Angeac had dispatched a very indignant letter to Graves at Placentia but received no sympathy from the governor. He decided to wait while Cook got on with the survey. No log or journal of Cook's survives from 1763, so exact details of his operations remain unknown but Douglas recorded some of Cook's movements in his own log:

2 JULY. pm Sent our Cutter under ye Command of a Midshipman to attend Mr Cook whilst he survey'd the Islands of Miquelon & Langley.

12 JULY. am Sent ye Longboat with 4 Days provisions for ye Men wth Mr Cook on ye Island of Langley. pm ye Longb^t return'd from Langley not finding Mr Cook there, he being gone to Miquelon.

25 JULY. Arriv'd here ye Shallop Tender & Cutter wth Mr Cook he having Finish'd ye Survey of that part of this Island Called Dunn.[15]

Cook completed the survey and Douglas was able to hand over the islands to d'Angeac on 31 July. Cook produced a chart, 'A Plan of the Islands of St Peter, Langly and Miquelong, Survey'd by Order of His Excellency Thomas Graves, Esq., Governor of Newfoundland &c, by James Cook'. Cook also produced sailing directions of which a part reads:

Island of Miquelon
From the North point of Langley, to the South point of Miquelon is about 1 mile; it is said that a few years since they joined together at this place by a neck of sand, which the sea has washed away and made a channel, wherein is 2 fathoms water. The Island of Miquelon is 4 leagues in length from North to South, but of an unequal breadth; the middle of the island is high land, called the high land of Dunn; but down by the shore it is low, except Cape Miquelon, which is a lofty promontory at the northern extremity of the island.

Cook and his assistants returned on board *Tweed* and Douglas carried them to Ferryland on the east coast of the Avalon Peninsula, whence Cook travelled to St John's to report to Graves. Edward Smart, Test's replacement as the surveying draughtsman employed to help Cook, had not yet arrived in Newfoundland.

Graves had, though, just purchased a small vessel on 7 August for Cook to use. This was a 68-ton schooner called *Sally* and now renamed *Grenville* after the prime minister. It had been built in Massachusetts in 1754 and 'together with her Boat, Tackle, Furniture and Apparell', cost £372 15s. It was forty-three feet long by seventeen feet wide and carried twelve 3-pounder guns and twelve ½-pounder swivels. Graves had the schooner prepared for service and Cook sailed from St John's as soon as the vessel was ready. Seven seamen from *Antelope* had been transferred to assist Cook sail it.

Graves had concerns about the activities of French fishermen at the tip of the Northern Peninsula, which was part of the French Shore. As the administration of Labrador had only recently been placed with Newfoundland, the British had only sketchy knowledge of the sides of the Strait of Belle Isle that separated Labrador from Newfoundland and Graves saw it as a priority to show the flag. Other concerns centred on the local native peoples, the Innu and Inuit, and their relationships with the French.

Graves's predecessor had been James Webb, whom he had replaced in 1762 after Webb's sudden death. Webb had visited the northern region in 1760 when he had named and described York Harbour on the Labrador shore. Webb had also fostered good relationships with the Inuit when he had taken three captured Inuit to Chateau Bay and released them. The grateful Inuit had then been prepared to trade whalebone.

Graves now wanted to build on that relationship and learn more about the area. He dispatched Cook to survey York Harbour, together with several of the more important French fishing harbours on the Northern Peninsula. As with St Pierre, no log survives from Cook so we only have vague details of his movements. He visited Croque, Quirpon and Noddy on the peninsula and surveyed each of the harbours.

Cook also produced sailing directions for the harbours:

Harbour of Great Quirpon

The passage into this harbour is on the N.W. side of the island of the same name, between it and Graves's Island, which is an island in the mouth of the harbour, in approaching the entrance you may make as free as you please with the Island Quirpon, there being no danger but what shews itself until you come to the entrance of the harbour, where there are shoals on your larboard side, which you avoid by keeping Black-head upon Quirpon open of all the other land, until Cape Raven is brought over Noddy Point; then haul in for the harbour, keeping about half a cable's length from the point of Graves's Island; it is every where good anchoring within the said island, and room and depth of water for any ships, and good ground; the best place is in 9 fathoms water, up towards the upper end of Graves's Island, abreast of Green Island, which lies about the middle of the harbour. The passage to the inner harbour on either side of Green Island, is very good for ships of a moderate draft of water, through which you will carry three fathoms; and above the island is exceeding good anchoring in 7 fathoms; there is a passage into this place through Little Quirpon, but it is too narrow and intricate for vessels to attempt, unless well acquainted: In and about Quirpon are excellent conveniences for great number of ships, and good fishing grounds about those parts: All the land about Griguet and Quirpon is mountainous and appears a barren rock.[16]

At Quirpon Cook named the island in the harbour after Thomas Graves, but the name has not been retained – it is now called Noble's Island. The name Quirpon is a corruption of the Basque name Cerpou, indicating the long association Basques had with the area. Cook moved across to Labrador, where he produced a plan for York Harbour and Chateau Bay with sailing directions and recommendations for future use.[17]

Cook then took *Grenville* back to St John's. It is possible that he was sent out again to contact Captain Ruthven in *Terpsichore*, who had been policing the terms of the treaty scrupulously and had burnt fishing vessels and stages. Graves recorded that 'The Schooner Grenville has since return'd from the Northward w^t our seeing the Terpsichore.'[18] Ruthven had sent in messages and Graves may have sent Cook with a response.

Spy, under Captain William Phillips, finally reached St John's from Britain, carrying Edward Smart, the draughtsman, who was to assist Cook in drawing up final versions of Cook's own rough charts. They also had all the charts and other information assembled by the other ships on the station, which had been passed on to Cook.

The 1763 season was now over and Graves began assembling the fishing fleet to escort them across the Atlantic to Spain and Portugal. *Grenville* would remain in St John's, so Cook was instructed to sail on *Tweed*. Graves and *Antelope* would take much longer to reach Britain than the other ships, so he wrote dispatches to be carried to the Admiralty, describing the events of the year in Newfoundland. Graves detailed Cook's activities:

> . . . Meanwhile the survey went on with all possible application on the part of Mr. Cook. At length, Mons. d'Anjac's patience being quite exhausted, I received a letter from him on the 30th of June, of which I enclose a copy together with my answer returned the same day. This conveyance brought me a letter fro Captain Douglas, expressing his uneasiness on the part of Mons. d'Anjac and pressing to receive his final instructions, and at the same time gave me the satisfaction to learn St. Peter's was completely surveyed, Miquelon begun upon and advanced so as to expect it would be finished before the French could be put in possession: so that any interruption from them was no longer to be apprehended.
>
> . . . and from thence to York Harbour to take a compleat survey of that or any other good harbour he shou'd fall in w^t on ye Labradore coast, and to employ himself in like manner on his return when ye Season shoud make it necessary to leave that Coast, this he has done with indefatigable industry haveing survey'd four harbours.[19]

The governor sent another letter to the Admiralty a few days later, on 30 October, again praising Cook's efforts:

> The Tweed sails with these dispatches and I hope to leave the country about the same time. As Mr Cook whose Pains and attention are beyond my description, can go no farther in surveying this year I send him home in the Tweed in preferance to keeping him on board [*Antelope*], that he may have the more time to finish the diff^t surveys allready taken of it to be layn before their Lordships – and to copy the different

sketches of ye Coasts and Harbours, taken by ye ships on the several stations by which their Lordships will perceive how extreamly erroneous ye present draughts are, & how dangerous to ships that sail by them – and how generally beneficial to Navigation the work now in hand will be when finished indeed I have no doubt in a Year or two more of seeing a perfect good chart of Newfoundland and an exact survey of most of ye good harbours in which there is not perhaps a part of the World that more abounds.

The inclosed Papers are the remarks made by the Captains of the Lark, Tweed and Pearl. Mr Cook will lay before their Lordsh: ye original Survey of St Peters Miquelon & Langley as allso Quirpon & Noddy harbours, Chateaux or York harbour & Croque, these though not so highly finished as a *Copy* may be, yet I am purswaded thier Lordships will think ye properest to be deposited in thier Office.[20]

Charles Douglas was keen to inform the Admiralty of his role in proceedings and to claim credit for charts and the like:

Be pleased to lay before my Lords Commissioners, the herewith-inclosed Sketch of the Magdalen Islands in the Gulph of St Laurence; where the Sea-Cow fishery is carried on. And be moreover pleased to acquaint their Lordships, that agreeable to the commands of the Right Honourable Board of last April, between the beginning of September and the middle of October I took an incompleat one, of the whole Coast of Newfoundland, within the limits of the station prescribed me by their Lordships; viz: between the Capes Race and Ray. Which Sketch is (pursuant to the desire of the Captain Graves of the Antelope) now in the hands of Mr James Cooke; who was last Summer employ'd to survey the Islands of St Peter and Miquelon: which Survey we were not able to compleat before the beginning of August. One of the reasons of the incompleatness of the Draught last mention'd.[21]

Tweed anchored at Spithead on 29 November 1763. Cook returned quickly to London in order to be with Elizabeth and their first child, James, born a few weeks earlier on 13 October. The family was still living in Shadwell.

Cook learned on his return that a new first lord had taken over at the Admiralty in September. The Earl of Sandwich had been moved to be a junior secretary of state and the Admiralty was offered to John Perceval, second Earl of Egmont on 16 September 1763. Egmont was not a popular politician but proved an effective first lord, even if he did use the office to reward his sons. Philip, a naval officer of no great ability, was promoted and Charles and Spencer were made registrars of the Admiralty (Spencer Perceval became prime minister in 1809 and was assassinated in 1812).

Cook, assisted by Edward Smart, set about producing neat versions of the charts he had drawn and the sailing directions he had written; Smart though died in March 1764. In doing so, Cook was completing a regimen of work that he would repeat each year over the next four years. Each year began with preparations for the return to Newfoundland and then he would cross the Atlantic. The summer months were taken up doing the practical survey work somewhere along the coast. Then, as winter approached about the end of September, Cook would sail back to Britain where he spent the winter drawing and writing.

Several manuscript charts survive from Cook's 1763 surveys. There are two charts from his survey of St Pierre et Miquelon: MS A701/14 is of St Peter Road and Harbour while MS B5299 is of St Peter, Langley and Miquelong. His time around the Strait of Belle Isle is represented by MS B188 York Harbour (Chateau Bay) and MS C54/6 Quirpon and Noddy Harbours. Cook submitted all these charts in 1766, when they were published, being incorporated into larger charts as insets.

Two more of Cook's charts are held in the Manuscripts Collection of the State Library of New South Wales. 'Original Sketches, Drawings, Maps etc., collected by Admiral Isaac Smith' (MS PXD 11) contains 'A Plan of the Harbour of St Johns in Newfoundland' (PXD 11 (f. ia)) and 'A Plan of the Harbour of Croque in Newfoundland' (PXD 11 (f. ib)).

At some time in 1763, probably for his own benefit and to acquaint himself with the geography of the island, Cook drew a map of Newfoundland. It is entitled 'A Sketch of the Island of Newfoundland. Done from the latest observations by James Cook 1763' and is held in the Admiralty Library of the United Kingdom Hydrographic Office at Taunton (Atlas Vv2, Vol. 1, item 21). While recognisable as Newfoundland, it highlights how poor was Britain's knowledge of the island. The south coast, especially, shows little detail, while nothing is shown in the interior. It does delineate the parts known as the French and English Shores. A year later Cook produced another map that already showed the benefits of his survey.

13

Northern Peninsula, 1764

January 1764 found James Cook living at home in Shadwell with his wife Elizabeth and their first child, young James. It was a rare piece of domestic life for Cook; even then, he was occupied with work concerns. He was expecting to return to Newfoundland but not until around April. Before that he had to complete the charts from his first year's survey and assemble supplies and equipment for the second year.

Early in 1764 Hugh Palliser was appointed the new Governor of Newfoundland, replacing Thomas Graves, who had not yet returned to Britain. There was some urgency for the appointment as the French had raised a problem that needed immediate attention. By the terms of settlement in 1763, French fishermen retained the right of access to the part of the Newfoundland coast termed the French Shore, which lay between Cape Bonavista in the southeast and Pointe Riche on the Northern Peninsula. The French were now disputing the extent of the French Shore.

A memorial from Claude-Louis-François de Régnier, Comte de Guerchy, the French ambassador, was forwarded by the Secretary of State for the North, George Montagu Dunk, second Earl of Halifax, to the Board of Trade. The French memorial now claimed that Point Riche was one and the same as Cape Ray, the south-western point of the island.[1] De Guerchy maintained that maps supporting the Treaties of Utrecht and Paris had contained errors, even though some of those maps had been drawn by French cartographers such as Bellin and d'Anville. His claim, if accepted, would have extended French access to the whole of the west coast. The British set about refuting the claim and Palliser was one of the people entrusted with the task. He employed Cook to find evidence to support the British viewpoint that the capes were two entirely different places, asking him to obtain all the maps and descriptions of Newfoundland he could find in London bookshops. Cook briefly set aside his surveys and preparations for returning to Newfoundland to become a detective and soon reported back to Palliser:

Wednesday Evening 5 o Clock 7 March 1764.

At the Book and Map seller at the large Gateway in Cheap-side Jno Senex's Map Pub. in 1710 names Cape Ray and calls Pt Rich Cape Pointu – this Map was drawn from the observations communicated to the Royl Society in London and the Academy at Paris –

Mitchel's Map – Pub 1755 – Cape or Point Rich, which is left out of the late French Maps as if there was no such place seemingly because it is the boundries of their prevelige of fishing which extend from hence Northward round to C. Bonavista.

The *Universal Traveller* or Compleat account of Voyages by Pat. Barclay – 1734–54, speaking of Newfoundland, I do not find he once mentions C. Ray or Pt Rich, but says their Journals was so confounded with names common to both sides of the Island that it was a difficult matter to tell which side there where [i.e. they were] upon, in the Gulf or on the NE side –

At Mr Vanbushels Gardener at Lambeth

In Ogilbys America Pub in 1671 is a Map without Date, that mentions Cape Ray only – this Historian doth not speak of Cape Ray but in one place, and there he must mean Cape Race –

I have seen no maps to day, but such as we see yesterday, except the above; neither have I met with any Historys or Voyages (and I have looked into several) that makes any mention of what we want –

Palliser was able to pass on this information, together with more from the likes of Thomas Jefferys, the map publisher and vendor, which showed that Point Riche and Cape Ray had always been two distinct locations at either end of the west coast.

SIR HUGH PALLISER (1722–96)

Hugh Palliser was born at Kirk Deighton in West Yorkshire on 22 February 1722. He entered the Royal Navy on *Aldborough*, his uncle's ship, at the age of eleven. In 1741 he became lieutenant and in 1746 a captain, commanding several ships towards the end of the War of the Austrian Succession. He commanded *Eagle* and *Shrewsbury* during the Seven Years' War.

In 1762 Palliser was sent to Newfoundland to help expel the French, who had captured St John's, but arrived the day after the French surrendered. Two years later he was appointed to succeed Thomas Graves as Governor of Newfoundland and arrived there in June 1764 on HMS *Guernsey*. For much of his term Palliser was concerned with French access to fisheries around Newfoundland and St Pierre et Miquelon; he had to keep the French within the limits set by the Treaty of Paris and prevent the British from disrupting the French. Palliser actively encouraged Cook in his survey of Newfoundland from 1764 until 1767. The two men became good friends and Palliser did much to champion Cook's career.

Palliser left Newfoundland in 1768 and from 1770 until 1775 he was comptroller of the navy. He was created a baronet in 1773 and elected to parliament in 1774. In 1778 he was promoted to vice admiral and made governor of Greenwich Hospital in 1780. In 1787 he was promoted to admiral. Palliser took part in a battle off Ushant in 1778, which led to accusations and courts martial. Even though he was acquitted, Palliser fared badly and was forced to retire from public life. He died at his house and estate at The Vache near Chalfont St Giles in Buckinghamshire, unmarried, in March 1796. Palliser erected a monument to Cook at The Vache, while Cook, in his turn, named a point in New Zealand, some islands in the Tuamotus and an inlet on Kerguelen after his friend. There is an entry for him in the *Oxford Dictionary of National Biography* and a portrait by Dance hangs at the National Maritime Museum in Greenwich.

Cook knew Palliser of old, having served under him on *Eagle* between 1755 and 1757, and they had both been at Quebec and St John's (in 1762). Even though Cook had only been one of his master's mates at the time, Palliser had been aware of Cook's abilities and would have approved of Cook's appointment as a surveyor of Newfoundland. Cook was, no doubt, looking forward to working again with the new governor but he obviously held the old one in very high regard, as he wrote to Graves:

> I learnt this day at the Admiralty of your arrival of which I give you joy, and have to acquaint you, that soon after my arrival, I gave my surveys into the board which was approved of, and was then order'd to draw a fair copie of St Peters and Miquelong to be laid before the King, these and the different Captains Sketches is finished and given in to the board. Those that you intend for the Board of Trade are ready. I had not the honour to see Mr Grenvill when I gave in the Plan, but am convinced it was well received, as he made me an offer soon after (by Mr Whatley Secretary to the Treasury) to go as one of the Surveyors to the Natral Islands, which I was obliged to decline, your favourable recommendation of me to this Gentleman, likewise, to the Admiralty, together with many other signal favours I have received during the short time I have had the honour to be under your command shall ever be had in the most gratfull rand tho' Captain Pallisser, who is appointed to the command in Newfoundland is a Gentleman I have been long acquainted with yet I cannot help being sorry that you do not enjoy that officer longer.
>
> It is more than probable the Survey of the Island will go on untill compleatly finished, this usefull and necessary thing the World must be obliged to you for. I shall do my self the honour to wait upon you as soon as you arrive in town and acquaint you with what has pass'd between Lord Egmont and me in regard to the North part of the Island.[2]

This letter is interesting in that it shows the circles Cook was now moving in and doing so with apparent ease. Graves and Cook had left for Newfoundland in 1763 at about the same time as the government changed. George Grenville, who had been first lord at the Admiralty, had become prime minister and first lord of the Treasury. Cook returned to Britain ahead of Graves with charts intended to be presented to Grenville so, presumably, he went to the Treasury to deliver them. As Cook stated, he did not see Grenville but he did see Thomas Whately, Grenville's private secretary and junior financial secretary at the Treasury. Grenville had appointed the Earl of Egmont as first lord of the Admiralty in September 1763 and Cook states that he met him. It is remarkable that a ship's master should meet personally with the first lord but Cook was able to report on the state of affairs around the Strait of Belle Isle. Cook later named the volcanic mountain in Taranaki, New Zealand, after the earl.

Palliser and Graves would have met so that Graves could brief his successor about the island. It is probable that Cook was party to some of the discussion since Palliser was writing to the Admiralty in early April 1764 with recommendations that would improve the operation of *Grenville:*

> I am informed by Captain Graves that the Grenville, schooner, employ'd by order of the R. Hon'ble my Lords Commissioners of the Adm'ty for surveying the coasts of

Newfoundland, is laid up at St. John's, and is in need of several stores (an amount of which is here inclos'd) for refitting and equiping her for that service. Be pleas'd to move their Lordships to give an order for them to be sent out by the first ship that may be dispatch'd for that station.

Be pleas'd also to represent to their Lordships that the vessell being laid up at St. John's in winter, and man'd in summer from the comanding officer's ship, occasions many great delays and interuptions to that and other services, for after the Comodore arrives she is to be refitted and equip't. After that she has a voiage to make to the place to be surveyed. This, together with the time necessary for her to return to be laid up and to return the men before the Comodore leaves the coast, expends the best part of the season in which the surveyor ought to be emp'd on that service; and the present method of maning her with men lent from the comanding officer's ship, her stores &c., charged to the boatswain of that ship, and no proper person appointed to have the comand and charge of the vessell, neither when employ'd or laid up, creates much confusion in acc'ts and many inconveniencys to the service, for remedy of which I humbly beg leave to offer to their Lordship's consideration whether it will not be more for the King's service to order that Mr. Cook, the surveyor, who is a master in the Navy, be appointed master of her, to be charged with all stores and materials belong to her, with the appointm't of a master of a 6th rate; the assistant surveyor to be seaman with some knowledge of surveying and drawing, to be mate of the vessell, with the pay of master's mate of a 6th rate, and an allowance of 3s. or 2s 6d a day assistant-surveyor. The vessell to bear 18 or 20 seamen, so many at lest being necessary for carrying on the service properly and with dispatch; but that number being necessary only when she is employ'd taking surveys, ten of them may be born as supernumereries belonging to the several ships on that station. At the end of the season the vessell to repair to the general randevouz at St. John's, return the men to the respective ships, and with the other ten, which is sufficient to sail and navigate her, to proceed to Portsmouth, where she will be properly refitted, and arrive the next season on her station much earlier and in better condition than if left at St. John's. I apprehend the best assistant the surveyor can have is such a person as is described in the above proposal for mate of the vessell; and I flatter myself their Lordships will think that such a person, who has been brought up in the Navy, is better intitled to encouragem't than any young man who has been brought up in the Tower, that is meerly a draftsman, no seaman, and without knowledge of either land or sea surveying.

From what is above propos'd, I apprehend the charge to the Government will not be incres'd above 2s. a day on the whole, but the service will be more compleatly perform'd, and with greater facility and dispatch.

I beg leave to observe to their Lordships that [by] the present method of man'ing this vessel from the comanding officer's ship, and likewise another small vessell allow'd to him as a tender to be always ready to send with dispatches along the coast, his ship will be reduced 30 men under her lowest complem't, when she may happen to be wanted on important service for protection of the fisherys and coasts under my care and government, all which I beg leave to submit to their Lordships' consideration.

[Admiralty Office note on back of above:] Navy B'd to cause them to be sent out by the Lark.[3]

THE ADMIRALTY AND THE NAVY BOARD

The Admiralty was responsible for running the British navy, which had become the Royal Navy, after the restoration of the monarchy under Charles II in 1660. In 1661 Sir William Penn and Samuel Pepys established the Naval Discipline Act, which included the articles of war and founded the Royal Navy by statute.

The navy was run by a series of boards, with, from 1628, the Lords Commissioners of the Admiralty – otherwise known as the Admiralty Board – the most senior, being responsible for the policy direction, operational control and maritime jurisdiction of the navy. The first lord of the Admiralty was in charge of the Admiralty Board and he had up to six Lords Commissioners to assist him. The first lord was also a member of the government and, therefore, the minister responsible for the navy. In Cook's time the Admiralty was situated at the north end of Whitehall. It is still called the Old Admiralty and a statue of Cook stands outside it in the Mall.

All Commissioners were political appointments, and membership of the Board changed as governments changed. Only a few Commissioners were or had been serving naval officers, though in Cook's time Anson, Hawke and Saunders served as first lords. All other Boards, including the Navy Board and the Victualling Board – which carried out administrative duties – were answerable to the Admiralty.

Serving alongside the Admiralty Board were the secretaries to the Admiralty, who exercised much power in their own right, often making decisions themselves without reference to the Board. John Clevland and Philip Stephens were the secretaries during the period 1755 to 1768, and they regularly dealt and corresponded with Cook.

The Admiralty dealt primarily with the fleet and especially its personnel. Everything, from orders for combat to officer appointments, emanated from Whitehall. All naval officers at the rank of lieutenant and above were commissioned officers; this term recognised that their appointments had been sanctioned by the Admiralty Commissioners.

The Navy Board, while subordinate to the Admiralty, oversaw the administrative affairs of the navy. It was located in Crutched Friars near the Tower of London. Various departments carried out the day-to-day operational activities, including the supervision of shipbuilding and repair, the purchase of ships, the purchase of naval stores and the administration of the dockyards. Warrants for positions such as master, gunner and carpenter were issued by the Navy Board and the control of naval expenditure also fell under its control. Other activities were looked after by related boards such as the Victualling Board and the Sick and Wounded Office but the Navy Board oversaw their financial control.

By the eighteenth century, the Navy Board comprised the controller (then spelled comptroller), the surveyor, the clerk of the Acts, and the controllers of the treasurer's, victualling and storekeepers' accounts. The controller was the senior naval officer represented on the Board and was usually in charge. The surveyor who, among other duties designed ships, was usually a master shipwright.

It was the Navy Board that acquired and arranged the fitting out of ships through the naval dockyards. While officers at the yards were appointed by the Board of Admiralty, the yards were under the administration of the Navy Board, represented at the yard by a resident Commissioner. Another junior official that Cook had regular dealings with was the clerk of the cheque. All ships' captains were required to maintain muster rolls listing their crews and this official would check the records on return to British ports.

One suspects that Cook was responsible for much of the content of the above letter. He would have been pleased that the Admiralty agreed to all of Palliser's recommendations. A proper complement for the schooner, comprising master, master's mate, master's servant and seven seamen, was set. The pay rates for the master and master's mate were agreed as if for a sixth rate – that is £4 and £2 2s a month respectively. A few days later Cook received his warrant from the Navy Board. He was now taking on all the responsibilities of command, whereby he would be charged with the provisions and stores supplied to the schooner and he would need to keep regular accounts as well as sailing the vessel and conducting a survey:

> By the Principal Officers and Commissioners Of His Majesty's Navy
> The Rt. Honbls the Lords Commissioners of the Admty having Directed us by their order of the 13th instant to Establish a Master on the Grenville Schooner Employ'd on the Survey of the Coast of Newfoundland; And having received a Certificate of the Corporation of the Trinity House of your Abilities to serve as Master of any of His Majesty's ships of the Fourth Rate; These are therefore to authorize and require you Forthwith to make your repair on Board the Grenville Schooner, and take Charge of her as Master During her intended Voyage, Officiating in all things proper to the Duty of your Place as becometh you, hereby willing & requireing all Inferior Officers and Seamen, as they under the Welfare of His Majesty's Service and will answer the Contrary their Peril, to observe your Directions in the full and Due Execution of this your Office. And you are to take Charge of all Provisions and Stores that shall from time to time be Supplied the said Schooner, and Pass regular accounts for the same, And for so Doing you will be Allowed the Pay of Master of a Sixth rate with a Servant. For which this shall be your Warrant Dated at the Navy Office this 18th April 1764.[4]

Cook quickly realised that he would have trouble finding men to crew *Grenville* in the short time available before crossing the Atlantic. He wrote to Philip Stephens requesting the authority to offer normal inducements. He asked the Admiralty to order '... that Number of men which I may raise here to be Allowed the Customary Allowance of Conduct money, and Carriage of their Chests and Bedding to Portsmouth'.[5] Stephens replied on 23 April: '... I am Commanded to acquaint you that Directions are Given to the Navy Board for the Said Purpose. And that the Captain of the Lark is Directed to Carry you & servant as well as the men to St. John's.'[6] To assist Cook make up his numbers on *Grenville*, the Admiralty issued instructions that ships on the Newfoundland station would each loan the schooner two men for the surveying season.[7] The captains of *Pearl, Tweed, Lark, Zephyr* and *Spy* duly complied.

Meanwhile, Palliser was receiving his commission as governor, and a lengthy set of instructions for Cook to carry out. Section 12 shows that the need for the production of correct charts of Newfoundland had been realised. It read:

> ... You shall also use Your best endeavours to procure accurate Draughts or Maps of the several Harbours, Bays and Coasts of Newfoundland, and the other Islands and Territories under Your Government, and you are more particularly to direct the Officer of any Vessel under Your Command, which may be appointed to visit that part of the Coast of Labrador which lyes between Hudson's Streights and the Streights of Bellisle, to search and explore the great Inlet, commonly known by the name of Davis's Inlet, in order to discover, whether the same has or has not any passage to Hudson's Bay or any other inclosed Sea.[8]

Now that he was officially appointed, Palliser was in a position to give formal orders to Cook, which he issued on 29 April 1764:

> You are hereby required and Directed to repair on Board His Majesty's ship Lark at Portsmouth, whose Captain has orders to Receive you on Board, together with the men belonging to the Grenville Schooner and to Carry you to St. John's in Newfoundland.
>
> On your Arrival there you are to use the utmost Dispatch in fitting out the said schooner, and get her in all Respects Ready for Service, against my Arrival there. In Case I should not arrive at St. John's, by the First Day of July you are to apply to the Captain of the Lark for a Supply of four months Provisions, and then Proceed on the Service of Surveying the Coast of Newfoundland, Beginning at the Island of Quorpont, and thence Proceed Down the West side of the Island, Making in your way an Exact survey of the coast, Islands, and Harbours, and Remark every thing that may be useful to the Trade and Navigation of all His Majesty's Subjects in those Parts.
>
> You are to Continue on this Service as Long as the Season is favourable for it, Taking Care to be at St. John's by the Middle of October.
>
> Whilst you are on this Service you are to be Particularly attentive to the State of the Fisherys Carried on by the French in those Parts, and Endeavour to get the fullest accounts thereof as, Nearly as may be Agreeable to the form used in the Returns made of the state of our own, To which you will add any other interesting Remarks of your own. But you are Strictly Required to give no Molestation, or Hindrance to any of them that may be Employ'd Fishing within the Proper Limits according to Treaty.[9]

By this time, paperwork was flowing in all directions and the Admiralty felt the need to inform Palliser:

> Mr Jas. Cook, who had been employed last year surveying the islands of St. Pierre and Miquelon and part of the coasts and harbours of the Island of Newfoundland, being appointed by the Navy Board Master of H.M. Schr. Grenville at Newfoundland and directed to follow your orders; I am commanded by my Lords Commissioners of the Admiralty to acquaint you therewith, and to signify their direction to you, to employ

the said Mr. Cook in surveying such harbours and parts of the coast, and in making fair and correct Charts and Draughts of the same as you shall judge most necessary during the ensuing season, and so soon as the season for surveying be over, you are to direct him to repair with the Schr. to Portsmouth and to transmit the Charts and Draughts to their Lordships.[10]

The other ships with Palliser in Newfoundland in 1764 were to be:

HMS *Solebay* – William Hay – to patrol from Quirpon to New Ferolle and along the Labrador coast;

HMS *Tweed* – Philip Perceval – to patrol from New Ferolle to Cape Race;

HMS *Lark* – Samuel Thompson – to patrol from Cape Race to Quirpon;

HMS *Pearl* – Charles Saxton – to patrol from Cape Race to Cape Ray including the Magdalen Islands;

HMS *Spy* – William Phillips – to patrol from Cape Race to Bay Bulls;

HM sloop *Zephyr* – John Hamilton;

HM schooner *Hope* – John Candler.

Cook arranged for some men to join *Grenville* before he left Portsmouth. However, William Barrall, Thomas James and Richard Stamp all deserted in May 1764 while still at Portsmouth. Cook and several others (James MacKenzie, Peter Flower, John Alder and Thomas Gerring, Cook's servant) joined *Lark,* which sailed from Portsmouth on 7 May 1764 for Newfoundland. After an uneventful crossing, Cook and his men arrived in St John's on 13 June and immediately repaired on board *Grenville.*

The other captains complied with their orders and the following men joined *Grenville*: John Johnston, Jonathan Hatchman and Andrew Shepherd (from *Lark*); Robert Barker and Christopher Heason (from *Tweed*); John Roche and Nathaniel Nation (from *Spy*); William Ball and Henry Jefferey (from *Pearl*) and Daniel Broad (from *Zephyr*). Alder, Nation and Johnston soon ran off and their places were taken by others: James Griffiths, Francis Gathman, John Young, Peter Cook, William Walsh, Richard McCarly and John Freeman. This meant a total of nineteen men, including Cook.

The final member of the crew was William Parker (see section 'Sir William Parker'), whom Palliser moved from *Guernsey* to be master's mate and assistant surveyor to Cook. Parker had received his lieutenant's passing certificate in 1762 but had not yet received his commission. As mate under Cook, Parker's role was to sail the schooner and make soundings and coastal observations while Cook went off in small boats to carry out inshore and onshore work. Parker ran the ship in Cook's absence and maintained the log and journal. Unfortunately, if Cook kept a separate journal recording his exploits ashore, it has not survived.

The first entry in *Grenville*'s log reads:

13 JUNE. At 1pm His Majesty's Ship the *Lark* anchored here in St. John's Harbour, Newfoundland from England on board of which came the Master and Company of this Schooner, went on board and took possession of her. Read over to the crew the Master's warrant, Articles of War and Abstract of the late Act of Parliament.

SIR WILLIAM PARKER (1743–1802)

William Parker was born on 1 January 1743 at Queenborough in Kent, the son of Augustine and Elizabeth Parker. He entered the navy in late 1756, serving briefly on *Portland* and *Ipswich* before joining *Centurion*, captained by William Mansell, on 18 February 1757. He remained on *Centurion* as midshipman and master's mate for the next six years and was present during the captures of Louisbourg in 1758 and Quebec in 1759. From 1760 until 1762 *Centurion* was in the West Indies, and on his return to Britain Parker passed his lieutenant's examination on 3 November 1762.

Parker joined HMS *Guernsey* and, in 1764, he was transferred to *Grenville* to be master's mate and assistant surveyor. Parker's role was to remain on board the schooner/brig and make soundings and coastal observations while Cook went off in small boats to carry out inshore work. Parker maintained the log and journal and so is rarely mentioned himself. He spent three years, from 1764 until 1766, working closely with James Cook as his assistant on *Grenville* surveying Newfoundland's coastline. Parker left *Grenville* at the end of 1766 when he was promoted to lieutenant on 29 November.

Parker also found time to marry Jane Collingwood on 28 December 1766 at Queenborough. He then joined HMS *Niger* and returned to Newfoundland waters and was promoted to commander in 1773 and captain in 1777. From 1787 to 1790 Parker was commander-in-chief on the Leeward Islands station, on board *Jupiter*. In 1792 Parker commanded *Audacious* in the Channel Fleet under Admiral Richard Howe.

Parker was promoted to rear admiral in 1794 and returned to the West Indies in early 1795 as commander-in-chief in Jamaica, with his flag in *Raisonnable*. Illness forced his return to Britain in 1796 but he recovered to take a squadron to reinforce Sir John Jervis, commanding the Mediterranean Fleet. Flying his flag in *Prince George*, Parker joined Jervis in time to take an active part in the battle of Cape St Vincent on 14 February 1797.

More rewards flowed Parker's way. He was made a baronet, presented with the freedom of the City of London and received the thanks of both houses of parliament. Parker remained with Jervis, becoming his second-in-command, but the two men fell out later. Parker became a vice admiral in February 1799 and was appointed commander-in-chief of the Halifax station in March 1800. He was recalled to Britain in 1801 for having sent two of his ships to the West Indies, contrary to orders. One of the ships was captained by his son-in-law, Joseph Bingham. Parker was court-martialled and acquitted of misconduct, but with the rider that he had been indiscreet.

Parker saw no further active service and he died of apoplexy at his home in Ham in Surrey on 31 December 1802 aged fifty-nine leaving a will.[11] William and Jane Parker, who died in 1815, had eight daughters before having a son, William George Parker, who followed his father into the navy, rising to be a vice admiral. Some features around Pistolet Bay on the Northern Peninsula in Newfoundland, such as Parker River and Parker's Pond, may honour Parker's time surveying the island.

The Articles of War (part of the late Act of Parliament referred to by Cook) set out all the rules and regulations (and punishments) by which a Royal Navy ship operated. They were a significant part of the Act for Amending, Explaining and Reducing into one Act of Parliament, the Laws Relating to the Government of His Majesty's Ships, Vessels and Forces by Sea, which had become law in 1749. Even though commonly known as the Articles of War, the Act itself specifically stated that the Articles and Orders 'shall be duly observed and put in execution as well in time of peace as in time of war'. Cook was asserting his authority.

Grenville had obviously suffered during the Newfoundland winter and was in need of repair, delaying Cook's departure. This delay, the state of the vessel and the lack of its own regular crew would lead Cook and Palliser to seek alternatives when they returned to Britain at the end of the year. Cook and his men immediately set about preparing the vessel for duty. On 18 June Palliser arrived in *Guernsey*:

> 18 JUNE. At 6am hauled alongside a wharf and got our stores out. At 11 came in here His Majesty's ships Guernsey and Tweed. The Lark and Tweed, with the garrison, saluted the Commodore, which he returned.

Palliser had no sooner arrived than he was issuing more orders to Cook:

> You are hereby required and Directed to Proceed with His Majesty's Schooner the Grenville to survey the Coasts of Newfoundland; Beginning at the Island of Quirpoon, thence Proceeding Down the West side of the Island, making in your way an Exact Survey of the coasts, Islands, and Harbours; and remark every thing that may be Useful to the Trade & Navigation of His Majesty's Subjects in those Parts; Particulary noting in your Drafts and Remarks the Beaches and Places fit for Stages and other Conveniences for Landing and Drying of Fish, as well such as have been, or may be used for that Purpose.
>
> In you Description of any good Port you are to Note whether there are any Situations which appear to you Covenient for Erecting Forts upon, to Defend the Entrances of the Harbours and the Fisherys in it.
>
> In your Drafts you are to make a Table of the Names of the Particular Places, Distinguishing those used by the English, and by the French.
>
> You are to be Careful that there not be not taken to the Vessel you are the Master of, any Seaman or others, than such as do belong to her, and as you are not to Land any of the Vessels Company to any of the Fishing Ships, So neither are you to Suffer to be taken on Board Her, any sort of Fish either by way of Merchandize, Freights, or otherwise excepting what shall be Necessary, and Spending of the Ship's Company.
>
> Whilst you are on this Service you are to be Particularly Attentive to the State of the Fishery Carry'd on in those Parts by the Subjects of France, and Endeavour to get the Fullest account thereof as nearly as may be agreeable to the Form used in the Reports of the State of our own, to which you will add any other Interesting remarks of your own; Taking Care not to give any Molestation or Hindrance to any of them that are Employ'd fishing within the Proper Limits According to Treaty.
>
> You are to Continue on this Service as Long as the season is Favourable for it, taking Care to be at St. John's by the 10th or Middle of October.[12]

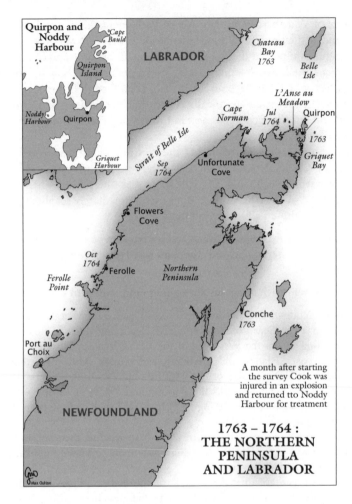

Quirpon and
Noddy
Harbour

Cape
Bauld

Quirpon
Island

LABRADOR

Chateau
Bay
1763

Belle
Isle

Noddy
Harbour   Quirpon

L'Anse au
Meadow

Cape
Norman

Jul
1764

Quirpon

1763

Griquet
Harbour

Strait of Belle Isle

Sep
1764

Unfortunate
Cove

Griquet
Bay

Flowers
Cove

Oct
1764   Ferolle

Northern
Peninsula

Ferolle
Point

Conche
1763

Port au
Choix

A month after starting
the survey Cook was
injured in an explosion
and returned tto Noddy
Harbour for treatment

NEWFOUNDLAND

1763 – 1764 :
THE NORTHERN
PENINSULA
AND LABRADOR

Max Oulton

The men were discharged from *Lark* on 25 June and the first muster for *Grenville* was taken the next day. On 4 July Cook sailed *Grenville* out of St John's Harbour:

> 4 JULY. At 5am weighed and ran out of the Harbour in company with His Majesty's Ships *Guernsey* and *Tweed*. At 10, parted company and stood to the northward.

They sailed past Funk Island and the Horse Islands, north-west of Cape St John, so that, on Sunday 7 July, *Grenville* anchored in the south-west arm of Carouge Harbour. They were in the heart of the French Shore and found four French fishing ships already at anchor. Carouge Harbour is situated on the east side of the Northern Peninsula, north of Conche, where Cook had been the previous year. The name Carouge is a corruption of Cap Rouge (Red Cape), a headland just to the north of the inlet. Cook would soon be surveying, so had his men preparing the tools of the trade:

10 JULY. am The people employed making signal flags for surveying.

Grenville sailed north on the 10th, rounding Quirpon Island, an island off the tip of the Northern Peninsula, to anchor on the 11th in Noddy Harbour, where they met more French fishing ships. Cook prepared sailing directions for Noddy Harbour:

> This harbour which lies a little to the Westward of Quirpon, runs in S.S.W. between Noddy Point and Cape Raven, which forms the entrance of the harbour; there is no danger in going in; the passage in is on the West-side of a small island that lies about three quarters of a mile within the heads, and you anchor as soon as above it in 5 fathoms water; or with small vessels you may run up into the bason, and anchor in 2 and a half or three fathoms; within the island, on the East side of the harbour, is a stage, and very convenient rooms for many fishing ships.[13]

Three of Parker's entries in the log mention activities that show the beginning of the season's survey. They also indicate the joint approach used by Cook, blending hydrographic charting with land surveying.

12 JULY. Set out with the boats to sound off Sacre.

13 JULY. pm Went into the Bay Sacre, measured a base line and fixed some flags on the different islands etc.

15 JULY. Employed sounding the Bay du Sacre and fixing flags on Cape de Ognon.

Cook took every opportunity to get ashore to set up base lines. He would then undertake a careful triangulation survey using his theodolite and marking each of his survey points with marker flags. Meanwhile, Parker in *Grenville* would be plying back and forth offshore, taking soundings and taking bearings on Cook's survey points. To complete the picture, Cook used the small boats to manoeuvre through the narrow and shallow channels (known locally as tickles), recording rocks, both visible and submerged, and any other features of possible interest. Back on the schooner, all the information was collated and turned into charts and sailing directions.

On 20 July, Cook finished surveying Sacred Bay and moved further west to survey Pistolet and Ha Ha Bays. *Grenville* anchored in Pistolet on the 23rd and two boats spent the next few days surveying the large bay. Cook named the river flowing into Pistolet Bay the Parker River after his deputy. However, the river was later renamed the Milan River. Parker's name has now been applied to a tributary and nearby pond. The schooner moved on the 30th to a new anchorage. This was called Cook's Harbour on the chart. It is not clear if Cook used an existing name or whether it represents one of the rare occasions where Cook applied his own name to a location. It still retains the name.

30 JULY. At 4pm anchored in a small harbour formed by the islands which lie to the SE of Cape Norman in 4 and a half fathoms water.

On 2 August *Grenville* stood off Cape Norman, the most northerly point of Newfoundland, while Cook went ashore, showing his growing ability and confidence in things astronomical, to take the sun's meridian altitude. This allowed him to calculate the cape's latitude. Cook's figure was 51° 39'N, a minute out from the correct figure, 51° 38'N. Cook was then able to use this base figure when calculating the latitude of other locations along the coast.

Cook resumed the survey along the coast to the south-west of Cape Norman. *Grenville*, though, was experiencing bad weather in the Strait of Belle Isle and, in trying to avoid trouble, was forced as far as Green Island in one direction and Quirpon Island in the other. Regaining the coast near Cape Norman on the 5th, Parker discovered there had been an accident involving Cook:

> 5 AUGUST. 2pm Came on board the cutter with the Master who unfortunately had a large powder horn blown up and burnt his hand which shattered it in a terrible manner and one of the people that stood hard by suffered greatly by the same accident. Having no surgeon on board, bore away for Noddy Harbour where a French fishing ship lay. At 8 sent the boat in for the French surgeon. At 10 the boat returned with the surgeon. At 11 anchored in Noddy Harbour in 6 fathoms water.

The location of the accident was named Unfortunate Cove. It had been Cook's right hand that was damaged; it did heal, but the hand bore a gash between the thumb and forefinger and a large scar as far as the wrist. Cook was careful to wear a glove to hide the scar when he had his portrait painted some years later. It would prove to be one of the identifying marks when his remains were recovered after his death in Hawai'i. Cook may have been hurt but his injuries were not going to stop the survey. While Cook recuperated, he sent Parker off on 9 August to the south, to Griquet, to survey that inlet and the coast and bays in the vicinity. The Bay of Griquet is an inlet on the eastern side of the Northern Peninsula, south of Quirpon.

Cook had his men brewing spruce beer at Noddy Harbour, and one of Cook's preoccupations during his career would remain the supply of 'beer' to his men. Whenever he was away from a supply of the real thing he would have his men set up a 'brewery'. Joseph Banks recorded a Newfoundland recipe for beer in 1766 and it is probable that Cook's men used something similar. On this occasion at Noddy Harbour there were repercussions, as several of the men overindulged and needed to be punished for drunkenness:

> 19 AUGUST. am Scraped and cleaned the vessel. 2 men employed brewing of spruce essence. pm Andrew Shepherd, Henry Jefferies and Peter Flower were confined to the deck for drunkenness and mutiny.
>
> 21 AUGUST. am Punished Andrew Shepherd (for the crimes before mentioned, he being the ringleader thereof) by running the Gantlope.

From 20 to 23 August Cook, still at Noddy Harbour, was visited by Jens Haven, a Moravian missionary, who was seeking assistance in reaching the Labrador coast. Governor Hugh Palliser had been under instruction to assist Haven and three other missionaries. Cook was unable to take Haven across himself or to authorise Haven to travel with French fishing boats, but, on the 23rd, Haven secured passage with some Irish fishing vessels then at Quirpon. The Moravians or United Brethren were a protestant church founded in Saxony in 1722 by Moravian refugees holding Hussite doctrines. Jens Haven's diary recorded his meetings with Cook:

> AUGUST 20. . . . so far that we went out from Carpoune [Quirpon]. We were scarcely out of the Harbour, when the Shallops began to scatter from each other, so that I was left alone, some went back again, some went to the island of Belisle but our boat carried me on board Capt. Cook because they dare not go any further by themselves. Capt. Cook receiv'd me very kindly.

> AUGUST 21. The French Capt. La Fouse sent me word that he would carry me with one of his boats to the Coast of Labradore. I sent him answer I could not go without an order from Capt. Cook, and I must have an English man with me which could speak French then I would be willing to go if it was only with two men but Capt. Cook would not Consent to it. August 23 Eight English Shallops was at Carpoune which was going to fish on the Coast of Labradore. I went overland about three milles to come to them, one of them took me in, but when he heard that my design was to speak with the Indians, then said he, I have no order to go there and put me back again on board Capt. Cook and return'd to St. Julian's, there was five Irish Shallops, to which Capt. Cook did speak that they should take me along with them, upon which they agreed if the Indians would come to them, but would not go to the Indians.[14]

Cook was finally ready to resume the survey on the 26th and *Grenville* left Noddy Harbour. Early on 30 August Cook went on shore to the west of Cape Norman while *Grenville* remained off the coast in the Strait of Belle Isle. For the next month they worked down this coast as far as Ferolle. Cook was regularly off in the small boats and

JOSEPH BANKS'S RECIPE FOR SPRUCE BEER

When chowder was mentioned something was hinted about spruce beer, the common liquor of this country. The receipt for making it, take as follows as perfectly as I can get it:

Take a copper that contains 12 gallons; fill it as full of the boughs of black spruce as it will hold, pressing down them down pretty tight. Fill it up with water. Boil it until the rind will strip off the spruce boughs which will waste it about one third. Take them out and add to the water one gallon of molasses. Let the whole boil till the molasses are dissolved. Take a half hogshead and put in nineteen gallons of water and fill it up with essence. Work it with barm or beergrounds and in less than a week it is fit to drink from this liquor. In itself very weak, are made three kinds of flip called here Callibogus, Egg Calli and King Calli. The first simply by adding rum, brandy, or gin if you cannot get either of the first, as much as is agreeable. The second by heating the first with the addition of an egg and some sugar. The third, King Calli, by adding spirit to the contents of the copper as soon as it is ready to put into the cask and drinking it hot.[15]

on shore, while Parker sounded the Strait and tried to keep *Grenville* in contact. The numerous rocks and ledges made Parker's task a difficult one and the vessel 'touched the ground' off Anse Savage Cove (Savage Bay) on 1 September. One of the British patrol vessels, *Solebay*, was sighted that day but did not return *Grenville's* signals (this was not *Solebay* on which Cook had sailed in 1757 but a later ship). On the 10th Parker had again to ride a storm and was forced as far as Quirpon. One of the little bays along this coast received the name Flowers' Cove after Peter Flowers, one of Cook's men, who had also been with him in 1763. St Barbe and St Genevieve Bays were surveyed before *Grenville* reached Old Ferolle. Parker recorded typical Cook movements as they worked down the coast:

13 SEPTEMBER. 4pm The Master with the cutter went ashore with six days provisions in order to continue the survey.

15 SEPTEMBER. 9am Saw our boat and people on shore to the eastward of us.

On the 23rd *Grenville* entered Old Ferolle Harbour, later moving on the 27th to anchor inside Ferolle Island. Cook dispatched Parker with the boats to continue the survey to the south:

23 SEPTEMBER. At 7am weighed and came to sail and sounded at small distances at about half a mile from the shore. Running toward Old Ferrol, the boat likewise employed sounding nearer the shore. At noon, lying to for the boat. The fish stages of Ferrol S by E half E, about 1 mile.

27 SEPTEMBER. pm Anchored inside Grat Ferrol off one of the stages in 2¾ fathoms water, and moored with both bowers.

28 SEPTEMBER. am The cutter with the Assistant went to survey the Bay of St. Margaret.

There was another incident on 1 October. The boats had gone to survey Ferolle Point but one of them struck a ledge, causing it to bilge and fill. Fortunately, the cutter managed to save all the boat's crew. Cook's instructions had required him to be back in St John's by the middle of the month, so he now prepared to finish the survey and return. *Grenville* sailed out past the Dog Peninsula on the afternoon of 5 October and headed up the Strait of Belle Isle. At noon on the 9th they passed Groais Island, and Cape Bonavista, the south-eastern end of the French Shore, was rounded on the 11th. At 8pm on 13 October, Cook anchored *Grenville* in St John's Harbour.

Palliser agreed for *Grenville* to sail to Britain, so the schooner was prepared for the Atlantic. Cook sailed in her on 1 November from St John's and, after a month's crossing, anchored in the Catwater at Plymouth on 4 December. Leaving again on the 7th, *Grenville* reached Woolwich on 12 December. Finally, on the 20th, the schooner tied up alongside the wharf at Deptford. Cook may have left the vessel early to rejoin his family in Shadwell as Elizabeth gave birth to their second son, Nathaniel, on 14 December 1764. With luck, Cook was at hand for the birth. Cook also reported in at the Admiralty.

The year 1764 proved very productive for Cook and several manuscript charts from around the Northern Peninsula and the Strait of Belle Isle survive. Some are in the

Admiralty Library at Taunton. MS C54/2 and MS C54/7 cover most of the year's survey from Griquet to Point Riche. Three smaller charts cover sections of the survey: MS C54/3 Unfortunate Bay to Flower Cove (approx.); MS C54/4 Griquet to Cape Norman (approx.); and MS 342 Flower Cove to Point Riche (approx.). Cook submitted all these charts in 1766, when they were published.

Cook also produced an updated version of his 1763 map of the whole island *A Chart of the Island of Newfoundland with Part of the Coast of Labradore Corrected from the Latest Observations by James Cook, 1764*. The original is held in The Royal Collection at Windsor Castle (710058.b). Cook incorporated the results of his 1764 surveys into this map, so the Northern Peninsula is more accurate; in other respects it is similar to the 1763 map. The Royal Collection also holds *A Chart of the Coasts, Bays and Harbours in Newfoundland between Griguet and Pt. Ferolle* (710058.a).

Sir Philip Stephens, secretary to the Admiralty from 1763 and a close colleague of James Cook

❀ 14 ❀

South Coast of Newfoundland, 1765

Sometime in early 1765 the Cooks moved from Shadwell to their own house in Mile End Old Town. The new house would remain the Cook home until about 1787 when Elizabeth Cook moved south of the river to Clapham to be near her cousins, the Smiths.

Cook had sailed *Grenville* schooner back from Newfoundland in late 1764 and it was now berthed at Deptford. He had misgivings about the vessel's seaworthiness and wrote to the Navy Board requesting that it be refitted as a brig. This, argued Cook, would improve its handling, especially close to shore:

> The masts sails and rigging of His Majesty's Schooner the Grenville being all or the most part of them Condemned by survey, Permit me to set forth the utility of having her rigged into a Brigg, as I presume it may now be Done without much additional expence to the Crown for Schooners are the worst of vessels to go upon any Discovery for in meeting with any unexpected Danger their staying cannot be Depended upon, and for want of sail to Lay a Back they run themselves ashore before they wear. This I experienced in the Grenville schooner Last summer in the Straights of Belle Isle. when I see the condition her Bottom is in it supprizeth me that she ever came off.
>
> A Brigg hath all these advantages over a schooner besides many more I could name, was I not applying to Gentlemen Better acquainted with those things than my self. I only mean to give some reasons for my request, and pray you will be pleas'd to take these into your Consideration, and if they appear reasonable to order her to be rigg'd into a Brigg, as I Cannot help thinking but that it will enable me to Carry on the Survey with greater Dispatch; and Less Danger of Loosing the Vessel than she is at present.[1]

The Navy Board was agreeable to Cook's request and replied a fortnight later: 'In return to your Letter of 22nd past, we acquaint you, that we have directed the Officers of Deptford Yard to cause the Grenville Schooner to be fitted and rigged as a Brigg as you have desired.'[2]

Cook was also worried about the number of crew he was assigned and the manner of their recruitment or appointment. In 1765 *Grenville* had been given an allocation of ten men, and the other ten required to sail the vessel had been acquired on a temporary basis from other ships on the Newfoundland station. Palliser took up Cook's case and wrote to the Admiralty on the matter:

> ... I pray you will also be pleas'd to inform their Lordships that the present method of furnishing the Grenvill schooner with men by detachments lent from the respective ships is attended with many inconveniencys, such as the difficulty of sending and returning them in due time, the discontent of the men serving on board a vessell they

do not belong to occasions them to desert, the difficulty the captains are under to know whether to discharge or run them, and when. Should their Lordships approve of establishing her compliment at 20 men, it would completely answer that service.[3]

Cook and Palliser were successful, and *Grenville's* complement was raised to twenty.

For 1765 James Cook and the following men were still on board from the previous year: William Parker (master's mate), Francis Gathman (now ranked midshipman), Peter Flower (for his third year with Cook), James Griffiths and William Walsh (all ABs). *Grenville* now qualified for a carpenter's mate, Thomas Smith, and Cook had a new servant, John Charlton. Twelve more ABs made up the crew that took the vessel across the Atlantic (Richard Barrow, John Cunningham, George Green, Thomas Hart, William Lamb, Thomas Lock, Nathaniel Lungley, James Mathews, Walter Price, Charles Roberts, James Willoughby and Morris Shortnell). Shortnell ran on arrival in Newfoundland and was replaced by Ruben Herbet.

Palliser was concerned about French naval ships on the south coast of Newfoundland operating from their base at St Pierre et Miquelon. In 1765 he therefore directed the efforts of his squadron along that coast to monitor the activity of the French and discourage British fishermen from contact with the French. Palliser ordered Cook into this region on his next assignment instead of continuing where he had left off in 1764:

> You are hereby required and directed to proceed with His Majestys schooner the Grenville to survey the Coasts of Newfoundland, beginning at the Harbour of St. Lawrence near the Red Hat Mountain thence to the Westwd. to Cape Ray, making in your way an exact survey of the Coasts Islands and Harbours, and remark every thing that may be useful to the Trade and Navigation of His Majesty's Subjects in those parts, particularly noting in your Drafts and remarks the Beaches and places fit for stages and other conveniences for landing and drying Fish as well as such as have been or may be used for that purpose.
>
> When you have finish'd the Harbour of St. Lawrence you are to leave a Copy thereof in the hands of some person there to be sent out to me in case of my arriving off there, or to be sent to Placentia in case of receiving advice of my being there.
>
> You are to be particular in Describing any place in any Harbour that from it's situation appearsto you for a Fortress that would secure the Harbour and Fishery and be advantageous for its own Defence.
>
> You are to be Careful that there be not taken into the Vessel you are Master of any seaman or others than such as do belong to her, and as you are not to lend any of the Vessel Company to any of the Fishing Ships, so neither are you to Suffer to be taken on board her any sort of Fish either by [the end of the letter is missing][4]

The *Grenville's* log for 1765 only begins at the beginning of April, with the news that the vessel has come out of the dry dock at Deptford, having been converted from a schooner to a brig. The crew were busy rerigging the brig and loading ballast and stores for the new season.

Palliser, meanwhile, was issuing orders to his captains. As governor, he had overall responsibility for the whole island, but his captains had authority in the sections of the island where they operated. They received surrogate commissions, which Palliser dispensed before he left Britain. The commissions had replaced the unofficial system of 'fishing admirals' (see section 'Fishing Admirals') that had operated in Newfoundland previously. A specimen commission is reads:

> By Virtue of the power and authority to me given by His Majesty's Letters made Patent, bearing date at Westminster the ninth day of April in the fourth year of the reign of our Sovereign Lord George III. by the Grace of God of Great Britain, France and Ireland, King Defender of the Faith I do hereby constitute and appoint you to be my Deputy or Surrogate with full power and authority to assemble Courts within to enquire into all such complaints as may be brought before you to hear and determine the same to all intents and purposes as I myself might or would do. By virtue of the power and authority vested in me you have likewise power and authority to seize and detain in order to proceed to condemnation all unaccustomed prohibited or run goods that may be found within the aforesaid limits or ports adjacent. And I do grant and give unto you full power and authority to administer the several oaths to any person or persons you shall think fit agreeable to the several Acts of Parliament made in that behalf. And I do strictly enjoin all Admirals of Harbours, all Justices of the Peace, all Officers Civil and Military, and all other His Majesty liege subjects to be aiding and assisting you the said and to obey and put into execution all such lawful orders as you shall give unto them as I myself might or would do by virtue of the power and authority vested in me.[5]

The surrogate commissions for 1765 were delivered to:

> Captain Charles Saxton of HMS *Pearl*, who was to patrol from Cape Ray to Ferryland;
>
> Captain Samuel Thompson of HMS *Lark*, who was to patrol from Trinity to Quirpon;
>
> Captain Sir Thomas Adams of HMS *Niger*, who was to patrol on the coast of Labrador from the entrance of Davis Strait to York Harbour;
>
> Captain John Hamilton of HM sloop *Zephyr*, who was to patrol from Point Riche to St Barbe on Newfoundland and from St John's River to Cape Charles on the coast of Labrador;
>
> Daniel Burr, Esq., on the coast of Newfoundland from Cape Bonavista to Cape St Francis.

By late April 1765 Cook and *Grenville* were ready to leave for Newfoundland and the pilot came on board to take the vessel out of the Thames to the Downs. In 1765 and 1766 the pilot taken on board *Grenville* at Deptford was John Blackburn. It is possible that this was James Cook's father-in-law.

21 APRIL. am A pilot came on board.

22 APRIL. am At half past 11 cast off the fasts and came to sail.

Given the French presence on the south coast of Newfoundland, *Grenville* was fitted with more armament when she stopped at Woolwich on her passage down the Thames. In the previous year the armament had been supplied from the flagship and had to be

FISHING ADMIRALS

The island of Newfoundland had had, for many years, an informal legal system, especially in outports (a Newfoundland term for small coastal settlements) away from St John's. The system, developed in the seventeenth century, involved 'fishing admirals'. Hardly anyone overwintered on the island in that period so, when the first vessel reached an outport at the start of the fishing season that year, the captain of that vessel (provided they were strong enough) was termed the fishing admiral. He would hold jurisdiction over fishermen at that location and would also have the first pick of fishing rooms in the harbour.

The code of law was developed slowly over time by the fishermen and seamen themselves but, since they had no legal training, the justice they dispensed was often wanting and there were many instances of abuse. Bribery and corruption were common and there was anarchy from October to April. The law was often unenforceable and so the situation became increasingly chaotic. By the late 1720s people such as William Keen were demanding that Britain introduce a formal and effective judicial system in Newfoundland. In 1729 the British government finally recognised the need for proper justice and one of its recommendations was to upgrade the naval convoy commander into a 'governor' with greater powers.

The governor only ruled directly for part of the year, though, as he continued to arrive in the spring and leave in the autumn. While he was present on the island, the governor sent out his surrogate officers, who held court around the island. He also appointed local justices of the peace, who would hear cases all year. This was the situation when Graves and Palliser held the office in the 1760s.

returned. The vessel was now established with '6 swivel guns, 12 Musquets, and powder and shot' of its own. *Grenville* proceeded down the Channel, passed Land's End on 6 May and headed across the Atlantic. While *Grenville* was crossing the Atlantic, Palliser received his instructions for the year. Section 10 comprised:

And in order that this Service may be more effectually performed, We have ordered the Commanders of the Ships & Sloop named in the margin [*Pearl, Lark, Niger, Zephyr* sloop] carefully to visit the several Harbours, Coasts, and Fishing Grounds, as well those upon the Coasts of Newfoundland, as those upon the Coasts of Labrador, & to the Northward, with Directions to them to prevent the French from drying their Fish, or continuing thereon, otherwise than is herein before-mentioned, between Cape Bonavista & Point Riche, or to fish nearer than the Distances allowed by the before-mentioned Treaties; and at the same Time We have ordered them to make Charts of all the said Coasts, with Drafts of the Harbors, noting the Depths of Water, Conveniences for Fishing, and whatever Observations may occur worthy of our Knowledge, which are to be transmitted by them to You, that they may be laid before Us.[6]

Cook sighted Newfoundland on 31 May and carried on to anchor in Great St Lawrence Harbour on the south side of the Burin Peninsula on 2 June. *Niger* was already there and they waited for Governor Palliser to arrive in *Guernsey*:

> 31 MAY. 1pm Saw the land from WNW to NNW. 2pm Cape Race and Cape Bollard in one bearing NE by E.

> 2 JUNE. 8am Half past standing in a bay discovered a ship at anchor. half past 9am anchored with the best bower in Great St. Lawrence Harbour. Found here His Majesty's Ship *Niger* and one merchant ship.

HMS *Niger* was a fifth rate of thirty-three guns, built in 1759 at Sheerness dockyard. It was under the command of Captain Sir Thomas Adams; William Munkhouse, who later sailed with Cook on *Endeavour*, was the ship's surgeon. The advantage of Cook having a self-contained ship and crew was shown, as he was able to begin surveying immediately in the twin harbours of St Lawrence.

> 3 JUNE. am Began surveying the harbour of St. Lawrence.

Cook tried to use local people as pilots to guide him, to warn of rocks and currents, and to provide existing local names for features. He took John Beck on board as pilot at Great St Lawrence. Cook used three other local Newfoundland pilots in 1765 as well as Beck: John Dawson (for Connaigre and Hermitage Bays), John Peck (in the Bay d' Espoir) and Morgan Snook (in Fortune Bay).

> 12 JUNE. am The cutter with the Master and pilot left the vessel to continue the survey along the coast.

Palliser and *Guernsey* arrived on the 13th. Cook had nearly finished the first piece of coast and *Grenville* moved on on the 16th. As well as the survey, Cook had prepared sailing directions for the St Lawrence Harbours:

> Close to the eastward of Cape Chapeau rouge are the harbours of Great and Little St. Laurence. To sail into Great St. Laurence, which is the westernmost, there is no danger but what lies very near the shore; taking care with Westerly, and particularly S.W. winds, not to come too near the Hat Mountain, to avoid the flerrys and eddy winds under the high land. The course in is first N.W. till you open the upper part of the harbour, then N.N.W. half W. the best place for great ships to anchor, and the best ground is before a cove on the East-side of the harbour in 13 fathoms water. A little above Blue Beach Point, which is the first point on the West-side; here you lie only two points open: you may anchor any where between this point and the point of Low Beach, on the same side near the head of the harbour, observing that close to the West shore, the ground is not so good as on the other side. Fishing vessels lay at the head of the harbour above the beach, sheltered from all winds.[7]

Adams then took *Niger* north to build a wharf at Chateau Bay in Labrador. Cook had surveyed the bay in 1763 so was probably consulted on where to place the wharf.

Cook worked past the Lamaline Islands to round the end of the Burin Peninsula at the beginning of July. The French islands of St Pierre et Miquelon lay twenty kilometres to the west. Cook was now entering Fortune Bay and would follow its southern shore to the bay's head at Grand le Pierre. On the 13th, two lost men were discovered wandering near the shore and close to death:

13 JULY. At 3pm anchored in a bay by Great Garnish. At 8pm took two men on board that had been lost in the woods for near a month. They came from Burin intending to go to St. Lawrence and were almost perishing for want of subsistance.

As usual, Parker kept *Grenville* off the coast, sounding as they went, while Cook stayed close to the shore in a small boat, landing regularly to take readings with the theodolite. They next surveyed Jacques Fontaine Cove and Bay l'Argent at the head of Fortune Bay. Turning west, they continued along the northern shore before entering Long Harbour on the 22nd, but at 11am disaster struck when they hit a rock:

22 JULY. At 11 am turning into Long Harbour ran ashore upon a rock. Struck the yards and topmasts. pm Employed shoaring the vessel with the yards, etc. And starting water and heaving ballast out. Got all the anchors from the bows and payed the cables out overboard. At midnight the water flowing got her off.

23 JULY. am Employed getting the cables and anchors on board and transporting the vessel. Cut 10 fathoms off the small bower cable, it being much rubbed in heaving off. At 1pm anchored with the small bower in 50 fathoms water. At 4 warped into a little cove where we moored with the small anchor.

Cook managed to get *Grenville* off the rock and nursed the brig to safety in Anderson's Cove on the west side of Long Harbour. Temporary repairs were carried out while the inlet was surveyed. They left Long Harbour on the 27th and continued round Belleoram and Boxey Harbours, some of the many inlets of Fortune Bay. In mid-August, Cook sailed past Sagona to anchor off Brunet Island in the middle of Fortune Bay. He produced sailing directions for Brunet Island:

The Island of Brunet is situated nearly in the middle of the entrance into Fortune Bay; it is about 5 leagues in circuit, and of tolerable height; the East end appears, at some points of view, like islands, by reason it is very low and narrow in two places. On the N.E. side of the island is a bay, wherein is tolerable good anchorage for ships in 14 and 16 fathoms, sheltered from Southerly and Westerly winds; you must not run too far in for fear of some sunken rocks in the bottom of it, a quarter of a mile from the shore; opposite this bay on the South-side of the island, is a small cove, wherein small vessels and shallops can lay pretty secure from the weather, in 6 fathoms water; in the middle of the cove is a rock above water, and a channel on each side of it. The islands lying at the West-end of Brunet, called Little Brunets; afford indifferent shelter for shallops in blowing weather; you may approach these islands, and the island of Brunet, within a quarter of a mile all round, there being no danger, but what lies very near the shore.[8]

Then it was back north to Harbour Breton and Connaigre Harbour, before sailing through Pass Island Tickle. Cook crossed Hermitage Bay to anchor in Great Jervis Harbour:

31 AUGUST. At 1pm anchored in the harbour of Grand Jervis, in the Bay Dispair.

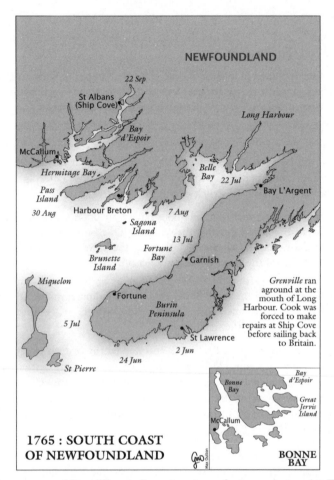

NEWFOUNDLAND

22 Sep

St Albans
(Ship Cove)

Long Harbour

*Bay
d'Espoir*

McCallum

*Belle
Bay* *22 Jul*

Hermitage Bay

Bay L'Argent

*Pass
Island*

30 Aug   Harbour Breton *7 Aug*

*Sagona
Island*

13 Jul

*Fortune
Bay* Garnish

*Brunette
Island*

Miquelon

Grenville ran
aground at the
mouth of Long
Harbour. Cook was
forced to make
repairs at Ship Cove
before sailing back
to Britain.

Fortune

*Burin
Peninsula*

5 Jul

St Lawrence

2 Jun

St Pierre   *24 Jun*

*Bay
d'Espoir*

*Bonne
Bay*

*Great
Jervis
Island*

McCallum

**1765 : SOUTH COAST
OF NEWFOUNDLAND**

**BONNE
BAY**

Grenville next entered Bay d'Espoir. In a nice piece of mistranslation this French name, meaning bay of hope, had been changed to Bay of Despair by the British, giving it quite the opposite meaning (the French name has now been reinstated). They worked their way up the long inlet to anchor on 21 September at Ship Cove (now called St Alban's), where Cook was able to repair the damage done to the vessel at Long Harbour:

> 21 SEPTEMBER. At 9pm anchored in Ship Cove in 5 fathoms water and moored with the hawser fast on shore.

> 29 SEPTEMBER. At 9am hauled on shore. Employed cleaning the bottom on the larboard side and boostoped with tallon. The carpenters employed about the fore foot which was damaged when run on shore in Long Harbour.

The forefoot is a timber curving upwards from the leading end of the keel to the lower end of the stem and forming part of both. All repairs were completed and *Grenville* departed on 9 October, anchoring the next evening in the mouth of the north entrance of Great Jervis Harbour. The surveying season was over for another year and Cook now headed for St John's, where his arrival and departure were noted by *Niger*:

21 OCTOBER. Anchored here his Majesty's Brig, Grenville.

5 NOVEMBER. Sailed for England, with Guernsey, Pearl, Spy and Brigg Grenville.

Palliser was still concerned about French activity and arranged for two of his ships to over winter in Newfoundland waters along the south coast.

Cook sighted the Scilly Isles on 28 October and two days later *Grenville* anchored at Spithead for Cook to report to Palliser:

30 NOVEMBER. 10am Anchored at Spithead. Found here the *Guernsey* and the *Aquilon*.

Cook then continued round to the river Thames where, after a short stopover at Woolwich, he moored the ship at Deptford dockyard on the south bank of the river, downstream from the centre of London:

16 DECEMBER. At 3pm made fast along side of ship off Deptford yard.

Having safely brought *Grenville* back to Britain, Cook quickly returned to his family in Mile End. Once again, he began drawing up the charts, the sailing directions and other reports from that year's survey of the Burin Peninsula, Fortune Bay and Bay d'Espoir on Newfoundland's south coast. One manuscript chart survives from 1765 in the Admiralty Library at Taunton. It is MS C58, covering from Burin Peninsula to Jervis Harbour. Cook submitted this chart in 1766, when it was published. Another manuscript chart, entitled 'A Chart of the Sea-Coast of Newfoundland Between St. Laurence and Point-May. Survey'd by Order of Hugh Palliser Esq Commodore &c. &c., by James Cook', was offered for sale in 2008. Its present whereabouts are unknown.

Palliser mentioned Cook in his reports to the Admiralty:

> Mr. Cook, the Surveyor, having been Employ'd under my Directions upon the Coasts where I have been Employ'd in His Majesty's Ship Guernsey, I beg leave to refer the Board to his Drafts and Remarks, & as the several Services I have had under my care have not allow'd me time to make such Surveys and Remarks myself, I desire you will be Pleas'd to move their Lordships to Signifie to the Navy Board that they have no Objection to their Paying my Wages.[9]

Of *Grenville*'s crew, nine men would return to Newfoundland in 1766, two men were discharged into sick quarters at Portsmouth (Charles Roberts and William Walsh); five men were discharged (Richard Barrow, George Green, Ruben Herbet, Thomas Lock and James Willoughby) and three men ran (Thomas Hart, James Mathews and Walter Price).

❧ 15 ❧

South-west Coast of Newfoundland, 1766

In 1766 nine men returned for another year with Cook on *Grenville* in Newfoundland. They were William Parker, Francis Gathman, Thomas Smith, John Cunningham, Peter Flower, James Griffiths, William Lamb, Nathaniel Lungley and John Charlton. Eight new men joined at Deptford, two at Woolwich and two men at the end of the season for the trip back across the Atlantic. The Deptford men were: Michael Brown, James Command, John Dunn, William Gilliard, Stephen Lyon, Timothy Rarden, Robert Turner and John Willoughby. Zachariah Stringer and John Williams joined at Woolwich.

At the beginning of 1766, *Grenville* was moored at Deptford and remained there until the end of February, when preparations were made to move the vessel into the dock for repairs and modifications. No major modifications were necessary so entries in the log were all concerned with the weather and being mustered by the clerk of the cheque. Cook was living at home in Mile End Old Town with his family, where he was occupied drawing up the charts from 1765. Palliser wrote to the Admiralty:

> Mr. Cook, appointed by the Right Hon'ble my Lords Commissioners of the Admiralty to survey the sea-coasts of Newfoundland under my direction, having finish'd his chart of that part of the south coast of Newfoundland adjacent to the islands of St. Pierre and Miquelow, including the said islands, upon a large scale of one inch to a mile, you will herewith receive the said chart, which be pleas'd to lay before the Right Hon'ble my Lords Commissioners of the Admiralty.
>
> He having also the last year deliver'd in to the Board his survey of the north part of Newfoundland upon the same scale, and having now prepar'd a chart of that part with the opposite part of the coast of Labradore, including the island and streights of Bell [Belle] Isle, likewise another of the above-mention'd survey of part of the south coast of Newfoundland, both upon a proper scale to be usefull to the trade and navigation of His Majesty's subjects, as a publication thereof, I am of opinion, will be a great encouragement to new adventurers on the fisherys upon these coasts, be pleas'd to move their Lordships to permit Mr. Cook to publish the same.[1]

The letter was endorsed: 'Their Lordships are pleased to comply with the request, By permitting Mr. Cook to publish them.' Cook, therefore, submitted copies of his manuscript charts. J Larken engraved the charts and they were printed and sold, together with sailing directions by Mount and Page of Tower Hill, London. The first chart (BL Add MS 17693A) was entitled *A Chart of the Straights of Belleisle with Part of the Coast of Newfoundland and Labradore, from Actual Surveys Taken by Order of Commodore Pallisser, Governor of Newfoundland, Labradore, &ca.* The second chart (BL Add MS 17693B) was *A Chart of Part of the South Coast of Newfoundland, Including the Islands St. Peters and Miquelon, from an Actual Survey Taken by Order of Commodore Pallisser, Governor of Newfoundland, Labradore, &c.* This chart was printed and sold by Thomas Jefferys and Andrew Dury as well as by Mount and Page. Both charts appeared later in 1766 and were published by Cook, so remained his property.

Two sets of sailing directions were also printed: *Directions for Navigating on Part of the North East Side of Newfoundland, and in the Streights of Bell-Isle, with a Chart Thereof, and a Particular Account of the Bays, Harbours, Rocks, Land-Marks, Depths of Water, Latitudes, Bearings and Distances from Place to Place, the Setting and Flowing of the Tides, etc. Founded on Actual Survey, Taken by Order of Commodore Pallisser, Governor of Newfoundland, Labradore, etc.*; and *Directions for Navigating on Part of the South Coast of Newfoundland with a Chart Thereof, Including the Islands of St. Peter's and Miquelon, and a Particular Account of the Bays, Harbours, Rocks, Land-Marks, Depths of Water, Latitudes, Bearings and Distances from Place to Place, the Setting of the Currents, and Flowing of Tides, etc. From an Actual Survey, Taken by order of Commodore Pallisser, Governor of Newfoundland, Labradore, etc.* Both were printed for the author, James Cook, and sold by Mount and Page.

Grenville was moved into the dock at Deptford on 2 March and remained there undergoing repairs until 22 March, when it was returned to moorings nearby. All the while repairs and maintenance were made to timbers, the sails and rigging. At the end of the month, stores began to be taken on board in readiness for sailing. Cook, anticipating longer stretches on shore in the coming season, asked to be issued with a tent, 'to serve as a covering to them in the night and in bad weather'.[2]

The Admiralty issued Palliser with fresh instructions:

Whereas His Majesty's Ships, Sloops, and Vessels named on the other side hereof are intended to be employed for the Convoy and protection of the Newfoundland Fishery this year; You are hereby required and directed to take them under your command, their Commanders being directed to obey your Orders; hoisting a Broad Pendant on board such of them as you shall think fit, And you are to employ them, as you shall judge best for the Service, conformable to the Orders and Instructions which you received last year and to such farther Instructions as you may receive from this Board before you leave for England.

And whereas it is intended that the Grenville Schooner, now refitting at Deptford, shall be continued on the service of surveying the Coasts of the Island of Newfoundland, you are to take her under your command also, and employ her, in such manner as you shall find best on the said Service; M[r] Cooke her Master being directed to obey your Orders.[3]

The vessels (and captains) named to be in Newfoundland waters in 1766 were: *Guernsey* (John Gell), *Pearl* (Charles Saxton), *Gilbraltar* (Richard Brathwaite), *Merlin* (John Hamilton), *Wells* (James Lawson), *Niger* (Sir Thomas Adams), *Favourite* (William Hamilton), *Zephyr* (Cornthwaite Ommanney), *Spy* (Thomas Allwright) and *Hope* (William Stanford).

During the early part of the month of April the crew of *Grenville* continued their preparation for the crossing back to Newfoundland to resume the survey. The brig left Deptford on 20 April and headed down the Thames via Woolwich, where it received its ordnance supplies. A few days later:

> 24 APRIL. At 6am moored with the kedge anchor. am Sent the boat with the men to Chatham to be paid their wages to the 30th September 1765.

Cook reached the Downs on the 28th and began sailing down the English Channel. The Scilly Isles, off Cornwall, were passed on 6 May and *Grenville* crossed the Atlantic, taking three weeks. On 29 May, Cape Race, the south-easternmost point of Newfoundland, was sighted through the icebergs. Cook worked his way along the south coast past St Pierre et Miquelon to enter Bonne Bay, west of Hermitage Bay, and anchored in Killbuck Cove on the west side of the main bay:

> 31 MAY. 7 Anchored in a little cove on the west side of Bon Bay in 7 fathoms water and moored with the hawser fast on shore.

The previous year Cook had surveyed from the south side of the Burin Peninsula at Great St Lawrence Harbour via Fortune Bay to the Bay d'Espoir. He was now intending to carry on, moving west from where he had left off. *Grenville* was carrying stores and provisions for the schooner *Hope*, which had spent the winter nearby at Great Jervis Harbour. *Hope*, purchased by Lord Colvill in 1765, carried thirty men under the command of Lieutenant William Stanford.

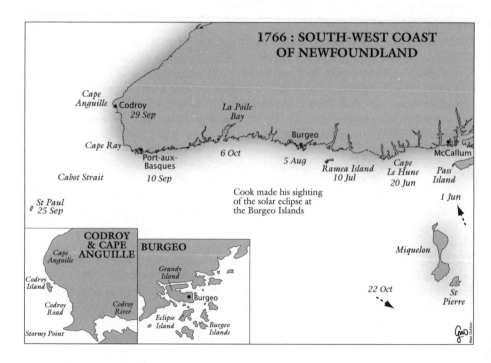

1766 : SOUTH-WEST COAST OF NEWFOUNDLAND

Cape Anguille
Codroy 29 Sep
La Poile Bay
Burgeo
Cape Ray
Port-aux-Basques
6 Oct
5 Aug
McCallum
Cabot Strait
10 Sep
Ramea Island 10 Jul
Cape Le Hune 20 Jun
Pass Island

St Paul 25 Sep

Cook made his sighting of the solar eclipse at the Burgeo Islands

1 Jun

CODROY & CAPE ANGUILLE
Cape Anguille
Codroy Island
Codroy Road
Codroy River
Stormy Point

BURGEO
Grandy Island
Burgeo
Eclipse Island
Burgeo Islands

Miquelon

22 Oct

St Pierre

2 JUNE. pm Began the survey. Employed overhauling the hold and platting the cable. Supplied His Majesty's schooner, the *Hope* with 293 lbs bread, 30 pieces of beef, 30 pieces of pork.

Cook immediately set off on the survey:

7 JUNE. At 5am came to sail. At noon Bon Bay NE 2 miles. Sounded the coast along.

11 JUNE. 6am The Master with the cutter and crew left the vessel to carry on the survey. 12 Noon Cape La Hune WNW 3 or 4 leagues.

Cook prepared sailing directions for Cape La Hune:

Cape La Hune is the Southernmost point of land on this part of the coast, and lies in the latitude 47° 31' 42" North. West Half North from Pass Island, and N.W. half N. 10½ leagues from cape Miquelon; it may be easily known by its figure, which much resembles a sugar loaf; but in order to distinguish this, you must approach the shore at least within 3 leagues, (unless you are directed to the Eastward or Westward of it) otherwise the elevation of the high land within it will hinder you from distinguishing the sugar loaf hill; but the cape may always be known by the High Land of La Hune, which lies one league to the Westward of it; this land rise directly from the sea, to a tolerable height, appears pretty flat at top, and may be seen in clear weather 16 leagues.[4]

Cook next investigated the Penguin Islands and La Hune Bay before reaching Fox Island Harbour in early July. He then crossed to the Ramea Islands, ten kilometres off Newfoundland's south coast. Cook anchored *Grenville* in Ship Cove on the south side of Ramea Island:

10 JULY. At 6pm anchored in a cove between the Ramea Islands in 5 fathoms water and moored with the hawser fast on shore.

11 JULY. am Employed on the survey.

Crossing back to the mainland, *Grenville* anchored in White Bear Bay before moving on to the Burgeo Islands, a group of many small islands, just off the south coast. The largest island, on which the modern settlement of Burgeo stands, is Grandy Island. Cook anchored *Grenville* in Grandys Cove, off Furber Point. On 5 August Parker's entry in the log was:

5 AUGUST. Employed as before.

This bland entry belies what happened that day, which proved a momentous one for Cook. Cook knew that a solar eclipse would occur that day and that southern Newfoundland was an ideal location from which to make observations. After several days of fog, conditions improved on the day of the eclipse and Cook was able to make his observation. He wrote up his findings and sent a report to the Royal Society that was presented at one of their meetings by John Bevis in London in April 1767 (see section 'Paper Read to the Royal Society'). The eclipse is now referred to as Cook's Eclipse and the small island on which the observation was made, just south of Grandy Island, was given the name Eclipse Island.

Cook continued with the survey, covering Connoire Bay before reaching La Poile Harbour on 16 August. The British knew the inlet as Tweed's Harbour (named after one of their ships) and another ship, HMS *Pearl*, was waiting there when *Grenville* arrived:

16 AUGUST. At 7am anchored with the small bower in 16 fathoms water in Tweed's Harbour and moored with the hawser fast on shore. Found here His Majesty's ship the Pearl.

After two weeks Cook was ready to move on. Parker and the crew had used the time to brew beer while Cook was out on the survey:

29 AUGUST. am Got the beer on board and unmoored. At 8am weighed and came to sail.

Anchored in Harbour Le Cou, they encountered a shallop belonging to the schooner *Hope* on 3 September. A week later they arrived at Port aux Basques, where the brig was overhauled while Cook surveyed:

16 SEPTEMBER. am Hauled ashore and scrubbed and boot topped with tallow. Employed about the rigging. At 6pm hauled off

17 SEPTEMBER. At 6am hauled a shore again. Scrubbed and boot topped the other side; and employed about the rigging. The cutter employed on the survey.

Cook was now nearing the south-western point of Newfoundland, Cape Ray. He left Port aux Basques on the 24th and crossed to the island of St Paul, situated in the Cabot Strait between Cape Breton Island and Newfoundland. He went ashore for a few hours:

25 SEPTEMBER. 4am The Isle of St. Pauls SW by W½W 3 or 4 miles. 5am The cutter, etc., went onshore on the island. 3pm The cutter came on board, hoisted her in and made sail.

By late September winter is on the way to Newfoundland and Cook was coming to the end of the survey season. He anchored behind Codroy Island and surveyed the Codroy River and the coast as far as Cape Anguille, but it was now time to return to St John's. They left Codroy on 4 October and rounded Cape Ray. *Grenville* put in again to La Poile Harbour for two weeks, before continuing along the south coast on the 21st. Cook brought *Grenville* into St John's Harbour on 27 October, where several other ships were already anchored:

27 OCTOBER. 5am Anchored in the Narrows of St. John's Harbour. 8 Anchored in St. John's Harbour and moored with the small anchor. Found here Commodore Palliser in the *Guernsey* with the *Niger, Favourite* and *Zephyr*.

Joseph Banks, who would sail with Cook on *Endeavour*, had spent the summer in Newfoundland on *Niger*. There has been speculation as to whether Cook and Banks met at St John's but is unlikely that they did. They only overlapped for twenty-four hours, during which time Cook was occupied with *Grenville* and Banks was preparing to sail the next day on *Niger* (see section 'The Itinerary of Joseph Banks in Newfoundland in

PAPER READ TO THE ROYAL SOCIETY

—An Observation of an Eclipse of the Sun at the Island of New-found-land, August 5, 1766, by Mr. James Cook, with the Longitude of the Place of Observation deduced from it: Communicated by J. Bevis, M.D., F.R.S. Read April 30, 1767.

Mr. Cook, a good mathematician, and very expert in his business, having been appointed by the Lords Commissioners of the Admiralty to survey the sea-coasts of New-found-land, Labradore, &c., took with him a very good apparatus of instruments, and among them a brass telescopic quadrant made by Mr. John Bird.

Being, August 5, 1766, at one of the Burgeo Islands, near Cape Ray, latitude 47° 36' 19", the south-west extremity of New-found-land, and having carefully rectified his quadrant, he waited for the eclipse of the sun; just a minute after the beginning of which, he observed the zenith distance of the sun's upper limb 31° 57' 00"; and allowing for refraction and his semidiameter, the true zenith distance of the sun's centre 32° 13' 30", from whence he concluded the eclipse to have begun at 0h. 4' 48" apparent time, and by a like process to have ended at 3h. 45' 26" apparent time.

N.B. There were three other observers, with good telescopes, who all agreed as to the moments of beginning and ending.

Mr. Cook having communicated his observation to me, I shewed it to Mr. George Witchell,[5] who told me he had a very exact observation of the same eclipse, taken at Oxford, by the Rev. Mr. Hornsby;[6] and he would compute, from the comparison, the difference of longitude of the places of observation, making due allowance for the effect of parallax and the earth's prolate spheroidal figure; and he has since given me the following result:—

5h. 23' 59" begun at Oxford.	7h. 7' 5" end at Oxford.
0h. 46' 48" begun at Borgeo Isles.	3h. 39' 14" end at Borgeo Isles.
-------------	---------------
4h. 37' 11"	3h. 27' 51"
- 51' 59" effect of parallax, &c.	+ 17' 35" effect of parallax, &c.
-------------	---------------
3h. 45' 22" diff. of meridians.	3h. 45' 26" diff. of meridians.[7]

J. Bevis.[8]

1766'). Cook prepared *Grenville* for crossing the Atlantic and Palliser gave him orders to proceed: 'You are hereby required and directed to proceed with His Majestys Brigg under your Command directly to Woolwich, and on your arrival you are to inform the Secretary of the Admiralty thereof.'[9]

Two new crewmembers, John Asget and William Dyer, were taken on at St John's on 1 November. Cook sailed from Newfoundland on 4 November. The Lizard was sighted on the 21st, and they were off Beachy Head on the 23rd. The log and journal both finish at this time so exact details for the rest of the year remain unknown.

At the end of 1766 only three crewmembers would remain on *Grenville* to return with Cook to Newfoundland in 1767. Nine men were discharged (James Command, John Cunningham, John Dunn, Francis Gathman, William Lamb, Nathaniel Lungley, Stephen Lyon, William Parker and John Willoughby); three men were discharged into sick quarters (William Gilliard, James Griffiths and Timothy Rarden) and six men ran (John Asget, Michael Brown, William Dyer, Zachariah Stringer, Robert Turner and John Williams). William Parker was one of those who left *Grenville*, having served for three summers; the question of a replacement arose and Hugh Palliser proposed Michael Lane, who had previously served as schoolmaster on *Antelope*:

> On a second conversation with Mr. Cook, I wish you to alow me to recommend for his assistant (in lieu of the young man I before mentioned) Mr. Michl. Lane, schoolmaster of the Guernsey, who draws well, is master of surveying, was brought up in the Bluecoat School, served afterwards as an apprentice to Capt. Denis, who is his friend and patron, at whose recomendation I took him into the Guernsey. Mr. Cook waits on you with this.
>
> P.S. —The other young man has a desire to go another way.[10]

THE ITINERARY OF JOSEPH BANKS IN NEWFOUNDLAND IN 1766

22 April 1766	Left Plymouth in *Niger*, Captain Sir Thomas Adams
12 May	Anchored St John's
11 June	Left St John's for Northern Peninsula
13 June	Arrived Croque
July	For most of the month Banks and Adams very sick, tended by Surgeon William Munkhouse
6 August	Left Croque; met Ommanney in *Zephyr* and Lawson in *Wells*
10 August	Anchored Pitt Harbour in Chateau Bay, Labrador
Remainder of August and September at Chateau Bay while small fort built	
3 October	Left Chateau Bay
4 October	Arrived Croque
11 October	Left Croque
13 October	Arrived St John's. *Guernsey, Pearl* and *Hope* already there; *Favourite* and *Zephyr* followed a day later. Banks reported population of St John's as 1,100
26 October	Ball hosted by Palliser for anniversary of king's accession to the throne
27 October	*Grenville* arrived in St John's
28 October	Banks and *Niger* left St John's
18 November	Arrived Lisbon
30 December	Left Lisbon
19 January 1767	Arrived Plymouth

As for Cook, he returned to Mile End to meet his first and only daughter, Elizabeth, who sadly died on 9 April 1771, aged only four, before Cook returned from his *Endeavour* voyage. Cook set about his usual task of preparing copies of his work from the surveying season he had just completed. One manuscript chart survives from 1766 in the Admiralty Library at Taunton. It is MS C54/5, covering from Jervis Harbour to Cape Anguille. Cook submitted this chart in late 1766 and it was published in 1767.

🎕 16 🎕

West Coast of Newfoundland, 1767

In January 1767, James Cook was at home in Mile End Old Town, London, working on his charts, enjoying being with his family and contemplating a new year. His vessel, the brig *Grenville*, was waiting moored at Deptford. Cook was about to cross the Atlantic for what would be his last season in Newfoundland; his intention was to resume at Cape Anguille and survey the west coast as far as Ferolle Point, the point at which he had finished in 1764.

After Cook had prepared his chart from 1766, he submitted it for publication. Once again J Larken engraved the chart and it was printed and sold by Mount and Page, Jefferys, Dury and Carrington Bowles. It was entitled *A Chart of Part of the South Coast of Newfoundland Including the Islands St. Peters and Miquelon: with the Southern Entrance into the Gulph of St. Laurence from Actual Surveys Taken by Order of Commodore Palliser, Governor of Newfoundland, Labradore, &c.* As well as drawing up the charts from 1766, Cook was still sorting out problems for his crew. He had written to the Admiralty seeking discharges for some of his men and received a reply from Philip Stephens:

> I have communicated to my Lords Commissioners of the Admiralty your Letter of this date informing them that the six men named in the Margin, belonging to the Schooner you command have applied to be discharged, on providing Able Seamen to serve in their room except Frans. Gathman, who desires to be discharged into the Scarborough on preferment, And I am commanded to Signify their Lordships direction to you to discharge the five first upon their procuring each an Able Sea-Man to serve in his room, and to acquaint you that it is necessary the Captain of the Scarborough should signify his request to have Gathman on preferment. [1]

The men mentioned in the margin of this letter were Nathaniel Lungley, John Cunningham, William Lamb, John Willoughby, Stephen Lyon and Francis Gathman. Lungley, Cunningham and Lamb had sailed on *Grenville* in 1765 and 1766. Willoughby and Lyon had only sailed on *Grenville* in 1766. All were discharged in March 1767. Francis Gathman (1744–67) had sailed on *Grenville* for three years: in 1764 as an AB, in 1765 and 1766 as a midshipman. He was successfully discharged onto *Scarborough* on 23 February 1767 but was dead within the year. Captain Robert Gregory of *Scarborough* sent documentation from Antigua, including monthly muster books and pay tickets for Francis Gathman and several other recently deceased crewmembers. [2] Gathman had been baptised on 9 December 1744 in Salem, Massachusetts, the son of Samuel and Mary Gahtman (the name had been changed from Gahtman after the family moved from Germany), who operated trading vessels on the American coast.

James Cook was joined on *Grenville* for 1767 by five men who had sailed with him in 1766: Thomas Smith (carpenter's mate); Peter Flower, William Gilliard and Timothy Rarden (ABs) and John Charlton (master's servant). New to the brig were Michael Lane (master's mate), Alexander Lind (midshipman) and William Coal, Simon Doughty, George English, William Grimshaw, Thomas Hardman, Isaac Hutchison, Edward Norris, John Simms, James Simpkins, Isaac Smith, James Surridge, Abraham Vandome and John Vincent (all ABs). John Smith was the new master's servant, and William Howson joined in Newfoundland as an AB.

Isaac Smith was a first cousin, once removed, of Cook's wife, Elizabeth (see sections 'Batts/Smith Family Tree' and 'Isaac Smith'). John Smith was most probably another cousin of Cook's wife through a different line of Smiths. Whether Thomas Smith was also a relation remains unknown.

Michael Lane (see section 'Michael Lane') replaced William Parker as master's mate and the vessel's second-in-command. The log for *Grenville* in 1767 begins on 2 March, in a new hand, that of Michael Lane who had assumed responsibility for maintaining the ship's record.

Since returning from Newfoundland late in 1766, *Grenville* had spent the winter moored at Deptford. The brig now needed to be repaired and fitted out for service in 1767 and was therefore moved into the dry dock.

2 MARCH. At 1pm hauled into dock.

On 10 March the crew received twelve months' wages. A few days later, *Grenville* was hauled out of the dock. The rest of the month was spent preparing the vessel and stowing stores and provisions for the new season; Cook had asked for new equipment, including a reflecting telescope. At the beginning of April the pilot went on board, which suggests that *Grenville* was about to sail, but neither the log nor the journal record the vessel unmooring and leaving Deptford. Instead, there was an accident while *Grenville* was still moored at the wharf. A collier, *Three Sisters,* caught *Grenville* as it sailed past:

4 APRIL. At 8pm a collier named *The Three Sisters,* Thomas Boyd, Master, of Sunderland in coming down the river fell athwart our hause and caried away our bow sprit cap and jib boom.

5 APRIL. am Hauled alongside the *David* sloop.

Three Sisters was one of many small ships employed to transport coal from the river Tyne south down the North Sea to London, similar to the ships that Cook had learnt to sail on out of Whitby. He may have sailed with or met Thomas Boyd, the master of *Three Sisters* at that time, as it is reported that the two men discovered that they knew each other. It has also been suggested that they had been schoolboys together in the Great Ayton days. The sloop *David* is not recorded as being a Royal Navy vessel. *Grenville* was finally able to sail on the 8th from Deptford down to Woolwich to collect her ordnance stores.

By 16 April *Grenville* was passing the Scilly Isles and heading out into the Atlantic. Newfoundland came into sight on 9 May. The records are not complete and are somewhat sloppy; there are differences between figures listed in the log and in the journal, possibly because Michael Lane was new to the task. The crossing in 1767 was completed a couple of weeks earlier than in previous years and as a result, as they approached Newfoundland, they encountered many icebergs or 'islands of ice' brought down by the Labrador Current from Greenland, Baffin Island and the Davis Strait.

Cook headed first for Capes Ray and Anguille, at the south-western corner of the island. On his passage there he had some difficulty rounding St Pierre et Miquelon, which Cook himself had charted four years previously in 1763. Cape Ray was sighted on 14 May and the next day Cook anchored in Codroy Road.

14 MAY. 12 noon Cape Ray ESE.

15 MAY. 7am Came to in Cod Roy Road. Stormy Point SW by S. Southern Point of Cod Roy Island W by S.

The south-western and western parts of Newfoundland had long been known to fishermen from the Basque region of north-eastern Spain and south-western France. Many of the features in the area had already received names and Cook recorded many of them, often in a corrupt form of the original; some names had even passed through an intermediate French stage before Cook used them on his charts. Cook hired pilots once again and this year they cost him £12 16s.[8] *Grenville* set off on the 18th to begin the survey.

18 MAY. At 6am weighed and came to sail. At noon Cape Anguille NE.

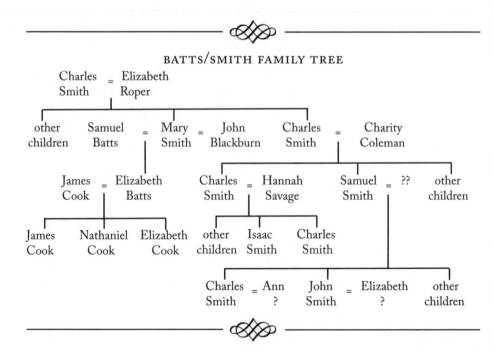

BATTS/SMITH FAMILY TREE

ISAAC SMITH (1753–1831)

Isaac Smith was born in 1753, the oldest of the seven children of Charles and Hannah Smith. Charles Smith was a cousin of Elizabeth Cook, and Isaac owed his first experience of sea life to Elizabeth, who probably persuaded her husband to take him on board. The thirteen-year-old Isaac accompanied Cook to Newfoundland as an AB on *Grenville* in 1767. He then joined Cook for the *Endeavour* expedition to the Pacific and was the first to land at Botany Bay. Cook is reported to have said 'Isaac, you shall land first,' and to have followed him ashore.

On 23 May 1770, Smith was made a midshipman and then on 26 May 1771, after Zachary Hicks's death, he became a master's mate. During the voyage, Smith became adept at drawing and copying charts for Cook, and later, Cook wrote, 'Mr Isaac Smith and Mr Isaac Manley, both too young for preferment, yet their behaviour merits the best recommendation. The former was of great use to me in assisting to make Surveys, Plans, Drawings &tc in which he is very expert.'[4]

Smith sailed on Cook's second voyage on *Resolution* as master's mate. As on *Endeavour*, he assisted with surveys, and Cook used him frequently to draw and copy charts. He obviously recognised his own limitations in writing prose when he put: 'As it will be impossible to describe the Situations of the Islands I have added a small map which I hope will Answer all Nautical Purposes, as farther Description I leave to Abler Hands.'[5] Nearing the end of the second voyage, on 24 May 1775, Cook sent ahead copies of his journals and charts via *Dutton*. In an accompanying letter, he mentioned Smith's journal, noting : '. . . and a Journal kept by one of ye Mates, this Journal is Accompanied by very accurate charts of all the Discoverys we have made, executed by a Young man who has been bred to the Sea under my care and who has been a very great assistant to me in this way, both in this and my former Voyage.'[6]

Smith became a lieutenant in August 1775 and joined the sloop *Weazle*. Over the next two years he served in West African waters and in the West Indies. He stayed in the West Indies, taking command of *Scourge*, an 8-gun sloop, in February 1781, and was promoted to commander on 13 May 1781. He remained on *Scourge* until May 1783, based at the Downs.

Smith was promoted to captain in December 1787 and, a year later, he was placed in command of HMS *Perseverance*, a fifth rate. In early 1789, they were ordered to join the British fleet that was about to leave for the East Indies. *Perseverance* later visited Madras, Bombay and Calcutta; the diarist, William Hickey, met Smith in Calcutta and reported: 'During Commodore Cornwallis's residence in Calcutta I became acquainted with two very fine fellows belonging to his fleet, Captain Smith, an old post-captain, who commanded the Perseverance, a noble frigate . . .'[7]

Smith returned to Britain in July 1793, which marked the end of Smith's active service. He was placed on the list of superannuated rear admirals in 1807, by which time he was severely afflicted with hepatitis. He went to live with Elizabeth Cook in Clapham, but also spent time in Merton with his brother Charles Smith and the children of their sister, Ursula Cragg.

Isaac Smith died on 2 July 1831, aged seventy-seven, leaving a will proven on 22 July 1831.[8] Elizabeth Cook erected a memorial to Isaac and Charles Smith in St Mary the Virgin Church, Merton. The memorial was sculpted by Richard Wyatt, whose sister Caroline had married Isaac Cragg, Isaac Smith's nephew.

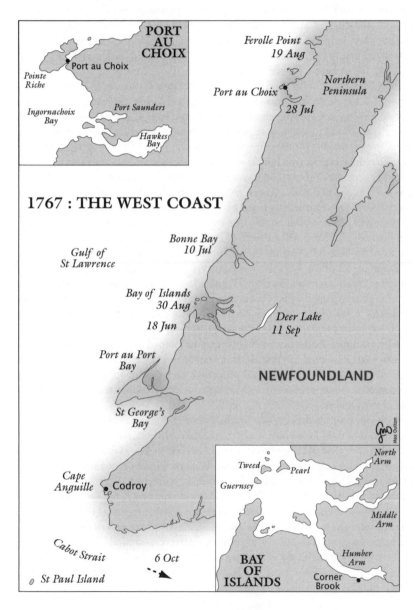

MICHAEL LANE (1739–94)

Michael Lane was baptised on 16 February 1739 at St Botolph without Aldgate, London, the third son of David and Anna Lane. He attended Christ's Hospital, the Bluecoat School, before joining the Royal Navy about 1757 under the patronage of Captain Peter Denis. He served on *Namur* and *Dorsetshire* with Denis.

The training Lane had received at Christ's Hospital marked him out and he served on several ships, including *Bellona* and *Antelope*, as schoolmaster, before joining Palliser on *Guernsey* in the same role. He remained on *Guernsey* for two and a half years before Palliser wrote to the Admiralty in December 1766 recommending Lane as Cook's assistant. Lane was master's mate and assistant surveyor on *Grenville* in 1767; he took over from Cook in 1768 and continued the survey of the Newfoundland and Labrador coasts. Many of his charts were published with those of Cook.

Lane served on *Grenville* for nearly seven years before becoming master of another survey vessel, HMS *Lion*. In 1776, much to Lane's annoyance, Richard Pickersgill was placed in command of *Lion* for a voyage west of Greenland in search of the Northwest Passage. Lane and Pickersgill quarrelled during the voyage and Lane called for Pickersgill to be court-martialled.

Lane finally became a lieutenant in 1777 after nineteen years' service. He served briefly on HMS *Conquistador* in 1778, and was in charge of a different HMS *Lion* from 1783. He returned to Newfoundland on *Lion*, which marks the end of his career. Lane died in 1794. In Rochester in 1768 he had married Susannah Moulden, who was one of several sisters to marry naval men associated with Newfoundland.

The vessel worked along the southern shore of St. George's Bay to the head of the bay, St George's Harbour. Here Lane recorded meeting a group of Mi'kmaq, a native American people:

> 20 MAY. At 8 came to in St. Georges Harbour in 10 fathoms water. Both boats employed on the survey. Found here a tribe of the Mickmak Indians.

The Mi'kmaq people were originally from Nova Scotia and Cape Breton Island, where they had lived relatively peaceably with the French Acadian settlers. When the British took over Nova Scotia the Mi'kmaq had sided with the French – as a result, in the late 1750s and early 1760s some of them had moved across to south-western Newfoundland to avoid the authorities in Nova Scotia. They were also looking for new hunting and fishing grounds.

Grenville next sailed west along the southern side of the Port au Port Peninsula to round Cape St George on 27 May. They passed Red Island and entered Port au Port Bay on the 31st. This is a bay formed behind a prominent peninsula on the west coast of Newfoundland; the peninsula is connected to the mainland by an isthmus and the bay lies to the north of the isthmus. A spit runs north from the isthmus to divide the bay partly into two.

31 MAY. pm Working into Port aux Port. At 6 came to in 9 fathoms water, body of the Island SW by W, point of beach. Employed on the survey.

The survey of Port au Port Bay took two weeks to complete. On 18 June Cook had moved out to survey around Shag Island, north of Port au Port, but the weather worsened and he took refuge the next day in York Harbour in the Bay of Islands.

5 JUNE. Landed on the isthmus and took the true bearing of Cape Anguille.

18 JUNE. Employed in sounding about the reef which lies off Shag Island.

19 JUNE. Employed sounding in the vessel only, it blowing too hard for the boat. At 1pm bore away for the Bay of Three Islands and at 9 anchored in York Harbour in that bay. Employed sounding the Harbour.

The Bay of Islands is a large inlet with several islands at its mouth; the name, or a close variant, had already been applied for some years, with Basque and French versions known too. The islands had been given British names three years earlier when Governor Palliser had visited the coast in *Guernsey*. Guernsey Island and its neighbours, Tweed and Pearl, honoured ships in Palliser's squadron. On the 23rd, Lane's log recorded the death of a member of the crew:

23 JUNE. Departed the life James Surridge seaman.

James Surridge, from Chipping Ongar in Essex, had joined *Grenville* at Deptford earlier that year. His death was the only one recorded during Cook's time in Newfoundland. The next day, William Howson was entered on the muster as an AB, a volunteer and fifteen years old. He must have been on board throughout but only now was his presence admitted when he was entered in place of Surridge. The bad weather had abated and Cook returned to finish off north of Port au Port. By the 29th the strong winds returned and Cook once more took refuge in the Bay of Islands.

29 JUNE. It blowing very hard obliged to put in the bay in the Bay of Three Islands.

This time Cook made for the northern and inner parts of the bay as the winds prevented his entering York Harbour. Joseph Gilbert (who would sail on *Resolution* with Cook in 1772) had been the master on *Guernsey* during Palliser's 1764 visit and he had charted the bay. Cook had a copy of Gilbert's chart on which the inner arms of the bay were called (from north to south) the River Medway, the River Thames and the River Humber. Cook now anchored by North Arm Cove at the entrance of the River Medway (now called the North Arm). By 3 of July he had moved on to survey the River Thames (now called the Middle Arm):

3 JULY. Employed surveying and sounding the River Thames.

On 9 July Cook anchored between the Shag Rocks and North Head as he began leaving the Bay of Islands to sail north. The next day he entered Bonne Bay (Cook called it Good Bay), the next large inlet to the north. It divides into two arms, and Cook moved to anchor off Woody Point at the entrance to the South Arm. By 20 July he had left the bay and resumed his journey up the coast surveying to the northward. On the 27th *Grenville* anchored in Ingornachoix Bay, a wide bay lying to the south of the prominent Point Riche:

27 JULY. At 9pm came to in Ingrenachoise in 10 fathoms water. Rocky Point [of] Island NNW½W. Found riding here a New England sloop.

Cook originally anchored off the western end of an island in the bay, which partly obscures three inlets lying further east. The names of the inlets honour three British naval heroes of the period. Keppel Island and Keppel Harbour behind it were named after Augustine Keppel, one of the naval officers who had captured Havana in 1762. The inlet to the north of Keppel Island was named Port Saunders after Sir Charles Saunders, who had commanded the British fleet at Quebec and who had transferred Cook to HMS *Northumberland*. The third and southern inlet was called Hawke's Harbour after Sir Edward Hawke, who had led the British victory at Quiberon Bay in 1759. It is not clear if Cook applied these names.

While Cook and *Grenville* were in the narrow part of Hawke's Harbour another of Palliser's ships, *Favourite*, came in. *Favourite*, a 16-gun sloop built at Shoreham in 1757, was under the command of William Hamilton, with Edward Pulliblank as master.

6 AUGUST. Employed surveying and sounding. am Came in here His Majesty's ship *Favourite*.

Cook left Ingornachoix Bay and rounded Point Riche to anchor in Port au Choix. While Lane remained with the vessel Cook went off to survey St John's Bay. Lane hauled *Grenville* ashore to clean and pay her bottom. During their stay here, the small boat from another of Palliser's ships, *Merlin*, arrived. *Merlin*, a 304-ton sloop with ten guns, built in Rotherhithe in 1757, was under the command of John Hamilton with William Paterson as master:

19 AUGUST. am The boat went away in order to survey and sound the Bay of St. Johns.

24 AUGUST. pm Anchored here a shallop from the *Merlin* sloop.

The northern end of St John's Bay is Ferolle Point, so Cook had reached his 1764 turning point and could now return south. He was close to the Labrador coast here, and the log mentions a group of mountains visible in the distance, which the British had named Our Ladies Bubbies. They include Colline's Black Mountain and Colline White East and lie just inside present-day Quebec, close to the Labrador border:

26 AUGUST. Employed sounding St. John's Bay both in the vessel and boat. At 12 noon Our Ladies Bubbies NE By N.

Grenville headed south so that Cook could finish the survey of the Bay of Islands where the southernmost arm, the River Humber, remained to be examined. She anchored in the bay on 30 August.

30 AUGUST. At 9pm came to in York Harbour in 35 fathoms water, and moored with a hawser fast ashore.

8 SEPTEMBER. am The boat went up the River Humber in order to survey and sound ditto.

The nature of the terrain of Newfoundland made access to the island's interior difficult and Cook rarely made such excursions. He now undertook a three-day trip up the Humber River and reached Deer Lake. The updated map of Newfoundland that Cook and Lane would produce is essentially one that depicts the coastline; however, it does show the upper reaches of the Humber River, for which Cook wrote directions:

The River Humber at about 5 leagues within the entrance, it becomes narrow, and the stream is so rapid in places for about 4 leagues up to a lake, that it is with great difficulty a boat can be got up it; and at some times quite impracticable; this lake which stretches N.E.½N. is in length 7 or 8 leagues, and from 2 to 5 miles broad. The banks of this river, and the shores of the lake are well clothed with timber, such as are common in this country. This river is said to abound with salmon, in which has been formerly a very great salmon fishery.[9]

Cook returned to Lark Harbour and rejoined *Grenville*, which was prepared for the voyage home. Cook finished off the survey along the southern edge of the bay. The schooner *Hope*, under William Stanford with John Turner master, joined them there on the 21st. *Grenville* and *Hope* tried to leave together on the 24th, but winds forced them back in to anchor again in Lark Harbour. They managed to leave on 27 September. Cook had finished the survey for the year and began his return to Britain via St John's.

There is no entry for Wednesday 30 September in the log. The journal is correct until 27 September, but then has several incorrect matchings of day with date before sorting itself out on Friday 2 October. On the 13 October, *Grenville* rounded Cape Race and anchored that evening in St John's Harbour:

13 OCTOBER. At 7pm got under weigh and turned up the Harbour. pm came to in 6 fathoms water with the small bower and best bower and moored with the kedge anchor. Found riding here Commodore Palliser in the *Guernsey* with the *Merlin* sloop and *Hope* schooner.

A mast was replaced during the stopover and *Grenville* took on board some artefacts that Captain Andrew Wilkinson had acquired for Joseph Banks. The brig left on 23 October and on 7 November they were informed they were south of Portland Bill in the English Channel:

23 OCTOBER. am Hove up and came to sail. At noon Cape Spear WSW about 5 miles.

7 NOVEMBER. 12 noon Spoke with an English ship who informed us Portland bore N 8 leagues distance.

Two days later they picked up a pilot at the Downs and entered the mouth of the Thames. Disaster struck on the afternoon of 10 November; during 'a hard storm of wind with excessive heavy squalls and showers of rain' *Grenville* slipped her anchor and was driven onto the Knock shoal, with dire results:

10 NOVEMBER. At 4pm anchored above the Nore Light (it bearing ESE) in 7 fathoms water. At 6 the best bower parted and we trailed into shoal waters. At 7 she struck very hard. Got a spring upon the small bower cable and cut the cable in order to cast her head to the southward and get her under weigh but the spring gave way and she cast to the northward directly ashore upon the shoal called the Knock. Got the topsails and crossjackyard down upon deck and she lay pretty easy until the flood made when the gales still continuing she struck very hard and lay down upon her larboard bildge. Hoisted out the boats and hove everything overboard from off the deck and secured all the hatchways. At 12 at night there being no prospect of the gale ceasing took all the people away in the boats. The cutter made the best of way to Sheerness for assistance.

11 NOVEMBER. At 10am the weather being moderate came on board with proper assistance from Sheerness Yard in order to get the vessel off and found she had received little damage. Began to lightening her by heaving out shingle ballast and pigs of iron ballast and to lay out anchors to heave her off. At high water pm the vessel floated. Hove her off and made sail for Sheerness. At 5 anchored between Sheerness and the Nore Light.

12 NOVEMBER. am Employed clearing the decks and putting the hold to right. pm Got from the Yard 2 topsail yards and a crossjack yard and such stores as we wanted. Discharged the Deal pilot and took on board a river pilot.

Cook hastily sent off two letters to the Admiralty describing his plight, but he was able to get underway again at noon on the 13th, having swapped the Downs pilot for a river pilot. They moored at Deptford two days later:

15 NOVEMBER. At 9 lashed along side the William & Mary Yacht off Deptford Yard.

Among the items lost overboard or jettisoned in the panic was a canoe, one of the items sent by Captain Wilkinson for Joseph Banks. Wilkinson told Banks about the loss and suggested he get in touch with Cook – but it is not known if he did so.

On his return to Britain Cook did some survey work for Palliser at his property, The Vache in Buckinghamshire: 'Mr Pownel has promis'd to fix a day when Mr Cook may go to the office to take a Sketch of our Estates, from the large plan, and I will apply for a Coppy of the conditions &c.'[10]

Cook's work from 1767 is represented by a manuscript chart in the Admiralty Library at Taunton. It is MS C54/1, covering from Cape Anguille to Ferolle Point. Cook submitted this chart in late 1767 and it was published in 1768.

✿ 17 ✿

HMB *Endeavour*, 1768

At the beginning of 1768 James Cook had little idea of what the year had in store for him. His life had entered a familiar pattern and he was expecting to repeat the events of previous years. To this end, he was preparing to return to Newfoundland to complete another season's survey. Over the winter Cook had once again prepared his chart from the previous season and had submitted it for publication in early 1768. Larken engraved the chart and it was printed and sold by Mount and Page, Jefferys and Dury. It was entitled *A Chart of the West Coast of Newfoundland, Surveyed by Order of Commodore Pallisser, Governor of Newfoundland, Labradore, &c. &c.* A set of sailing directions entitled *Directions for Navigating the West-Coast of Newfoundland with a Chart Thereof, and a Particular Account of the Bays, Harbours, Rocks, Sands, Depths of Water, Latitudes, Bearings and Distances from Place to Place, the Flowing of Tides, etc. From an Actual Survey, Taken by Order of Commodore Pallisser, Governor of Newfoundland, Labradore, etc.* accompanied the chart and was sold by the same printers.

The copyright on the four chart engravings and three sets of sailing directions for Newfoundland still rested with Cook in early 1768. However, it appears that before he left on his *Endeavour* voyage he conveyed his rights to Thomas Jefferys as, when Jefferys published a portfolio of charts of Newfoundland and Labrador, *A Collection of Charts of the Coasts of Newfoundland and Labradore, etc.*, they were now the property of the printer. Many of its charts had been drawn by Cook, while others were contributed by Michael Lane and Joseph Gilbert. Of particular note is a chart of Newfoundland entitled *A General Chart of the Island of Newfoundland with the Rocks and Soundings. Drawn from Surveys Taken by Order of the Right Honourable the Lord Commissioners of the Admiralty* and jointly attributed to James Cook and Michael Lane. It is interesting to compare this chart with Cook's earlier versions from 1763 and 1764. The amount of detail around the coast has increased dramatically, especially along the south coast, while some rivers and lakes in the interior are also displayed.

A companion volume of sailing directions was also issued by Jefferys. This work, *The Newfoundland Pilot: Containing a Collection of Directions for Sailing Round the Whole Island, Including the Streights of Bell-Isle, and Part of the Coast of Labradore, Giving a Particular Account of the Bays, Harbours, Rocks, Land-Marks, Depths of Water, Latitudes, Bearings and Distance from Place to Place, the Setting and Flowing of Tides, etc. Founded on Actual Surveys, Taken by Surveyors that Have Been Employed by the Admiralty, and Other Officers in the King's service. Published by Permission of the Right Honourable the Lords Commissioners of the Admiralty*, contained Cook's work and was published in 1769. An early version of the *Collection of Charts* was issued in 1769 but without the general chart of Newfoundland.

The full edition, complete with the general chart, seems to have appeared after May 1770, as an Act of Parliament of that date is included on the chart.

Thomas Jefferys died in 1771 and his plates for Cook's charts passed to Robert Sayer and John Bennett. In 1775 Sayer and Bennett combined the charts from the *Collection of Charts* with others for a new production, *The North-American Pilot for Newfoundland, Labradore, the Gulf and River St. Laurence: Being a Collection of Sixty Accurate Charts and Plans*. This work, together with accompanying sailing directions, appeared several times over the next twenty-five years. Cook was presented with a copy of the *North-American Pilot* in 1775 by Sayer and Bennett and asked to write a letter of commendation, and a copy of his letter was included with later copies of the work:

Mile End, Feb, 26, 1776
Sir,
   I am greatly obliged to you for the Perusal of the NORTH AMERICAN PILOT ... I am much pleased to see a Work, in which I have had some Hand, so likely to prove useful to Navigation. – From the Knowledge I have of these Parts (which is not a little), I shall not hesitate to Declare, that as much Faith may be put in the CHARTS, together with the Sailing Directions, as ought to be put in any Work of the Kind.

During the 1760s the Royal Society in London had determined that it would sponsor observers of the transit of Venus expected in June 1769 and, at a council meeting of the society held in November 1767, a sub-committee was set up: 'To consider the places proper to observe the ensuing Transit of Venus, and the method, the persons fit, and other particulars relative to the same.'[1]

The sub-committee reported back that Alexander Dalrymple was: 'A proper person to send to the South Seas, having a particular turn for discoveries, and being an able navigator, and well skilled in Observation ...'[2]

The Royal Society was, however, without funds of its own and could not afford to equip ships to transport the various observers to locations around the world, so it petitioned the king in early 1768 for financial assistance. Lord Shelburne informed the Admiralty on Monday 29 February that the king and government were prepared to allocate £4,000 and that they should acquire a vessel to take an observer to the Pacific.

A further meeting of the Royal Society, held on Sunday 3 April 1768, received a letter from the Admiralty informing the society that a vessel had been purchased for the expedition and enquiring who was to go and what instructions the society had for her commander. The president, Lord Morton, reported that Alexander Dalrymple had already been recommended as commander, but that their nomination had been rejected with horror by the Admiralty. The first lord, Sir Edward Hawke, is supposed to have said that he would rather have his right hand cut off than allow a civilian to command a naval vessel. Dalrymple, present at the meeting, reacted with equal disgust and withdrew from the expedition. He had expected to lead it; a letter written by him in December 1767 shows his position: 'It is necessary to Observe that I have no thoughts of making this voyage as a passenger nor in any other capacity than having total management of the Ship intended to be sent.'[3]

THE TRANSIT OF VENUS

The transit of a planet occurs when one of the two inner planets, Mercury and Venus, which lie between the Sun and Earth, passes across the face of the Sun, as seen from Earth. Transits of Venus occur in a clear pattern of recurrence at intervals of 8, 121.5, 8 and 105.5 years. They are only possible during early December and June when Venus's orbital nodes pass across the Sun. In 1639, Jeremiah Horrocks and William Crabtree became the first to observe a transit of Venus scientifically.

In 1716, Edmond Halley published a paper describing exactly how transits could be used to measure the distance from the Earth to the Sun. Halley had realised that a transit of Venus could be used to estimate the parallax to the Sun and that, having observed the transit from many widely separated locations on the Earth, the data could be collated for the Sun's distance from the Earth to be calculated with unprecedented precision. Halley formulated a detailed plan for how the next transits of 1761 and 1769 should be observed.

A transit occurred on 6 June 1761 and observations were made from selected points. The next transit was scheduled for 3–4 June 1769, and bodies such as the Royal Society dispatched astronomers around the world. The Royal Society negotiated with the navy to organise an expedition to take an astronomer to the central South Pacific, which had been determined to be an optimum location for observations. In 1768 Wallis returned from the Pacific with news of the island of Tahiti, which was then selected.

James Cook led the expedition to Tahiti in *Endeavour*, with Cook himself and Charles Green being the astronomers (during the voyage, Green trained several officers in making observations). They reached Tahiti in April 1769 and set up an observatory at Point Venus in Matavai Bay. Cook arranged for two other parties to make observations elsewhere in case Matavai Bay was cloudy. Hicks went east to Motu Taaupiri and Gore took a party across to Motu Irioa on Moorea. The observations were made relatively successfully.

The analysis of the transit data proved to be worth the great price paid by the astronomers who travelled the world to observe it. In 1771, the French astronomer Lalande used the combined 1761 and 1769 transit data to compute a distance from the Earth to the Sun of 153 million kilometres, which compares with a modern radar measurement of 149.6 million kilometres.

An important figure then emerges. Captain John Campbell already had a distinguished naval career, having served with Anson on his Pacific adventure and as Hawke's flag captain at the battle of Quiberon Bay in 1759. He had also been interested in navigational instruments and had worked with John Bird to develop the sextant in the late 1750s. His scientific interests had led to him being elected a fellow of the Royal Society in 1764. Campbell, therefore, acted as a mediator over the following days; Cook would acknowledge Campbell by naming a headland in Cook Strait, New Zealand, after him.

Someone was needed who would be acceptable to both sides. A naval officer with interests and abilities in astronomy was required, and it is probable that Philip Stephens, the Admiralty secretary, put Cook's name forward. Stephens had been dealing with Cook for several years and knew his qualities; Hugh Palliser was approached and would have given Cook a good reference. Cook then needed to be presented to the Royal Society, and Campbell was the man for this task, taking Cook to a meeting of the Royal Society on Thursday 5 May. Banks's notes for that meeting record: 'The Society were informed that Mr Js Cooke appointed by the admiralty to the Command of the vessel was a proper person to be one of the Observers was called in & accepted the Office in Consideration of Such a gratuity as the Society should think fit & £120 a year for victualling himself.'[4]

If Cook was unknown in person at the Royal Society at least his name was familiar, his paper of observations on the solar eclipse in August 1766 having been read before the society in 1767 by John Bevis. That, together with Bevis's support, would have counted a great deal in the society's acceptance of him as being capable of making astronomical observations. A fortnight later Cook attended another meeting at the Royal Society. Banks reported:

Captn Cooke attended & accepted the sum of one hundred Guineas as a Gratuity for his trouble as one of the Observers.

Ordered that £120 be paid to Captn Cooke on account of the Expence of Victualling the Ship before he Sets out & that he be at liberty to draw upon the Society for any sum not exceeding £120 whilst on his Voyage.[5]

In accordance with the king and the British government's backing for the expedition, the Admiralty instructed the Navy Board to find a suitable ship:

His Majesty has been graciously pleased to express his Royal inclination to defray the expense of conveying such persons as it shall be thought proper to send to make the observations [of the passage of the planet Venus over the disk of the sun] ... I am commanded by their Lordships to signify their directions to you to propose a proper vessel to be fitted for this service.[6]

The Navy Board initially suggested *Tryal*, a two-masted sloop built in 1744, which was at Deptford being repaired. It was realised, though, that repairs would take too long and HMS *Rose*, a sixth rate built in 1757, was proposed instead, on Thursday 10 March; it was quickly rejected as being unable to carry sufficient stores. The Navy Board then suggested using a cat-built vessel, similar to the many ships sailing in the North Sea coal trade: they were roomy and examples could be found locally. The Admiralty assented immediately: 'We do signify to you our approval of the employing of a cat-built vessel instead of a ship of war on the aforesaid service, and we desire and direct you to purchase such a vessel for the said service accordingly.'[7] The Board was ordered to inspect two vessels, *Valentine* and *Earl of Pembroke*, which were both then moored at Shadwell.

... doubt of her [*Rose*] being able to stow the quantity of provisions required on such an occasion, but if their Lordships incline to make choice of a cat-built vessel for the said service, which in their kind are roomly and will afford the advantage of stowing and carrying a large quantity of provisions so necessary on such voyages . . . a vessel of this sort of about 350 tons, may now be purchased in the River Thames if wanted.[8]

Officers from Deptford dockyard led by Adam Hayes, the master shipwright, promptly surveyed both vessels and even inspected a third vessel, *Ann and Elizabeth*. Within a week Hayes reported back recommending *Earl of Pembroke*:

The *Earl of Pembroke*, Mr Thos. Milner, owner, was built at Whitby, her age three years nine months, square stern back, single bottom, full built and comes nearest to the tonnage mentioned in your warrant and not so old by fourteen months, is a promising ship for sailing of this kind and fit to stow provisions and stores as may be put on board her.[9]

The report valued *Earl of Pembroke* at £2,307 5s 6d and she was purchased for £2,800. The Navy Board needed to know what to call the vessel and how to register her. They also wanted instructions on what special fittings were required for her new role. In anticipation, the vessel was taken down to the dry dock at Deptford:

. . . inform their Lordships that we have purchased a cat-built bark, in burthen 368 tons, and of the age of three years and nine months . . . and pray to be favoured with their Lordships' directions for fitting her for this service accordingly, in which we presume it may be necessary to sheath her bottom . . . and that we may also receive their commands by what name shall she be registered on the list of the Navy.[10]

The Master Attendant and the Pilot went on board the Earl of Pembroke lately purchased for his Majesty's service at Mr Bird's Ways this morning, in order to bring her down to be unmasted and docked [at Deptford].[11]

The name 'Endeavour' was chosen and the ship was to be registered as a bark (there already being another vessel, a cutter, with the same name): '. . . you are to cause the said vessel to be registered on the List of the Royal Navy as a bark by the name of the *Endeavour* . . .'[12]

Work was needed on the vessel and the dockyard began sheathing and filling to provide extra protection against the *teredo* worm that ruined ship's hulls in the tropics. For sheathing, a layer of tar and hair was applied to the hull and then a further outside layer of boards was added. While copper was starting to be used for sheathing it was not used on *Endeavour*. Filling involved completely covering the sheathing with broad-headed nails.

It was also found that most of the masts and yards needed replacing, while various modifications were required, including the installation of new cabins; new decks were also created. The cost of repairs and alterations was £5,394 15s 4d. By Monday 18 May *Endeavour* was out of dry dock.

Some authors have attributed the choice of *Earl of Pembroke* to Cook, either by himself or with Hugh Palliser, but it is safe to say that neither man was involved. Cook was still preoccupied with *Grenville* when vessels were being inspected in late March, while Palliser was still Governor of Newfoundland and not yet comptroller of the navy as some have suggested (that appointment came in 1770). At this stage neither man had any connection with the planned transit of Venus expedition. Cook would have certainly applauded the choice of the Navy Board and Deptford dockyard, but he played no role in it.

While all the activity was taking place over the acquisition of a ship for the expedition and the choice of the person to command that expedition, James Cook was still working with *Grenville*, preparing to depart for North America. At the same Admiralty meeting where *Endeavour's* name was sanctioned, the matter of reimbursement for Cook was being discussed:

> Mr Cook's vouchers amounting to £12-16s-od for the money he paid in hiring men well acquainted with the coast of Newfoundland, to point out to him the hidden dangers therein, to be transmitted to the Navy Board with orders to repay it, also vouchers for the repairing of Mathematical Instruments and stationary ware for the ensuing summer, amounting to £28.[13]

Cook's own accident in 1764, when he had his hand damaged in an explosion, and the death of James Surridge in 1767 had highlighted the need for a surgeon on *Grenville* to deal with sickness and emergencies. Cook wrote to Philip Stephens on 9 April, asking for the appointment of a surgeon's mate. The minutes of an Admiralty meeting of 12 April show that his request was granted: 'Mr Cook, commander of the *Grenville* schooner, desires she may be allowed a surgeon's mate, as she is employed at places distant from any of His Majesty's ships. To be allowed accordingly.'[14] Those same Admiralty minutes, though, are one of the first indications of the upheaval that was surrounding James Cook. Palliser was seeking a replacement for Cook: 'A letter was read from Commodore Palliser, that he understands Mr Cook who is master of the *Grenville* schooner, is to be employed elsewhere, and desiring that Mr Lane, mate of the said vessel, may be appointed to succeed him. Resolved that he be directed to appoint Mr Lane accordingly in Mr Cook's absence.'[15]

The following day Cook was discharged from *Grenville*, together with his servant, John Smith, and several other members of *Grenville* crew who would follow him to *Endeavour*. William Howson, Isaac Smith, Peter Flower, John Charlton, Alexander Weir and William Grimshaw would accompany him, while Timothy Rarden, who was disqualified ill on 29 April 1768, and Thomas Hardman, who was listed as running on 4 March 1768, also followed Cook to *Endeavour*.

In Cook's place, Michael Lane assumed command of *Grenville* on 14 April 1768. He was accompanied by William Richardson as master's mate, who transferred from *Guernsey*. Thanks to Cook's application the brig also now had a surgeon's mate, George Rossant.

So, instead of returning to Newfoundland, Cook was about to set off on a voyage to the Pacific, but many things needed to be sorted out first. There was the small matter of Cook's rank to overcome. While it had been acceptable to have a ship's master in charge of a surveying brig in Newfoundland, it was not permissible for him to lead an expedition to the Pacific. For that role a commissioned officer with at least the rank of lieutenant was necessary. Fortunately, Cook now met the requirements to become a lieutenant as he was well over twenty-one and had more than the requisite six years' experience in the Royal Navy. He attended an examination on Wednesday 13 May, where he answered questions and presented examples of his logs and references from several of his previous commanders. It was a formality, and Cook easily gained his lieutenant's certificate, signed by George Cockburn, Captain Robert Man and Captain Abraham North. It may have been one of the most informal sessions ever as North was a neighbour of Cook in Mile End Old Town. North had lived on Redman Row since 1765 and his garden backed on to that of Cook, so the men were most probably friends.

By 18 May *Endeavour* was ready to receive her crew, and on 25 May Cook received his lieutenant's commission:

> Whereas we have appointed you First Lieutenant of his Majesty's bark the Endeavour, now at Deptford, and intend that you shall command her during her present intended

LIEUTENANT'S CERTIFICATE FOR JAMES COOK

In pursuance, etc of the 6th May 1768, we have examined Mr. James Cook who by certificate appears to be more than 39 years of age, & find he has gone to sea more than 11 years in the Ships and qualities undermentioned (viz)

Ship	*Quality*	Y	M	W	D
Eagle	Able seaman	0	1	1	2
Eagle	Master's mate	0	7	0	3
Eagle	Master's mate	1	4	3	2
Solebay	Master	0	1	1	5
Pembroke	Master	1	11	3	3
Northumberland	Master	3	1	3	0
Grenville schooner	Master	3	12	3	5
	Total	11	2	0	6

He produceth Journals kept by himself in the Eagle, Northumberland, and Certificates from Captains Craig, Palliser and Bateman of his diligence, etc. He can splice, knot, reef a sail, etc and is qualified to do the duty of an Able Seaman and Midshipman. Dated 13 May 1768. George Cockburn, Captain Robert Man, Captain Abraham North.[16]

voyage; and whereas we have ordered the said bark to be fitted out and stored at that place for foreign service, manned with seventy men (agreeable to the scheme of the back hereof), and victualled to twelve months of all species of provisions (for the said number of men at whole allowance), except beer, of which she is to have only a proportion for one month, and to be supplied with brandy in lieu of the remainder. You are hereby required and directed to use the upmost dispatch in getting her ready for the sea accordingly, and then falling down to Galleons Reach to take in her guns and gunners' stores at that place, and proceed to the Nore for farther order.

Given, &c., 25 May 1768

Ed. Hawke, C. Townshend, Py. Brett.[17]

The Admiralty minutes recorded the fact: 'Resolved that Mr James Cook 2d be appointed first Lieutenant of the *Endeavour* Bark.'[18] He was called James Cook the second as that other James Cook – whom Cook had met at St John's in 1762 – had become the first. The muster for *Endeavour* was opened with James Cook appearing as #1. He made his appearance on 27 May, accompanied by William Howson from *Grenville* in 1767 as his servant (#2). The *Endeavour* log for Friday 27 May records:

At 11am hoisted the Pendant and took charge of the Ship agreeable to my commission of the 25th Instant, She lying in the Bason in Deptford Yard.

Now he was in place, Cook could begin assembling a crew, and Deptford was a hive of activity for the next few weeks as *Endeavour* was made ready. On 21 July she sailed down to Gallions Reach to collect the ordnance stores.

In Mile End, Elizabeth Cook was nearing the end of her fourth pregnancy, and Cook had arranged for a cousin of his to come down from the north-east to help her. Frances Wardale was part of the Pace family and a relation to Cook's mother. Elizabeth gave birth only a few days after Cook left Plymouth, but Joseph Cook, their third son, died within a month. Cook was still making sure that the family finances were in order and asking for back wages to be paid: 'Having Passed all my accounts for His Majestys Schooner the Grenville, Please to move my Lords Commissrs of the Admiralty to order me to be Pay due to me as Master of the said Schooner.'[19]

Finally on Saturday 30 July Cook received his instructions from the Admiralty and left the Thames to begin his new adventure.

Conclusion

On 26 August 1768 James Cook sailed from Plymouth in command of HMB *Endeavour*, leading an expedition into the unknown. The departure was largely unheralded and of interest only to a small group of scientists and some people at the Admiralty. For those who did know about it, the voyage was regarded as significant, as it would help Britain's ambitions to take a more prominent role in the world. The original object of the expedition was to observe a transit of Venus from Tahiti in the South Pacific, and it was hoped that this would increase British prestige in the scientific community. The second object reflected Britain's desire to increase its overseas trade and influence: *Endeavour* would search for new lands that were believed to exist in the South Seas, which might offer rich rewards. Britain had effectively gained control of the seas by the end of the Seven Years' War and the government felt it was now time to exploit that position. The voyage would prove to be one of the first steps in the creation of the British Empire. To the existing colonies in North America and India would be added knowledge of Australia, New Zealand and the Pacific Islands.

The voyage might change the world, but Cook's personal world had already just undergone a massive upheaval: only five months earlier he had been preparing his brig, *Grenville*, for their return to return to Newfoundland to continue the survey of the island's coastline. No doubt part of Cook would have been reluctant to leave incomplete the task he had been set in 1763. However, he could rest easy in what he had already achieved and in the knowledge that Michael Lane, his successor, would continue his work to the same high standard. Indeed, the charts of Cook and Lane would continue to be used long after those of their contemporaries (and some of their successors) had been dismissed.

It might seem that Cook had been selected for this voyage to the Pacific out of the blue. But was the choice really such a haphazard one? In considering why Cook had been chosen it may prove useful to imagine a report card for Cook in 1768, as shown opposite.

Cook, therefore, can be seen to have possessed all the qualities that the Admiralty would have been looking for in a captain, and he was exceptionally gifted in most of those qualities. Indeed, there would have been few rivals in the navy who could have matched him. Possessing such talent, though, did not necessarily count for much; achieving promotion and success in the Royal Navy in the eighteenth century was much like achieving promotion and success anywhere in the twenty-first century. As well as a combination of skills and experience, patronage was needed and, in the end, it was often the patronage that counted the most. Some men waited years after passing their lieutenant's examination before they received their commission while others, well

Cook's 'Report Card'

Skill	Ability	Comments
Navigation	Excellent	Cook's time on the North Sea laid the grounds for his exceptional skill as a navigator.
Seamanship	Excellent	Cook's time as an able seaman and master's mate in both the Royal and merchant navies meant he had first-hand knowledge of handling sails and rigging. He had done the work himself and had also directed crews. Men would know that he knew how hard and boring it could be.
Astronomy	Proficient	Possibly Cook's weakest skill. His observation of the solar eclipse in 1766 counted for him and he was well grounded in the basics of astronomy. Cook had also recently learned to use Meyer's Lunar Tables. He appears to have known his limitations and was prepared to act as back-up to Charles Green on the expedition.
Surveying	Excellent – developing	Cook had only learned to survey in 1758 but he had quickly blended the techniques of land surveying with traditional marine charting to produce charts of exceptional quality. The expedition was expected to find new lands and Cook was the man most able to prepare charts of those discoveries.
Cartography	Good	Cook only drew his first chart in 1758 and since then had become a proficient cartographer. His charts of Newfoundland were good enough to be used for many years, when those of most of his contemporaries had been superseded. As leader of the expedition Cook realised he would have little time to draws his own charts so trained his 'young gentlemen' in the work.
Leadership	Good – developing	As master of HMS *Northumberland*, a third rate with a crew of over four hundred men, Cook had demonstrated his leadership skills. The time with *Grenville* had been with a much smaller crew but had involved isolation and the need to be self-sufficient – experience likely to be crucial in the forthcoming voyage.
Medical knowledge	Basic	Not really one of Cook's skills, but he had a far greater awareness than many of his contemporaries that a healthy crew was essential for a long voyage. He therefore insisted on cleanliness both of the men's quarters and of the men themselves. Added to which were dietary considerations and the regular brewing of beer.

connected or well related, were promoted at the first opportunity. Promotion was more likely during times of war, as officers were killed in action, creating vacancies, but 1768 was a time of peace and many captains and lieutenants were already on half-pay waiting for employment.

It is not known who the Admiralty's first choice was for *Endeavour*. It probably was not Cook, given that he was not a captain or even a lieutenant at the time, but he must have soon entered the reckoning. He had begun in the navy as a complete unknown in 1755 and it has been suggested that he was chosen because he was still a nobody with no social standing and, should the expedition come to grief, he would not be missed. While it is true that he had little social importance, he had amassed a huge reputation in the Admiralty and among people who recognised talent and potential. To that end, the Admiralty would not want to lose one of its greatest assets. If they did consider the possibility of the expedition coming to grief, they would have been far readier to lose one of those many surplus officers idly sitting around on half-pay than a man of Cook's ability.

Philip Stephens, the Admiralty secretary, had been dealing directly with Cook for several years, so was well aware of Cook's abilities. The two men had become friends through their contact and correspondence, and Cook would later name features after Stephens. The position of Admiralty secretary was a powerful one and Stephens was able to shape and influence the decisions of the Lords Commissioners and Sir Edward Hawke, the first lord. In that way, it was most probably Stephens who proposed Cook for the expedition. For endorsement, Stephens turned to Hugh Palliser, Governor of Newfoundland and soon to be comptroller of the Navy, whose own reputation was growing and whose recommendations already carried weight. Further endorsements could have come from Admirals Graves, Saunders and Colvill, all men of influence, who had dealt closely with Cook and are known to have thought highly of him. So, while Cook was not known by the public at large (or even by large sections of the navy), he was highly thought of by the very people who made decisions.

The period that Cook was about to enter is the one in which he accomplished his great deeds in the Pacific and for which he is rightly famous. However, I feel he deserves to be equally well known for what he achieved in Canada and Newfoundland. He may not have made comparable 'discoveries', but the charts and sailing directions he produced were no less important.

In the introduction to this book I posed the question that has been asked by some writers: 'Why was James Cook chosen to lead the *Endeavour* expedition?' The simple answer is that he was by far the best candidate for the job. I hope that after reading this book you will agree with that answer. I will conclude by posing two alternative questions: 'Why would the Admiralty have chosen anyone else to lead the expedition?' and 'Who else could they have chosen?', which I feel are more appropriate.

APPENDIX I

Cook's Ships, 1755–1767

	Eagle	Solebay	Pembroke	Northumberland	Grenville
Ship's rating	Fourth rate	Sixth rate	Fourth rate	Third rate	Schooner/brig
Built – by	Barnard	Veale	HM Dockyard	HM Dockyard	?
Built – where	Harwich	Plymouth	Plymouth	Plymouth	Massachusetts
Keel laid	24 Jun. 1744	11 Jul. 1740	1 Jan. 1753	14 Aug. 1744	
Launched	2 Dec. 1745	20 Jul. 1742	2 Jun. 1757	1 Dec. 1750	1754
Commissioned	Dec. 1745	Jul. 1742	May 1757	1753	
Cost	£14,767 0s 5d	£7,269 15s 4d	£24,734 10s 4d	£25,564 3s	
Length gundeck	147ft 0in	106ft 0in	156ft 0in	160ft 0in	54ft 11in
Keel length	119ft 9in	87ft 0in	128ft 7in	131ft 4in	43ft 0 5/8in
Breadth	42ft 1½in	30ft 5½in	42ft 3¼in	45ft 0in	17ft 2½in
Depth in hold	18ft 2in	9ft 5in	18ft 0in	19ft 4in	7ft 4in
Tonnage (bm)	1,130 29/94	429 29/94	1,122 9/94	1,414 56/94	67 76/94
Men – total	~420	~160	~420	~520	20
Officers	4	3	4	5	
Warrant officers	~53	~35	~53	~62	2
Midshipmen	10	2	10	16	1
Seamen	~286	~83	~286	~360	17
Marines	~67	~38	~67	~77	
Guns – total	60	24	60	68	24
32-pounders				26	
24-pounders	24		24		
18-pounders				28	
12-pounders	26		26		
9-pounders		22		14	
6-pounders	10		10		
3-pounders		2			12
½-pounders					12
Year – sold/ broken up/sank	1767 (sd)	1763 (sd)	1793 (bu)	1780 (sk)	1775 (bu)

❀ APPENDIX 2 ❀

Masters' Regulations and Instructions (from *c*1750)

I When a master is warranted to serve in any of His Majesty's ships he is to repair on board and observe the orders of his captain or commanding officer for the dispatch of what is to be done towards the fitting her out, and to give his constant attendance for that purpose, unless otherwise employed by him on the service.

II He is to be present at the coming on board of the stores and provisions and to take care that the same be hoisted in speedily and carefully, to prevent damage; and if any of the said stores or provisions are not good, to represent the same to the captain or chief officer on board, in order to their being surveyed and returned.

III He is to observe whether the hoys which bring the ballast on board be laden up to their marks and are clear of water, and to see the ballast all taken into the ship and that it be clean, sweet and wholesome and no fraud committed therein and to sign to the quantity delivered. He is to take care in returning ballast, that the vessels do carry away their full lading.

IV He is to be present and give his directions in stowing the hold, and to see the same done skillfully, as well for making the most room as with regard to the trim of the ship, and also for preserving the provisions from damage, and the oldest provisions are to be stowed so as to be first expended.

V He is frequently to inspect into the condition of the rigging and sails, to be present at all conversion of stores and to sign the boatswain's and carpenter's expense book, taking great care not to sign any undue allowances thereupon. He is to take care that the compasses, glasses, log and lead lines be preserved in good order, that the cables be well coiled upon the orlop, and when convenient opportunities offer, to wet them in salt water, if the same shall be necessary.

VI He is to have the care of navigating the ship under the directions of his superior officer, and to see that the log and log book be duly kept and to keep a good lookout.

VII He is to apply himself to observe the appearances of coasts and how they show themselves in different points of view and if he discovers any new shoals or rocks underwater, to note them down in his journal, with the bearings and depth of water.

VIII When the ship is at anchor he is to be watchful that the hawse be kept clear, that she be not girt with her cables, and that they do not chafe or rub for want of sufficient service; and to be very careful to keep the anchor clear when single.

IX It is to be expected that he do provide himself with the proper instruments, maps and books of navigation, and keep an exact and perfect journal, taking care to note therein the coming in and going out of all stores and provisions, and when the ship is ordered to be laid up he is to deliver a copy of the same into the Navy Office together with his log book, signed by himself.

X He is to be very careful not to sign any accounts, books, lists or tickets before he has thoroughly informed himself of the truth of every particular contained in the same.[1]

Notes

1 Captain Cook's War, 1755–1762

1 Gerald S. Graham, *Empire of the North Atlantic: The Maritime Struggle for North America*, 2nd edn, Toronto: University of Toronto Press, 1958, p. 151.
2 Voltaire, *Candide*, France: 1759, ch. 23, author's translation.
3 From the Treaty of Paris, 1763.
4 Horace Walpole, *The Letters of Horace Walpole, Earl of Orford*, edited by Peter Cunningham, London: Bohn, 1861, vol. 3, p. 259.
5 R. Sedgwick (ed.), *Letters from George III to Lord Bute, 1756–1766*, London: Macmillan, 1939.
6 Newcastle MSS, BL, Add. MS 32931, fol. 46.

2 Joining the Royal Navy, 1755

1 Andrew Kippis, *The Life of Captain James Cook*, London: 1788, p. 4.
2 John Cawte Beaglehole, *The Life of Captain James Cook*, London: A&C Black, 1974, p. 15.
3 Clifford Thornton, personal communication.

3 HMS Eagle, 1755–1757

1 Edward Hawke to Admiralty, 1755, TNA Adm 1/89.
2 Hugh Palliser to Admiralty (Clevland), 15 June 1756, TNA Adm 354/153/33.
3 TNA Adm 354/157/13.
4 See John Rathby (ed.), *The Statutes at Large of England and Great Britain*, 10 vols, London, 1811, Anno 6° Anne, c. 13, 1707.
5 TNA HCA 32/249.

4 HMS Solebay, 1757

1 Master's certificate for James Cook, 29 June 1757, Trinity House minute book.

5 HMS Pembroke, 1757–1758

1 Letter, 28 July 1749, *London Magazine*, 1749.
2 James Cunningham to Lord George Sackville, 30 May 1758, reproduced in JS McLennan, *Louisbourg: From its Foundation to its Fall*, Halifax: The Book Room, 1979, p. 238.

6 Louisbourg, 1758

1 James Cunningham to Lord George Sackville, 30 May 1758, reproduced in McLennan, *Louisbourg*, p. 240.
2 Augustin de Boschenry de Drucour, 'Journal ou relation sur ce qui se passera des movements pour l'attaque et la defense de la Place de Louisbourg pendant la presente année 1758', France, Archives Nationales, Archives des Colonies, C11B vol 38, 6 April 1758, ff. 57–103 v. All quotations from Drucour are taken from this source.

3   Drucour, 'Journal'.
4   Boscawen's journals, 1758, TNA CO 325.
5   James Wolfe to Lord George Sackville, August 1758, reproduced in Beckles Willson, *The Life and Letters of James Wolfe*, London: Heinemann, 1909.
6   Drucour, 'Journal'.

7 Surveyor, 1758

1   17 August 1770, James Cook, *The Journals of Captain James Cook on his Voyages of Discovery: The Voyage of the Endeavour, 1768–1771*, edited by JC Beaglehole, London: Hakluyt Society, 1955–68, p. 380.
2   Samuel Holland, 'Letter 11 Jan. 1792 to Lieutenant-Governor John Graves Simcoe', *Ontario Historical Society, Papers and Records*, vol. 21, 1924, pp. 18–19.
3   Ashley Bowen, *The Journals of Ashley Bowen (1728–1813) of Marblehead*, Boston, MA: Colonial Society of Massachusetts, 1973, pp. 62–3. All quotations from Bowen's journals are from this source.
4   Holland, 'Letter 11 Jan. 1792 to Lieutenant-Governor John Graves Simcoe', p. 19.
5   Samuel Holland, 'Letter 14 May 1789 to Right Honble Mr. Pitt', *Ontario Historical Society, Papers and Records*, vol. 21, 1924, p. 77.
6   Samuel Holland, 'Enclosure in Letter 14 May 1789 to Right Honble Mr. Pitt', *Ontario Historical Society, Papers and Records*, vol. 21, 1924, p. 78.
7   ERG Taylor, *Navigation in the Days of Captain Cook,* London: National Maritime Museum, 1980, p. 1.
8   Ibid.
9   WO51/201 and WO51/205.
10   James Cook to Admiralty, 27 July 1768, Adm 1/1609.
11   Cook, *Journals* , p. 79.
12   17 August 1770, Cook, *Journals* , p. 413.
13   James Wolfe to Jeffery Amherst, 30 September 1758, quoted in Francis Parkman, *Montcalm and Wolfe*, Part II, London: Macmillan, 1884. p. 81.
14   NLA MS 1627.
15   NA Adm 346/14/18.
16   Governor Francklin to President of the Board of Trade, 1766, TNA CO 217/19.
17   HLHU MS Can 63, #28.

8 Quebec, 1759

1   Philip Durell to Admiralty, Halifax, 19 March 1759, in CH Little (ed.), *Despatches of Rear-Admiral Philip Durell 1758–1759 and Rear-Admiral Lord Colville 1759–1761*, Halifax: Maritime Museum of Canada, 1958, p. 7.
2   Philip Durell to Admiralty, Halifax, 19 March 1759, in ibid., p. 7.
3   Horace Walpole, *Memoirs of King George II*, edited by John Brooke, New Haven, CT: Yale University Press, 1985, vol. 3, p. 81.
4   Master's log, *Eagle*, HMS, Bisset, TNA Adm 52/578.
5   Charles Saunders, *Despatches of Vice-Admiral Charles Saunders, 1759–1760: The Naval Side of the Capture of Quebec*, edited by CH Little, Halifax: Maritime Museum of Canada, 1958, p 14.
6   James Wolfe, reproduced in Charles Stacey, *Quebec, 1759: The Siege and Battle*, edited and with new material by Donald E Graves, Toronto: Robin Brass Studio, 2002, p. 90.
7   James Wolfe, Manifesto issued 28 June 1759, reproduced in John Knox, *An Historical Journal of the Campaigns in North America for the Years 1757, 1758, 1759, and 1760*, vol. 1, London: 1769.
8   James Wolfe, reproduced in Stacey, *Quebec, 1759*, p. 103.

9 Charles Holmes (*Lowestoff* off Foulon above Quebec), 18 September 1759, University of Waterloo Archives GA 141.
10 Holland, 'Letter 11 Jan. 1792 to Lieutenant-Governor John Graves Simcoe', pp. 18–19.
11 Saunders, *Despatches of Vice-Admiral Charles Saunders*, pp. 17–19
12 Townshend to Pitt, 18 September 1759, reproduced in Stacey, *Quebec, 1759*, p. 90.

9 HMS Northumberland, 1759–1761

1 Alexander Colvill to Admiralty, 16 October 1759, in Alexander Colvill, *The Recapture of St. John's Newfoundland: Dispatches of Rear-Admiral, Lord Colville,1761–1762*, edited by CH Little, Halifax: Maritime Museum of Canada, 1959.
2 Charles Saunders to Admiralty (Clevland), 22 April 1760, TNA Adm 1/482.
3 Lévis to Bigot, 15 May 1760, Collection des Manuscrits de Lévis, France, Archives Nationales, Archives des Colonies, C11a.
4 Little (ed.), *Despatches of Rear-Admiral Philip Durell 1758–1759 and Rear-Admiral Lord Colville 1759–1761*, pp. 15–16.
5 Alexander Colvill, TNA Adm 1/482, reproduced in Bowen,*The Journals of Ashley Bowen,* p. 111.
6 Little (ed.), *Despatches of Rear-Admiral Philip Durell 1758–1759 and Rear-Admiral Lord Colville 1759–1761*, pp. 19–21.
7 *The Gentleman's Magazine,* 1780.
8 Little (ed.), *Despatches of Rear-Admiral Philip Durell 1758–1759 and Rear-Admiral Lord Colville 1759–1761*, pp. 15–16.
9 Beaglehole, *The Life of Captain James Cook,* p. 54.
10 Donald Macintyre, *Admiral Rodney,* London: Davies, 1962, p. 122.
11 Court Martial minutes, TNA PRO 30/20/18.
12 Little (ed.), *Despatches of Rear-Admiral Philip Durell 1758–1759 and Rear-Admiral Lord Colville 1759–1761*, pp. 19–21.
13 TNA Adm 346/14/ 17.

10 St John's, Newfoundland, 1762

1 Alexander Colvill (*Northumberland* at Halifax) to Admiralty, 17 January 1762, in Colvill, *The Recapture of St. John's, Newfoundland.*
2 Alexander Colvill (*Northumberland* at Halifax) to Admiralty, 12 May 1762, in ibid.
3 Alexander Colvill (*Northumberland* at Mauger's Beach near Halifax) to Admiralty, 24 July 1762, in ibid.
4 Alexander Colvill (*Northumberland* at Mauger's Beach near Halifax) to Admiralty, 30 July 1762, in ibid.
5 Alexander Colvill (*Northumberland* at Mauger's Beach near Halifax) to Admiralty, 6 August 1762, in ibid.
6 Alexander Colvill (*Northumberland* in Placentia Road) to Admiralty, 17 August 1762, in ibid.
7 William Amherst, *The Recapture of St. John's, Newfoundland, in 1762: As Described in the Journal of Lieut.-Col. William Amherst,* edited by John Clarence Webster, n.p.: the author, 1928.
8 Ibid.
9 Alexander Colvill (*Northumberland* in St John's Harbour) to Admiralty 20 September 1762, in Colvill, *The Recapture of St. John's, Newfoundland.*
10 Amherst, *The Recapture of St. John's, Newfoundland.*
11 Alexander Colvill at Spithead to Admiralty, 25 October 1762, TNA Adm 1/482, in Colvill, *The Recapture of St. John's, Newfoundland.*
12 Essex County Record Office St Margaret's Church, Barking. Register.

13 Alexander Colvill to Admiralty, 30 December 1762, TNA Adm 1/482, in Colvill, *The Recapture of St. John's, Newfoundland.*
14 UKHO MSS 20/book 3.

11 Captain Cook's Peace, 1763–1768

1 Derek Morris, *Mile End Old Town, 1740–1780: A Social History of an Early Modern London Suburb*, 2nd edn, London: East London History Society, 2007, p. 16.
2 JG Boulton, *Admiral Bayfield*, Quebec: Literary and Historical Society of Quebec, 1909.
3 Ibid.
4 Charles Douglas (*Tweed* at Spithead) to Admiralty, 8 December 1763, TNA Adm 1/1704.

12 Newfoundland, 1763

1 Thomas Graves (HMS *Antelope*, River Tagus, Portugal) to John Clevland, 2 January 1763, TNA Adm 1/1836.
2 Board of Trade to the King, 29 March 1763, University of Michigan Archives, Shelbourne MSS.
3 Thomas Graves to Philip Stephens, 5 April 1763, TNA Adm 1/1836.
4 Thomas Graves to Philip Stephens, 12 April 1763, TNA Adm 1/1836.
5 Thomas Graves to Philip Stephens, 15 April 1763, TNA Adm 1/1836.
6 Thomas Graves to Philip Stephens, 18 April 1763, TNA Adm 1/1836.
7 Admiralty to Navy Board, 26 April 1763, NMM Adm/A/2546.
8 Admiralty (Stephens) to James Cook, 19 April 1763, Adm 2/90.
9 Admiralty Instructions to Captain Thomas Graves as Commander-in-Chief of His Majesty's Ships on the Newfoundland Station, Adm. Sec. Out Letters, vol. 90, pp. 174–84.
10 Lord Colvill to Philip Stephens, 25 October 1763, TNA Adm 1/482.
11 Thomas Graves (at Plymouth) to Admiralty, 8 May 1763, TNA Adm 1/1836.
12 *Tweed*'s muster book, 13 June 1763, TNA Adm 36/6901.
13 Adm 1/1704, n.d.
14 Charles Douglas to Admiralty, 3 May 1764, TNA Adm 1/1704.
15 Captain's log, *Tweed*, HMS, Douglas, TNA Adm 51/1016.
16 James Cook, *Directions for Navigating on Part of the North East Side of Newfoundland, and in the Streights of Bell-Isle, with a Chart Thereof, and a Particular Account of the Bays, Harbours, Rocks, Land-Marks, Depths of Water, Latitudes, Bearings and Distances from Place to Place, the Setting and Flowing of the Tides, etc. Founded on Actual Survey, Taken by Order of Commodore Pallisser, Governor of Newfoundland, Labradore, etc.*, London: Printed for the author, and sold by J Mount and T Page, etc, 1766.
17 UKHO B 188.
18 Thomas Graves to Admiralty, 30 October 1763, NMM GRV/106.
19 Thomas Graves to Admiralty, 20 October 1763, GRV/106, MSS. 9365.
20 Thomas Graves to Admiralty, 30 October 1763, GRV/106, MSS. 9365.
21 Charles Douglas (*Tweed* at Spithead) to Admiralty, 8 December 1763, TNA Adm 1/1704.

13 Northern Peninsula, 1764

1 TNA CO 194/27 166-166v, 29 March 1764.
2 James Cook to Thomas Graves, 15 March 1764, NMM GRV/106, MSS. 9365.
3 Hugh Palliser to Admiralty, 4 April 1764, TNA Adm. 1/2300.
4 Navy Board warrant to James Cook to take charge of *Grenville*, 18 April 1764, ATL Holograph Letters qMS-0526.

5 James Cook to Admiralty (Stephens), 21 April 1764, ATL Holograph Letters qMS-0526.
6 Admiralty (Stephens) to James Cook, 23 April 1764, TNA Adm. 2/724 and ATL Holograph Letters qMS-0526.
7 Admiralty to Navy Board, 24 April 1764, NMM, ADM/A/2558.
8 TNA CO195, Vol. 9, 10 April 1764, pp. 276–89.
9 Hugh Palliser to James Cook, 29 April 1764, ATL Holograph Letters qMS-0526.
10 Admiralty to Hugh Palliser, 2 May 1764, TNA Adm. 2/537.
11 TNA PRO PROB11/1387.
12 Hugh Palliser (St John's Harbour) to James Cook, 19 June 1764, ATL Holograph Letters qMS-0526.
13 James Cook, *Directions for Navigating on Part of the North East Side of Newfoundland, and in the Streights of Bell-Isle, with a Chart Thereof, and a Particular Account of the Bays, Harbours, Rocks, Land-Marks, Depths of Water, Latitudes, Bearings and Distances from Place to Place, the Setting and Flowing of the Tides, etc. Founded on actual survey, taken by order of Commodore Palliser, Governor of Newfoundland, Labradore, etc.* London: Printed for the author, and sold by J Mount and T Page, etc., 1766.
14 From Jens Haven's diary, 1764, 'An Account of an Interview between Mr. Jens Haven, a Moravian, and the Esquimeaux Savages', reproduced in AM Lysaght, *Joseph Banks in Newfoundland and Labrador, 1766,* London: Faber and Faber, 1971.
15 From journal entry of Joseph Banks for 2 September 1766 on his tour of Newfoundland, reproduced in Lysaght, *Joseph Banks in Newfoundland.*

14 South Coast of Newfoundland, 1765

1 James Cook to the Commissioners of the Navy [22 January 1765], SLNSW DLMSQ 140.
2 Commissioners of the Navy to James Cook, 6 February 1765, SLNSW DLMSQ 140.
3 Hugh Palliser to Admiralty (Stephens), 6 March 1765, TNA Adm 1/2300.
4 Hugh Palliser to James Cook, 1765, SLNSW DLMSQ 140.
5 Hugh Palliser to captains on the Newfoundland station, 13 April 1765, Privy Council. Correspondence, Documents and Papers relating to the History of the Administration of the Coast of Labrador, 1927, vol. 3, no. 217.
6 Admiralty instructions to Hugh Palliser, 14 May 1765, TNA CO194/27, p. 32.
7 Cook, *Directions for Navigating on Part of the South Coast of Newfoundland with a Chart Thereof, Including the Islands of St. Peter's and Miquelon, and a Particular Account of the Bays, Harbours, Rocks, Land-Marks, Depths of Water, Latitudes, Bearings and Distances from Place to Place, the Setting of the Currents, and Flowing of Tides, etc. From an Actual Survey, Taken by order of Commodore Pallisser, Governor of Newfoundland, Labradore, etc.,* 1766.
8 Ibid.
9 Hugh Palliser to Admiralty (Stephens), 14 December 1765, TNA Adm 1/2300.

15 South-west Coast of Newfoundland, 1766

1 Hugh Palliser to Admiralty (Stephens), 3 February 1766, TNA Adm 1/470.
2 Admiralty to Navy Board, 17 March 1766, TNA Adm. 2/236.
3 Admiralty Secretary to Hugh Palliser, 1 April 1766, Out letters, vol. 93, p. 182. TNA Adm 2/726.
4 Cook, *Directions for Navigating on Part of the South Coast of Newfoundland,* 1766.
5 George Witchell, an astronomer, was Master of the Naval Academy at Portsmouth.
6 Thomas Hornsby was appointed Savilian Professor of Astronomy at Oxford in 1763. He was involved in the planning for the observations of the transit of Venus in 1769.

7   The point of greatest eclipse was near Sept Îles in Quebec on the north side of the St Lawrence (50° 11' 04"N, 66° 54' 08"W), only about 725 kilometres WNW of Burgeo.

8   *Philosophical Transactions of the Royal Society of London*, vol. LVII, part 1, 1767, pp. 215–16, XXIV.

9   Hugh Palliser to James Cook, 29 October 1766, Essex Peabody Museum.

10 Hugh Palliser to Admiralty (Stephens), 2 December 1766, TNA Adm 1/2300.

16 West Coast of Newfoundland, 1767

1   Philip Stephens to James Cook, 28 January 1767, Essex Peabody Museum.

2   23 October 1767, TNA Adm 106/1152/373.

3   Admiralty minutes, 5 April 1768, TNA Adm 3/76.

4   James Cook to Admiralty Secretary, August 1771 TNA Adm 1/1609.

5   Cook, *Journals*, p. cxxxiv.

6   James Cook to Admiralty Secretary, May 1775, TNA Adm 1/1610.

7   William Hickey, *Memoirs of William Hickey*, edited by Alfred Spencer, 4 vols, London: Hurst & Blackett, 1913–25.

8   TNA PRO PROB11/1788.

9   James Cook, *Directions for Navigating the West-Coast of Newfoundland with a Chart Thereof, and a Particular Account of the Bays, Harbours, Rocks, Sands, Depths of Water, Latitudes, Bearings and Distances from Place to Place, the Flowing of Tides, etc. From an Actual Survey, Taken by Order of Commodore Pallisser, Governor of Newfoundland, Labradore, etc.*, London: Printed for the author, and sold by J Mount and T Page, etc, 1768.

10 Hugh Palliser to Admiralty, 30 November 1767, TNA Adm 1/2300.

17 HMB Endeavour, 1768

1   Royal Society, Council Minutes, 17 November 1767.

2   Royal Society, Transit Committee, Council Minutes, 19 November 1767.

3   Royal Society, Council Minutes, 18 December 1767.

4   Royal Society, Council Minutes, 5 May 1768.

5   Royal Society, Council Minutes, 19 May 1768.

6   Admiralty secretary to Navy Board, 5 March 1768, NMM Adm/A/2605.

7   Admiralty secretary to Navy Board, 21 March 1768, NMM Adm/A/2605.

8   Navy Board to Admiralty secretary, 21 March 1768, NMM Adm/B/180.

9   Deptford Yard officers to Navy Board, 27 March 1768, TNA Adm 106/3315.

10 Navy Board to Admiralty secretary, 29 March 1768, NMM Adm/B/180.

11 Deptford Yard officers to Navy Board, 27 March 1768, TNA Adm 106/3315.

12 Admiralty minutes, 5 April 1768, TNA Adm 3/76.

13 Admiralty minutes, 5 April 1768, TNA Adm 3/76.

14 Admiralty minutes, 12 April 1768, TNA Adm 3/76.

15 Admiralty minutes, 12 April 1768, TNA Adm 3/76.

16 Lieutenant's passing certificates, TNA Adm 6/86-7 and Adm 107/3-4.

17 Admiralty to James Cook, 25 May 1768, TNA Adm 2/94.

18 Admiralty minutes, 25 May 1768, TNA Adm 3/76.

19 James Cook to Admiralty secretary, 27 July 1768, TNA Adm 1/1609.

Appendix 2

1   Brian Lavery (ed.), *Shipboard Life and Organisation, 1731–1815*, Aldershot: Ashgate, for the Navy Records Society, 1998, pp. 25–7.

Bibliography

Published Works

Amherst, William, *The Recapture of St. John's, Newfoundland in 1762: As Described in the Journal of Lieut.-Col. William Amherst,* edited by John Clarence Webster, n.p.: the author, 1928.

Bannister, Jerry, *The Rule of the Admirals: Law, Custom, and Naval Government in Newfoundland, 1699–1832,* Toronto: University of Toronto Press, 2003.

Barkham, Selma Huxley, *The Basque Coast of Newfoundland,* St John's, Newfoundland: Great Northern Peninsula Development Corporation, 1989.

—— 'Between Cartier and Cook: The Contribution of Fishermen to the Early Toponymy of Western Newfoundland', *Northern Seas Yearbook,* 1999, pp. 23–31.

Baugh, Daniel A, *British Naval Administration in the Age of Walpole,* Princeton: Princeton University Press, 1965.

Beaglehole, John Cawte, *The Life of Captain James Cook,* London: A&C Black, 1974.

Bonner Smith, David, 'Cook and the Grenville', *Mariner's Mirror,* vol. 23, no. 2, April 1937, p. 233 plus tables.

Bowen, Ashley, *The Autobiography of Ashley Bowen (1728–1813),* edited by Daniel Vickers, Peterborough, ON: Broadview Editions, 2006.

—— *The Journals of Ashley Bowen (1728–1813) of Marblehead,* Boston, MA: Colonial Society of Massachusetts, 1973.

Carrington, Arthur Hugh, *Life of Captain Cook,* London: Sidgwick & Jackson, 1939.

Charnock, John, *Biographia Navalis or, Impartial Memoirs of the Lives and Characters of Officers of the Navy of Great Britain, from the Year 1660 to the Present Time,* 6 vols, London: R Faulder, 1794–8.

Chartrand, René, *Louisbourg 1758: Wolfe's First Siege,* Oxford: Osprey, 2000.

Chipman, Willis, 'The Life and Times of Major Samuel Holland, Surveyor-General, 1764–1801', *Ontario Historical Society, Papers and Records,* vol. 21, 1924, pp. 11–90.

Colledge, JJ, *Ships of the Royal Navy: The Complete Record of All Fighting Ships of the Royal Navy,* rev. edn, London: Greenhill Books, 2003.

Colvill, Alexander, Lord, *The Recapture of Saint John's, Newfoundland: Dispatches of Rear-Admiral, Lord Colville, 1761–1762,* edited by CH Little, Halifax: Maritime Museum of Canada, 1959.

Cook, James, 'Capt. James Cook's Description of the Sea-coast of Nova Scotia, Cape Breton Island and Newfoundland', in *Annual Report of the Trustees of the Public Archives of Nova Scotia for 1958,* Halifax: Queen's Printer, 1959.

—— 'An Observation of an eclipse of the sun at the Island of Newfoundland, August 5, 1766', *Philosophical Transactions of the Royal Society,* vol. 58, 1767, pp. 215–16.

—— *James Cook, Surveyor of Newfoundland Being a Collection of Charts of the Coasts of Newfoundland and Labradore, &. Drawn from Original Surveys Taken by James Cook and Michael Lane . . . with an Introductory Essay by R. A. Skelton,* facsimile edition of original published in London in 1769-70 by Thomas Jefferys, David Magee; San Francisco, 1965.

—— *The Journals of Captain James Cook on his Voyages of Discovery: The Voyage of the* Endeavour, *1768–1771*, edited by JC Beaglehole, London: Hakluyt Society, 1955–68.

David, Andrew CF, 'Captain Cook's First Chart', *The Map Collector*, no. 60, 1992, pp. 10–11; no. 61, 1992, p. 56.

—— 'Further Light on James Cook's Survey of Newfoundland', *International Hydrographic Review*, vol. 1, no. 2, December 2000, pp. 6–12.

—— *James Cook's Manuscript Sailing Directions in Nova Scotia, Newfoundland and the St. Lawrence River*, n.p., 1979.

—— 'James Cook's 1762 Survey of St John's Harbour and Adjacent Parts of Newfoundland', *Terrae Incognitae*, vol. 30, 1998, pp. 63–71.

Dictionary of Canadian Biography, 15 vols, Toronto: University of Toronto Press, 1966–.

Fryer, Mary Beacock, and Christopher Dracott, *John Graves Simcoe, 1752–1806: A Biography*, Toronto: Dundurn Press, 1998.

Gradish, Stephen F, *The Manning of the British Navy During the Seven Years' War*, London: Royal Historical Society, 1980.

Graham, Gerald S, *Empire of the North Atlantic: The Maritime Struggle for North America*, 2nd edn, Toronto: University of Toronto Press, 1958.

Holland, Samuel, 'Letter 11 Jan. 1792 to Lieutenant-Governor John Graves Simcoe', *Ontario Historical Society, Papers and Records*, vol. 21, 1924, pp. 18–19.

Janzen, Olaf Uwe, 'Hugh Palliser, the Royal Navy, and the Projection of British Power in Newfoundland 1764–68', paper presented at the XIXth International Congress of Historical Sciences, Oslo, Norway, 6–13 August 2000.

—— 'Showing the Flag: Hugh Palliser in Western Newfoundland, 1764', *The Northern Mariner*, vol. 3, July 1993, pp. 3–14.

Kippis, Andrew, *The Life of Captain James Cook*, London: 1788.

Kitson, Arthur, *The Life of Captain James Cook the Circumnavigator*, London: John Murray, 1912.

Knox, John, *An Historical Journal of the Campaigns in North America for the Years 1757, 1758, 1759, and 1760*, 2 vols, London: 1769.

Lavery, Brian (ed.), *Shipboard Life and Organisation, 1731–1815*, Aldershot: Ashgate, for the Navy Records Society, 1998.

Leadbetter, Charles. *A Compleat System of Astronomy*, 2 vols, London: 1728.

—— *The Young Mathematician's Companion*, 2nd edn, London: 1748.

Little, CH (ed.), *Despatches of Rear-Admiral Philip Durell 1758–1759 and Rear-Admiral Lord Colville 1759–1761*, Halifax: Maritime Museum of Canada, 1958.

Lysaght, AM, *Joseph Banks in Newfoundland and Labrador, 1766*, London: Faber and Faber, 1971.

Macintyre, Donald, *Admiral Rodney*, London: Davies, 1962.

McLennan, John Stewart, *Louisbourg: from its Foundation to its Fall*, Halifax: The Book Room, 1979.

Marston, Daniel, *The Seven Years' War*, Oxford: Osprey, 2001.

Middleton, David, *The Bells of Victory: The Pitt–Newcastle Ministry and the Conduct of the Seven Years' War, 1757–1762*, Cambridge: Cambridge University Press, 1985.

—— 'British Naval Strategy, 1755–1762', *Mariner's Mirror*, vol. 75, no. 4, November 1989, pp. 349–67.

Morris, Derek, *Mile End Old Town, 1740–1780: A Social History of an Early Modern London Suburb*, 2nd edn, London: East London History Society, 2007.

Olson, Donald W, et al., 'Perfect Tide, Ideal Moon: An Unappreciated Aspect of Wolfe's Generalship at Quebec, 1759', *William and Mary Quarterly*, vol. 59, no. 4, October 2002, pp. 957–74.

Oxford Dictionary of National Biography, edited by HCG Matthew and Brian Harrison, 60 vols, Oxford: Oxford University Press, 2004.

Parkman, Francis, *Montcalm and Wolfe*, 2 vols, London: Macmillan, 1884.

Rae, Julia, *Captain James Cook Endeavours*, London: Stepney Historical Trust, 1997.

Reid, Stuart, *Quebec 1759: The Battle that Won Canada*, Oxford: Osprey, 2003.

Robson, John, *The Captain Cook Encyclopaedia*, London: Chatham Publishing, 2004.

—— *Captain Cook's World: Maps of the Life and Voyages of James Cook, R.N.*, Auckland: Random House NZ, 2000.

Rodger, Nicholas AM, *The Command of the Ocean: A Naval History of Britain, 1649–1815*, London: Penguin, 2005.

—— *The Wooden World: An Anatomy of the Georgian Navy*, London: Fontana Press, 1988.

Saunders, Charles, *Despatches of Vice-Admiral Charles Saunders, 1759–1760: The Naval Side of the Capture of Quebec*, edited by CH Little, Halifax: Maritime Museum of Canada, 1958.

Sherrard, Owen Aubrey, *Lord Chatham: Pitt and the Seven Years' War*. London: Bodley Head, 1955.

Skelton, Raleigh Ashlin, 'Captain James Cook as a Hydrographer', *Mariner's Mirror*, vol. 40, 1954, pp. 92–119.

—— 'Cook's Contribution to Marine Survey', *Endeavour*, vol. 27, 1968, pp. 28–32.

—— 'James Cook, Surveyor of Newfoundland', introductory essay in Cook, *A Collection of Charts of the Coasts of Newfoundland and Labradore*, facsimile edition, 1965.

—— and RV Tooley, 'The Marine Surveys of James Cook in North America, 1758–1768, Particularly the Survey of Newfoundland: A Bibliography of Printed Charts and Sailing Directions', *Map Collector's Circle*, vol. 4, 1967.

Stacey, Charles Perry, *Quebec, 1759: The Siege and Battle*, edited and with new material by Donald E Graves, Toronto: Robin Brass Studio, 2002.

Suthren, Victor, 'Creating the Instrument: The Transformation of James Cook in North American Waters, 1758–1767', *Soundings*, issue 2, Spring 2005.

—— *To Go Upon Discovery: James Cook and Canada, 1758–1767*, Toronto: Dundurn Press, 1999.

Syrett, David, and RL DiNardo (eds), *The Commissioned Officers of the Royal Navy, 1660–1815*, Aldershot: Scolar Press, for the Navy Records Society, 1994.

Thornton, Cliff, *Captain Cook in Cleveland*, Stroud: Tempus, 2006.

Trevelyan, George Macaulay, *A Shortened History of England*, London: Penguin, 1959.

Vickers, Daniel, 'An Honest Tar: Ashley Bowen of Marblehead', *New England Quarterly*, vol. 69, no. 4, December 1996, pp. 531–53.

Walpole, Horace, *The Letters of Horace Walpole, Fourth Earl of Orford*, edited by Peter Cunningham, 9 vols, Edinburgh: J Grant, 1906.

Warner, Oliver, *With Wolfe to Quebec: The Path to Glory*, Toronto: Collins, 1972.

Whiteley, William H, 'James Cook and British Policy in the Newfoundland Fisheries 1763–7', *Canadian Historical Review*, vol. 54, no. 3, September 1973, pp. 245–72.

—— *James Cook in Newfoundland, 1762–1767*, St John's, Newfoundland: Newfoundland Historical Society, 1975.

—— 'James Cook, Hugh Palliser and the Newfoundland Fishery', *Newfoundland Quarterly*, vol. 69, no. 2, October 1972, pp. 17–22.

Willson, Beckles, *The Life and Letters of James Wolfe*, London: Heinemann, 1909.

Winfield, Rif, *British Warships in the Age of Sail, 1714–1792: Design, Construction, Careers and Fates*, Barnsley: Seaforth Publishing, 2007.

Wood, William H, *The Logs of the Conquest of Canada*, Toronto: Champlain Society, 1909.

Online Tools

Oxford Dictionary of National Biography, Oxford University Press, 2004, http://www.oxforddnb.com/

Dictionary of Canadian Biography Online, http://www.biographi.ca/EN/index.html

Acts of Parliament

from Rathby, John (ed.), *The Statutes at Large of England and Great Britain*, 10 vols, London: 1811.

Anno 6° Anne. c.13. 1707. Act for the Better Securing the Trade of this Kingdom by Cruisers and Convoys.

Anno 22° George II. c.33. 1749. An Act for Amending, Explaining and Reducing into One Act of Parliament, the Laws Relating to the Government of His Majesty's Ships, Vessels and Forces by Sea.

Anno 31° George II. c.10. 1758. An Act for the Encouragement of Seamen Employed in the Royal Navy; and for Establishing a Regular Method for the Punctual, Frequent and Certain Payment of their Wages; and for Enabling them More Easily and Readily to Remit the Same for the Support of the Wives and Families; and for Preventing Frauds and Abuses Attending Such Payments.

Published Charts

Cook, James, *To the Right Hon.ble the Master and Wardens of the Trinity House of Deptford Strond This Draught of the Bay and Harbour of Gaspee in the Gulf of St. Laurence Taken in 1758 is Humbly presented by their most obed.t hum.le Serv.t James Cook Master of his Majesty's Ship the Pembroke.* Sold by W. & I. Mount T. & T. Page in Tower Hill / London. [2 sheets; overall 16¼ x 37 in; scale 2 in=1 mile (1:31,680). No original MS is known]

—— *A New Chart of the River St. Laurence, from the Island of Anticosti to the Falls of Richelieu: with all the Islands, Rocks, Shoals, and Soundings. Also Particular Directions For Navigating the River with Safety. Taken by Order of Charles Saunders, Esq.r Vice-Admiral of the Blue, and Commander in Chief of His Majesty's Ships in the Expedition against Quebec in 1759.* Engraved by Thomas Jefferys Geographer to his Royal Highness the Prince of Wales. Published by Command of The Right Honourable the Lords Commissioners of the Admiralty. [12 sheets; overall 35 x 90 in; Scale 1 in=2 leagues (approx. 1:380,000)].

—— *A Chart of the Straights of Belleisle with part of the coast of Newfoundland and Labradore, from actual surveys Taken by Order of Commodore Pallisser, Governor of Newfoundland, Labradore, &ca. by James Cook, Surveyor.* Larken, sculp. 1766. Published by permission of the Right Honourable the Lord Commissioners of the Admiralty, by James Cook, and Sold with a Book of Directions, by I. Mount and T. Page, on Tower Hill London. [Chart was based on Hydro. Dept., X54, and eight plans; B.M., Add. MS 31360, two plans (from 1763), and Hydro. Dept., C54/3, C54/4, C54/7, 342; B.M., Add. MS 31360.11 (from 1764)]

—— *A Chart of Part of the South Coast of Newfoundland, including the islands St. Peters and Miquelon, from an actual survey Taken by order of Commodore Pallisser, Governor of Newfoundland, Labradore, &c.* by James Cook, Surveyor. Larken, sc. Published by permission, of the Right Honble. the Lord Commissioners of the Admiralty, by James Cook, and Sold by I. Mount and T. Page … Thos. Jefferys … Andw. Dury. London. 1766.

—— *A Chart of Part of the South Coast of Newfoundland including the islands St. Peters and Miquelon: with the Southern Entrance into the Gulph of St. Laurence from actual surveys Taken by Order of Commodore Pallisser, Governor of Newfoundland, Labradore, &c.* by James Cook; Larken, sculp., 1767. Published by permission, of the Right Honble. the Lord Commissioners of the Admiralty, by James Cook, and Sold by J. Mount and T. Page, Thos. Jefferys, Andw. Dury and Carrington Bowles. London. 1767. [Chart was based on (from 1763) Hydro. Dept., B5299 and one plan; B.M., Add. MS 31360.21, K. Top. CXIX.III, and four plans; (from 1765) Hydro. Dept., C58. (from 1766) Hydro. Dept., C54/5; B.M., Add. MS 31360, two plans)]

—— *A Chart of the West Coast of Newfoundland, Surveyed by Order of Commodore Pallisser, Governor of Newfoundland, Labradore, &c.&c.* by James Cook, Surveyor. Larken sculpt. Published by

permission, of the Right Honble. the Lord Commissioners of the Admiralty, by James Cook, and Sold with a book of directions by J. Mount and T. Page, Thos. Jefferys and Andw. Dury. London. 1768. [Chart was based on (from 1767) Hydro. Dept., C54/1; B.M., Add. MS 17693.D]
—— and Michael Lane, *A General Chart of the Island of Newfoundland with the rocks and soundings. Drawn from surveys taken by order of the Right Honourable the Lord Commissioners of the Admiralty. James Cook and Michael Lane, Surveyors, and others. Publish'd according to Act of Parliament, 10th May 1770 by Thomas Jefferys Geographer to the King.*

Sailing Directions

[Cook, James], *Directions for Navigating the Gulf and River of St. Laurence, with a particular Account of the Bays, Roads, ..., Tides &c* ... by Order of Charles Saunders, Esq; Vice-Admiral of the Blue, and Commander in Chief of the British Naval Forces in the Expedition against Quebec, in 1759. Published by Command of the Right Hon. the Lords Commissioners of the Admiralty. London Printed for Thomas Jeffreys, Geographer to his Royal Highness the Prince of Wales. 1760.

Cook, James, *Directions for Navigating on part of the North East Side of Newfoundland, and in the Streights of Bell-Isle, with a Chart thereof, and a particular account of the Bays, Harbours, Rocks, Land-Marks, Depths of Water, Latitudes, Bearings and Distances from Place to Place, the Setting and Flowing of the Tides, etc.* Founded on actual survey, taken by order of Commodore Pallisser, Governor of Newfoundland, Labradore, etc. London: Printed for the author, and sold by J. Mount and T. Page, etc, 1766.

—— *Directions for Navigating on part of the South Coast of Newfoundland with a Chart thereof, including the Islands of St. Peter's and Miquelon, and a particular account of the Bays, Harbours, Rocks, Land-Marks, Depths of Water, Latitudes, Bearings and Distances from Place to Place, the Setting of the Currents, and Flowing of Tides, etc.* From an actual survey, taken by order of Commodore Pallisser, Governor of Newfoundland, Labradore, etc. London: Printed for the author, and sold by J. Mount and T. Page, etc, 1766.

—— *Directions for Navigating the West-Coast of Newfoundland with a Chart thereof, and a particular account of the Bays, Harbours, Rocks, Sands, Depths of Water, Latitudes, Bearings and Distances from Place to Place, the Flowing of Tides, etc.* From an actual survey, taken by order of Commodore Pallisser, Governor of Newfoundland, Labradore, etc. London: Printed for the author, and sold by J. Mount and T. Page, etc, 1768.

The Newfoundland Pilot: containing a collection of Directions for sailing round the whole Island, including the Streights of Bell-Isle, and part of the Coast of Labradore, giving a particular account of the Bays, Harbours, Rocks, Land-Marks, Depths of Water, Latitudes, Bearings and Distance from Place to Place, the Setting and Flowing of the Tides, etc. Founded on actual surveys, taken by Surveyors that have been employed by the Admiralty, and other Officers in the King's service. Published by permission of the Right Honourable the Lords Commissioners of the Admiralty. London: Printed for Thomas Jeffreys, 1769.

Manuscripts

Admiralty
Letters to:
Cook: 13, 18 April 1763, TNA Adm 2/722; 19 April 1763 TNA Adm 2/90; 23 April 1764, TNA Adm 2/724 and ATL qMS-0526; 18 December 1764, TNA Adm 2/725 and SLNSW DLMSQ 140; 5 April 1765, TNA Adm 2/725; 15, 17 March, 27 November 1766, TNA Adm 2/726; 24 March, 12, 13 November 1767, 11 April 1768, TNA Adm 2/727; 25 May 1768, TNA Adm 2/94

Navy Board: 22, 26 April 1763, NMM Adm/A/2546; 4 January 1764, NMM Adm/A/2555; 13, 23, 24, 27 April 1764, NMM Adm/A/2558; [June] 1764, NMM Adm/A/2561; 17 March 1766, Adm. 2/236; 12 February 1767, NMM Adm/A/2592; 5 March 1768, NMM Adm/A/2605; 21 March 1768, NMM Adm/A/ 2605; 15 January 1773, NMM Adm/A/2663.

Palliser: 7, 13, 30 April 1764, TNA Adm 2/724; 1 April 1766 TNA Adm 2/726.

Minutes: 5, 12 April 1768, TNA Adm 3/76.

Orders and Instructions to:

Cook: 19 April 1763, TNA Adm 2/90; 11 April 1765, SLNSW DLMSQ 140.

Graves: 19 April, 2, 3, 27 May 1763, TNA Adm 2/90; 2 May 1763, NMM GRV/106, Section 9.

Captains of HM *ships Spy, Pearl and Tweed*, 24 April 1764, TNA Adm 2/90.

Captain of HMS *Lark*, 24 April 1764, TNA Adm 2/91.

Colvill, Alexander, Lord
Letters to Admiralty: 10 April 1761, 25 October, 30 December 1762, TNA Adm 1/482.

Cook, James
Grenville Letter-Book: Stray leaves survive bearing correspondence between Cook and Admiralty, Navy Board and Victualling Board, also Palliser's Instructions [1764]. There are three leaves possibly torn from the letter-book in the SLNSW DLMSQ140 (Palliser's Instructions form the first item); one leaf is inserted at the beginning of Zachary Hicks's *Endeavour* log, ATL; one leaf is in ATL qMS-0526.

Letters to:

Admiralty: 21 April 1764, ATL qMS-0526; 9 March 1765, SLNSW DLMSQ 140; 27 July 1768, TNA Adm 1/1609.

Graves: 15 March 1764, NMM GRV/106.

Navy Board: 14 January 1765, SLNSW DLMSQ 140; [22 January 1765], SLNSW DLMSQ 140.

Palliser: 7 March 1764, TNA Adm 1/2300.

Victualling Board: 12 January 1765, SLNSW DLMSQ 140.

Sailing directions:

Harbour of Louisbourg in Cape Breton, 1758, HLHU MS Can 63, #28.

Louisbourg to Quebec, TNA Adm 346/14/18 and OD 791.

Death certificates signed by Cook: John Grigg, 8 December 1759, SLNSW DLMSQ 140.

Deptford Yard
Letter books, Series 1, TNA Adm 106/3315.

Douglas, Sir Charles
Letter to Admiralty: [1763], 3 May 1764, TNA Adm 1/1704.

Drucour, Augustin de Boschhenry de
'Journal on Relation sur ce qui Se passera des movements pour L'attaque et la defense de la Place de Louisbourg pendant la presente année 1758', France, Archives Nationales, Archives des Colonies C11B vol. 38, 6 April 1758, ff. 57 - 103 v.

Graves, Thomas, Baron
Letters to Admiralty: 2 January, 5, 12, 15, 18, 21, 29 April, 8 May 1763, TNA Adm 1/1836; draft of letter 20 October, letter 30 October 1763, NMM GRV/106.

High Court of Admiralty
Prize Court: Papers: 1592–1855. Standing Interrogatories. *Triton*, TNA HCA32/249.

Navy Board
Letters to:
Admiralty: 4 March 1746/7, NMM Adm/B/135, 12 February 1747/8, NMM Adm/B/137; 2 December 1763, NMM Adm/B/173; 21 March 1768, NMM Adm/A/ 2605; 29 March 1768, NMM Adm/B/180.
Cook: 16 January 1765, SLNSW DLMSQ 140; 6 February 1765, SLNSW DLMSQ 140.
Warrant to James Cook to take charge of *Grenville*, 18 April 1764, ATL qMS-0526.

Palliser, Sir Hugh
Instructions to Cook: [1764], SLNSW DLMSQ140.

Letters to:
Admiralty: 27 November 1755, TNA Adm 1/2292; 13 April, 3, 4, 17 June, 6, 18 July, 2 August 1756, TNA Adm 1/2293; 15 June 1756, TNA Adm 354/153/33; 6, 13 January, 17 April, 5 June 1757, TNA Adm 1/2294; 7 March, 4, 7 April 1764, 6 March, 14 December 1765, 2 December 1766, 30 November 1767, TNA Adm 1/2300; 3 February 1766, TNA Adm 1/470.
Cook: 29 April, 19 June 1764, ALT qMS-0526.

Saunders, Sir Charles
Letters to Admiralty: 5 September 1759, 22 April 1760, TNA, Adm 1/482.

Simcoe, John
Letters to Admiralty: 19 April, 14 May, 2 June 1757, TNA, Adm 1/2471.

Trinity House
Master's certificate for James Cook, Minute Books, 29 June 1757.

Admiral's Journal
Northumberland, HMS, Colville, TNA Adm 50/22.

Captain's Journal
Endeavour, HMB, Cook, TNA Adm 55/40.

Captains' Logs
Eagle, HMS, Hamar, Palliser, TNA Adm 51/292.
Niger, HMS, Adams, TNA Adm 51/.
Northumberland, HMS, Adams, Bateman, TNA Adm 51/3925.
Pembroke, HMS, Simcoe, Wheelock, TNA Adm 51/686.
Solebay, HMS, Craig, TNA Adm 51/908.
Tweed, HMS, Douglas, TNA Adm 51/1016.

Lieutenants' Logs
Eagle, HMS, 1755–8, NMM Adm/L/E/8B-10.
Northumberland, HMS, 1757–62, NMM Adm/L/N/168-171.
Pembroke, HMS, 1756–63, NMM Adm/L/P/78-79.

Solebay, HMS, 1755–8, NMM Adm/L/S/309.

Masters' Logs
Diana, HMS, Hawkins, TNA Adm 52/829.
Eagle, HMS, Bisset, TNA Adm 52/578.
Grenville, HM schooner, Cook (14 June 1764–15 November 1767), TNA Adm 52/1263.
Hunter, HM sloop, Wood, TNA Adm 52/881.
Northumberland, HMS, Cook (30 September 1759–11 November 1762), TNA Adm 52/959.
Pembroke, HMS, Cook (27 October 1757–30 September 1759), Cleader, TNA Adm 52/978.
Solebay, HMS, Cook (30 July–7 September 1757), TNA Adm 52/1033.

Musters
Antelope, HMS, (1762–4), TNA Adm 36/4887 and 36/4889.
Eagle, HMS, (July 1755), TNA Adm 36/5533.
Grenville, HM schooner, (1764 June–1771), TNA Adm 36/7103 and 36/9921.
Lark, HMS, (April 1763–January 1766), TNA Adm 36/7615 and 36/7617.
Pembroke, HMS, (May 1758–April 1759), TNA Adm 36/6347.
Stirling Castle, HMS, (July 1761–1762), TNA Adm 36/6738-39.
Tweed, HMS, (January–December 1763), TNA Adm 36/6901.

Master's Mates' Logs
Eagle, HMS, Cook (27 June 1755–31 December 1756), ATL qMS-0537.

Lieutenants' Passing Certificates
1712–76, TNA Adm 6/86-7 and Adm 107/3-4.

Manuscript Charts
1758 Harbour of Gaspey (UKHO A306).
1759 A Plan of the Traverse or Passage from Cape Torment into the South Channel of Orleans, BL Add Ms. 31360 f.14.
1759–62 [Halifax Harbour], BL Add Ms. 31360 f.9.
1762 Various charts in Cook's log book (MSS 20/book 3) (UKHO), including:
Plan of Carbonere Harbour and Harbour Grace in Conception Bay in Newfoundland, surveyed by order of the Right Honble. the Lord Colvill, by James Cook. 1762 (UKHO).
A Plan of the Bay of Bulls and Harbour of St. John's, Newfoundland, by James Cook. 1962 (UKHO).
A Plan of the Road of the Harbour of Placentia in Newfoundland; with a Plan of the Fort on Castle Hill, by James Cook. 1962 (UKHO).
A Sketch of the Sea Coast of Newfoundland between Cape Spear and Cape St. Francis, by James Cook. 1962 (UKHO).
A Sketch of Harbour Grace and Carbonere in Newfoundland, by Jas Cook. 1762, NLA MS 5.
A Plan of the Harbour of Croque in Newfoundland. By James Cook. Original Sketches, Drawings, Maps etc., collected by Admiral Isaac Smith. Drawings and watercolours, mainly of Captain Cooks Second Voyage (1772–1775). [1762]. SLNSW PXD 11 (f. ib).
1763 A Plan of York Harbour on the Coast of Labradore. Survey'd by Order of his Excellency Thos Graves Esqr Governor of Newfoundland &c &c &c by James Cook. 1763 (UKHO A701/5).

A plan of the Road and Harbour of Saint Peters. Survey'd by Order of His Excellency Thos Graves Esq Commander of His Majesty's Ship Antelope and Governor of Newfoundland &c &c &c by James Cook (UKHO A701/14).

A Plan of York Harbour on the Coast of Labradore; Surveyed by Order of His Excellency Thos Graves Esqr Governor of Newfoundland &c &c &c by James Cook, 1763 (UKHO B188).

A plan of the Island of St Peter, Langly and Miquelong Surveyed by Order of His Excellency Thomas Graves Esq. Governor of Newfoundland &c by James Cook, 1763 (UKHO B5299).

A plan of the Harbours of Quirpon Noddy in Newfoundland. Surveyed by order of His Excellency Thos. Graves Esq. Governor by James Cook, 1763 (UKHO C 54/6).

A Sketch of the Island of Newfoundland. Done from the latest observations by James Cook, 1763. Atlas Vv2, Vol. 1, item 21 (UKHO).

A Plan of the Harbour of St Johns in Newfoundland, by J. Cook. Original Sketches, Drawings, Maps etc., collected by Admiral Isaac Smith. Drawings and watercolours, mainly of Captain Cooks Second Voyage (1772–1775), 1763. PXD 11 (f.ia) (SLNSW).

1764 A Chart of Part of the Coast of Labradore from Shecatica to Chateaux Including the Island and Straights of Bellisle. Surveyed by Order of the Honble; Commodore Byron Governor of Newfoundland, Labradore &c &c by Michael Lane in the year 1769. To which is Added Part of the Coast of Newfoundland from Quirpon to Point Ferolle Surveyed by Order of Commodore Palliser Governor of Newfoundland, Labradore &c &c, by James Cook in the year 1764. With Sailing Directions &c notes. (UKHO C 54/2) (see also C54/7 below).

A chart of the Sea Coast Newfoundland between Open Bay and Green Island. Survey'd by order of Hugh Pallisser Esqr Commodore &c by James Cook, 1764. (UKHO C 54/3).

A chart of the coast, bays, and harbours in Newfoundland between the White Cape and Boat Harbour. Survey'd by order of Hugh Pallisser Esqr Commodore &c by James Cook, 1764. (UKHO C 54/4).

A chart of the Coasts, Bays and Harbours in Newfoundland between Griguet and Pt Ferolle. Survey'd by Order of Hugh Pallisser Esqr Commodr &c &c by James Cook. (UKHO C 54/7) (see also C54/2 above).

A Chart of the Sea coast, Bays, and Harbours, in Newfoundland between Green Island and Point Ferrolle. Surveyed by order of Hugh Pallisser Esq Commodore &c, by James Cook (UKHO 342).

A Chart of the Island of Newfoundland with part of the Coast of Labradore Corrected from the latest Observations by James Cook, 1764 (W 710058.b).

1765 A chart of the Sea-coast, Bays, Harbours and Islands in Newfoundland between the Bay of Despair; and the Harbours of St Laurence. Survey'd by Order of Hugh Pallisser Esqr. Commodore &c &c by James Cook (UKHO C58).

1766 A Chart of the Sea-Coast, Bays, Harbours and Islands in Newfoundland between Cape Anguille and the Harbour of Great Jervis, including the Island of St Paul and Cape North on the Island of Cape-Briton. Survey'd by Order of Commodore Palliser, Governor of Newfoundland, Labradore &c by James Cook, 1766. (UKHO C 54/5).

1767 An exact trigonometrical survey of the West Coast of the Island of Newfoundland taken by Order of Commodore Palliser, Governor of Newfoundland, Labradore etc etc by James Cook, 1767. Signed by James Cook (UKHO C 54/1).

Index

Adams, George 68
Adams, Captain Sir Thomas 158, 160, 165, 170
Adams, Tomlin 97
Adams, Captain William 89, 95, 97–8, 101, 104–5, 107
Admiralty 144–5
Adventure, HMS 20
Aix-la-Chapelle, Treaty of (1748) 7, 15, 49, 52
Alcide, HMS 101
Aldborough, HMS 30, 141
Alder, John 147
Algonquin peoples 83, 128
Allen, George 46, 77
Allwright, Thomas 165
Amherst, General Jeffrey 51, 55, 57–9, 66, 70–1, 78–9, 103–5, 114–15, 117–19
Amherst, Colonel William 115
Anderson's Cove 161
Ann and Elizabeth (GB) 186
Angeac, François-Gabriel d' 134–5, 137
Anse au Foulon 79, 90, 92, 100, 102
Anse de la Cormorandiere *see* Kennington Cove
Anse aux Meadows 128
Anse aux Sables 53
Anse Savage Cove *see* Savage Bay
Anson, Admiral Lord George 9–10, 13, 15, 19–20, 34, 76, 144, 184
Antelope, HMS 114–15, 126, 131–3, 136–8, 177
Anticosti Island 134
Aquaforte 114

Aquilon, HMS 163
Arethuse (Fr) 55–6
Articles of War 149
Asget, John 169–70
astronomy 60, 63–4, 67, 151, 169, 183–4, 191
Atalante (Fr) 102
Atkinson, Jonathan 26
Audacious, HMS 148
Austria 7, 9–10
Avalon Peninsula 114, 118, 129, 133

Baie des Chaleurs 104
Baie de Gaspé *see* Gaspé Bay
Balfour, Captain George 56–7
Ball, William 147
Banks, Sir Joseph 152–3, 168, 170, 180–1
Barker, Robert 147
Barrall, William 147
Barrow, Richard 157, 163
Bateman, John 107
Bateman, Captain Nathaniel 97–8, 103, 105–7, 188
Batts, Elizabeth *see* Cook, Elizabeth (wife)
Bay l'Argent 161
Bay Bulls 113, 116, 147
Bay d'Espoir 160, 162–3, 166
Bay of Islands 178–80
Bayfield, Admiral Henry William 125
Beauport 79, 86–91, 93
Bechinoe, Lieutenant Benjamin 46, 77
Beck, John 160
Bedford, Duke of 121
Bedford Bason 109
beer 152–3, 168

Belle Isle 134, 136, 139
Belle Isle, Strait of 54, 128, 146, 152–4, 156, 164–6, 182
Belleoram Harbour 161
Bellona, HMS 177
Bennett, John 183
Beothuk people 128
Bevis, John 167, 185
Bic 102, 112
Biddon, James 133–4
Bienfaisant (Fr) 104
Bird, John 69, 184
Bisset, Thomas 19, 21, 26, 41, 43, 46, 48, 84, 86–8, 93
Blackburn, John 119, 124, 158
Blandford, HMS 17, 24
Bonne Bay 166, 178–9
Boscawen, Admiral Edward 9, 16–17, 25, 29, 32–4, 48, 50–1, 55, 58–9, 70, 74, 77, 86, 97
Bougainville, Louis-Antoine de 77, 83, 89, 92, 104
Bouville, Captain Louis Jubert de 24
Bowen, Ashley 74–5, 80, 83, 103
Bowen, Emmanuel 120
Boxey Harbour 161
Boyd, John 95, 98
Boyd, Thomas 173
Braddock, Major-General Edward 8, 16
Brathwaite, Richard 165
British–Prussian alliance 7
Broad, Daniel 147
Brodrick, Admiral Thomas 34
Brown, Michael 164, 170
Brown, Sarah 120–1

Brunet Island 161
Burgeo Islands 167, 169
Burin Peninsula 160, 163, 166
Burnett, Captain 112
Burr, Daniel 158
Bute, Earl of 12–13, 121, 130
Byng, Admiral John 12–13, 24–5, 27, 47
Byron, Captain John 104, 114, 134

Cabot, John 128
Cabot Strait 168
Campbell, Captain John 69, 184–5
Canada 8, 10, 83, 99, 192
Candler, John 147
Cap Rouge/Red Cape 150
Cape Anguille 168, 171–2, 174, 178, 181
Cape Bonavista 140, 154, 158
Cape Breton Island 168
Cape Charles 158
Cape La Hune 167
Cape Norman 151–3
Cape Race 134, 147, 166
Cape Raven 136, 151
Cape Ray 140–1, 147, 157–8, 168–9, 174
Cape St Francis 117, 158
Cape St George 177
Cape Spear 117
Carbonear 118–19
Carouge Harbour 150
Carteret, Captain Joseph 40
Cartier, Jacques 83
Centurion, HMS 81, 84, 88, 148
Chabert de Cogolin, Joseph-Bernard 110
Chads, Captain James 92
Chaffault, Capitaine Louis-Charles du 54
Champernowne, Lieutenant Rawlin 42–3
Charlton, John 157, 164, 173, 187
Charming Nancy (GB) 113
Chateau Bay 136–9, 142, 160, 164–5, 170
Choiseul, duc de 13, 113
Cleader, John 46

Cleland, Captain 93
Clevland, John 131–2, 144
Coal, William 173
Cockburn, George 188
Codroy Island 168
Collins, Lieutenant 80
Columbine, Lieutenant Edward 46
Colvill, Admiral Alexander, Lord 93–7, 101–3, 105–8, 110–15, 117–21, 133, 166
Command, James 164, 170
Compagnie des Indes 33
Conception Bay 118
Concord (Fr) 116
Connaigre Bay 160–1
Connoire Bay 168
Connolly, Charles 43
Conquistador, HMS 177
Cook, Elizabeth (daughter) 124, 171
Cook, Elizabeth (wife) 3–4, 119–20, 123–5, 138, 140, 154, 156, 173–6, 189
Cook, Captain James
  charts and sailing
    directions 62–3, 69–73, 76, 82, 86, 97–8, 106, 108–10, 116–23, 125–7, 129, 132, 134–5, 145–7, 149, 154–5, 163, 171–2, 177–8, 181–3, 190–1
  childhood 1–3
  death 125, 152
  early sea experience 3–4, 14–15
  health 27, 152
  joins Royal Navy 7, 11, 14–15, 17–21
  leadership 14, 191
  promotions 39–40, 188–9
  surveying 11, 21, 60–3, 66–73, 82, 86, 97–8, 108–10, 116–19, 122–3, 125–7, 129–32, 134–8, 142, 145–55, 157, 160–2, 166–8, 174, 177–80, 191
Cook, James (father) 1–2, 17, 123
Cook, James (son) 124, 138, 140

Cook, James (James Cook #3) 120
Cook, Lieutenant James (James Cook #2) 118, 120
Cook, Joseph (son) 189
Cook, Nathaniel (son) 124, 154
Cook, Peter 147
Cook's *Eclipse* (1766) 126, 167, 169, 185
Cook's Harbour 151
Cornwallis, Colonel Edward 49
Courserac, Marie Anne Aubert de *see* Drucour, Madame
Craig, Captain Robert 42, 44–5, 188
Croque 136, 138–9, 170
Cruizer (cutter) 28–9
Cumberland, Duke of 9, 13, 21, 78
Cunningham, John 157, 164, 170, 172

Dalrymple, Alexander 183
David (GB) 173
Davis Inlet 146
Davis Strait 158
Dawson, John 160
Deane, Captain Joseph 102, 105
Deer Lake 180
Denis, Captain Peter 177
Denne, Lieutenant William 98
DesBarres, Lieutenant JFW 117–19
Devonshire, Duke of 12–13, 34
Devonshire, HMS 80–2, 106
Diana, HMS 86–7, 97, 102–3, 105–6
Discovery, HMS 114
disease *see also* scurvy 11, 15, 17, 48, 100, 112
Dog Peninsula 154
Dolphin, HMS 114
Dorsetshire, HMS 177
Doughty, Simon 173
Douglas, Captain Charles 114, 126, 133–5, 137–8

Drucour, Augustin de
    Boschenry de 51, 53,
    55–7
Drucour, Madame 53, 55
Dubois de la Motte, Admiral
    Emmanuel-Auguste de
    Cahideuc 16, 21, 24–5,
    34, 48
Duc d'Aquitaine (Fr) 34–8
Dugdale, Lieutenant Robert
    98
Dunk, George Montagu,
    second Earl of Halifax
    121, 140
Dunn, John 164, 170
Durell, Commodore Philip
    48–9, 65, 73–7, 79–80, 93
Dyer, William 169–70

Eagle, HMS 11, 17–30, 32–8,
    41, 48, 66, 118, 141–2,
    188, 193
Earl of Pembroke (GB) *see also*
    Endeavour 185–6
Eclipse Island 167
Egmont, second Earl of 138,
    142
Elizabeth (GB) 113
Elphinston, Captain John
    97, 103
Endeavour, HMB 69, 123, 125,
    133, 160, 168, 175, 182,
    184, 186–90
English, George 173
Enterprise, HMS 118–19
Esperance (Fr) 24–5
Eurus, HMS 97, 101, 103, 105,
    107
Eveille (Fr) 115
Everrest, William 120–1
Everitt, Captain Michael 84

Falkland, HMS 106
Falmouth, HMS 28
Fame, HMS 104
Favourite, HMS 165, 168, 170,
    179
Ferdinand, Duke of
    Brunswick-Luneberg 9
Ferguson, Captain James 95,
    103

Ferolle Island 154
Ferolle Point 154–5, 172, 179,
    181
Ferrior, Lieutenant Samuel
    98, 101
Ferryland 158
Fishing Admirals 158–9
Flamborough, HMS 20
Fleck, Margaret (sister) 124
Flower, Peter 133–4, 147, 152,
    154, 157, 164, 173, 187
Flowers Cove 154–5
Fontainebleau, Treaty of
    (1762) 121
Forster, William 134
Fort Duquesne 8, 13, 16
Fort Levis 104
Fort Pitt *see* Fort Duquesne
Fortune Bay 160–161, 163, 166
Fox, Henry 130
Fox Island Harbour 167
Freelove (GB) 3
France 7, 9, 12–13
    colonies 10, 52, 83, 88, 113,
    127
    fisheries 12, 24, 52, 113,
    127–9, 133, 136, 140–1,
    146, 149, 157–9, 165
French Indies Company *see*
    Compagnie des Indes
Frederick II, of Prussia 7–9, 13
Frederick, Prince of Wales 12
Freeman, John 147
French and Indian War *see*
    Seven Years' War
French-Austrian-Russian
    alliance 7
French Shore 127, 129, 136,
    140–1, 150, 152–4
Friendship (GB) 3, 14
Funk Island 150

Gabarus Bay 51, 54, 58, 62,
    78–9
Garonne (Fr) 115, 134
Gaspé Bay 48, 71, 74, 105, 110
Gathman, Francis 147, 157, 164,
    170, 172
Gell, John 165
George II, of England 7, 12,
    30, 106

George III, of England 13,
    106, 121
Gerring, Thomas 147
Gibraltar, HMS 165
Gilbert, Sir Humphrey 128
Gilbert, Joseph 178, 182
Gilliard, William 164, 170, 173
Giraudais, François Chenard
    de la 134
Gordon, Captain William
    80–1
Gore, Lieutenant Hamilton
    23
Gore, John 28
Gosport, HMS 115–16, 118, 120
Gouttes, Marquis des 54–6
Gramont, HMS 113–14
Grand Banks 113, 127–128, 134
Grandy Island 167
Graves, Samuel 47
Graves, Governor Captain
    Thomas 96, 114–15,
    126–7, 129–32, 134–8,
    140–2, 159
Graves's Island *see* Noble's
    Island
Great Ayton 2, 17
Great Jervis Harbour 161,
    163, 171
Great St Lawrence Harbour
    see St Lawrence
    Harbour
Green, Charles 184
Green, George 157, 163
Green Island 136, 152
Gregory, Captain Robert 172
Grenville, HM schooner/brig
    123, 126, 136–7, 142–3,
    145–54, 156–9, 161–4,
    167–8, 170, 172–5, 177,
    179–81, 187, 190, 193
Grenville, George 121, 130, 142
Grenville, Richard, Earl
    Temple 34
Griffith, Captain Walter 23,
    30, 35
Griffiths, James 147, 157, 164,
    170
Grimshaw, William 173, 187
Griquet 152, 155
Groais Island 154

Guernsey, HMS 141, 147–50, 160, 163, 165, 170, 178, 180, 187
Guernsey Island 178

Ha Ha Bay 151
Halifax 11, 48–52, 63, 65–6, 73–4, 76–7, 79–80, 93, 95–7, 99, 101, 103, 106, 108–9, 112–15, 120
Halifax, second Earl of *see* Dunk, George Montagu
Halifax, HMS 53
Hamar, Captain Joseph 19–20, 22–3
Hamilton, Captain George 97, 103
Hamilton, John 147, 158, 165, 179
Hamilton, William 165, 179
Hanover 7, 9
Harbour Breton 161
Harbour Grace 118–19
Harbour le Cou 168
Hardman, Thomas 173, 187
Hardy, Sir Charles 48, 51, 58, 70
Harmood, Lieutenant James 98
Harrison, Rear Admiral Henry 32, 35
Harrison, John 60
Hart, Thomas 157, 163
Haswell, Lieutenant Robert 95
Hatchman, Jonathan 147
Haussonville, Colonel Joseph-Louis-Bernard de Cléron d' 113, 115, 118
Havana 118, 121, 179
Haven, Jens 152–3
Haviland, Brigadier William 104
Hawke, Admiral Sir Edward 9, 17–18, 21–2, 27, 29, 144, 179, 183–4, 189, 192
Hawke's Harbour 179
Hay, William 147
Hayes, Adam 186
Heason, Christopher 147

Herbert, Ruben 157, 163
Hermitage Bay 161, 166
Hicks, Zachary 175
Holburne, Admiral Francis 29
Holland, Samuel Johannes 47–8, 61–6, 70, 73, 87, 92, 97
Holmes Admiral Charles 79, 87, 89–90, 93
Hope, HMS 147, 165–8, 170, 180
Hopewell (GB) 3
Horse Islands 150
Howe, Colonel William 92
Howe, Admiral Richard 148
Howson, William 173, 178, 187, 189
Hubertusburg, Treaty of (1763) 12
Hudson Bay 146
Humber River *see* Bay of Islands
Hunter, HMS 89–90, 95, 97, 101, 103
Hutchison, Isaac 173

Île au Coudres 103, 105
Île-aux-Noix 104
Île d'Orléans 80–1, 84, 86, 92, 103
Île du Bic 102, 112
Île Royale 110
India 7, 13
Ingornachoix Bay 179
instrumentation 68–9, 131, 184
Innu people 136
Inuit people 128, 136
Ipswich, HMS 148
Isis, HMS 28

Jacques Fontaine Cove 161
James, John 98
James, Thomas 147
Jefferey, Henry 147, 152
Jefferys, Thomas 182–3
Jervis, Captain John 114–15, 120, 148
Johnston, John 147
Jones, James 95, 98
Jupiter, HMS 148

Kennington, HMS 53
Kennington Cove 47, 51–3, 61–3, 66, 70
Keppel, Augustine 179
Keppel Harbour 179
Keppel Island 179
Kerfoot, Nathaniel 40
Killbuck Cove 166
King George, HMS 115
Klosterseven, Convention of (1757) 13
Knight, Gowin 68–9
Knowles, Vice Admiral John 34

Labrador 127, 134, 136–7, 146–7, 155, 158, 164
Laforey, Captain John 56–7
Lamaline Islands 160
Lamb, William 157, 164, 170, 172
Lane, Michael 125, 170, 173–4, 177, 179, 182, 187, 190
La Pérouse, Jean-François de Galaup de 54, 113
La Poile Harbour 168
Lark Harbour 180
Lark, HMS 132, 134, 138, 143, 145–7, 149–50, 158–9
Latitude *see* navigation
Lawrence, Charles 51–3
Lawson, James 165, 170
Leadbetter, Charles 67
Lemesurier, Nicholas 112
Lemesurier, William 112
Leopard, HMS 22
Leopold Josef, Graf Daun 9
Lizard, HMS 106
Levis, Brigadier Francois de 99–102, 104
Ligonier, Sir John 78–9
Lind, Alexander 173
Lion, HMS 177
Lock, Thomas 157, 163
Long Harbour 126, 161–2
Longitude *see* navigation
Louisbourg 8, 11, 13, 24, 39, 47–8, 51–9, 61–2, 66, 70–4, 77–81, 86, 96–7, 104, 117
Lovely, Edward 95, 106

Lowestoffe, HMS 89–90, 92, 102–3, 105
Lungley, Nathaniel 157, 164, 170, 172
Lyon, Stephen 164, 172

Macartney, Captain John 100, 103
McCarly, Richard 147
McDonald, Captain 117
Machault (Fr) 104
Mackenzie, James 147
McKenzie, Murdoch 69–70
McMillard, William 103
McNabs Island 114
Magdalen Islands 138
Major, John 98, 119
Man, Captain Robert 188
Manley, Isaac 175
Mansell, William 148
Maria Theresa, Empress of Austria 7
Marquis de Malauze (Fr) 104
Marton (birthplace) 1–2
Marechal de Belle-Isle (Fr) 44–5
Mars, HMS 120
Mary (GB) 3
Masters' regulations 194
Mathews, James 157, 163
Mayer, Tobias 60
Medway, HMS 34–7
Medway River *see* Bay of Islands
Mercury, HMS 120
Merlin, HMS 165, 179–80
Middle Arm *see* Bay of Islands
Mike, James 103–4
Mi'kmaq people 128, 177
Mile End Old Town 124–5
Miller, Captain George 100, 103
Milligan, Captain John 23
Milner, Thomas 186
Missionaries 152–3
Monckton, Brigadier General Robert 89, 92, 98
Monmouth, HMS 24
Monongahela River, battle of (1755) 16

Montagu, John, fourth Earl of Sandwich 130, 138
Montcalm, Louis-Joseph de 79, 83, 86, 89, 91–3, 99–100
Montmorency 86, 88–9
Montreal 83, 89, 93, 99–100, 102–5, 113
Moravians 152–3
Mordaunt, Sir John 78
Mouat, Alexander 114
Mouat, Captain Patrick 114
Munkhouse, William 160, 170
Murray, Brigadier General James 89, 98–105

Namur, HMS 177
Nation, Nathaniel 147
Navigation 60, 67–9, 160, 182–3, 191
Navy Board 144–5, 156, 185–7
Neptune, HMS 84, 107
New Ferolle 147, 153
New France *see* Quebec
New York 48, 50, 61, 79, 81, 98, 103, 107, 110, 115
Newcastle, Duke of 12–13, 16, 34, 121, 130
Newfoundland 11, 64, 68–9, 105, 110, 113, 120–3, 125–9, 131–4, 136–41, 145–9, 155, 159, 162–6, 174, 180, 182, 192
Niger, HMS 148, 158–60, 163, 165, 168, 170
Noble's Island 136–7
Noddy Bay/Harbour 136, 138–9, 151–3
Norman, James 46
Norris, Edward 173
North, Captain Abraham 125, 188
North America 8, 10, 16
North Arm *see* Bay of Islands
North Head 178
North Sea coal trade 3, 14–15, 41
Northumberland, HMS 11, 41, 75, 77, 81, 93–7, 101–8, 110–14, 117–20, 129, 179, 188, 193

Office of Ordnance 68, 130
Old Ferolle 154
Ommanney, Captain Cornthwaite 165, 170
Osbaldstone, William 37
Osborne, Admiral 27
Osborne, Captain Henry 129
Our Ladies Bubbies (Quebec) 179

Palliser, Governor Captain Hugh 22–3, 25–6, 28, 30, 32, 34–5, 37–9, 93, 118, 125, 140–3, 145–7, 149, 152, 154, 156–7, 159–60, 163–4, 168, 170, 177, 180–1, 185–8, 192
Panther, HMS 26
Paris, Treaty of (1763) 127, 129, 140–1
Parker, Admiral Sir William 126, 147–8, 151–2, 154, 157, 164, 167–8, 170, 173
Pass Island Tickle 161
Paterson, William 179
Pearl, HMS 132, 134, 138, 146–7, 158–9, 163, 165, 168, 170, 178
Peck, John 160
Pelham, Henry 12, 15–16
Pembroke, HMS 11, 21, 41, 43, 46–51, 54–6, 62–5, 67–8, 70–1, 73–5, 77, 80–2, 84–8, 94–5, 101–3, 105, 125, 193
Penguin Islands 167
Penzance, HMS 106
Perceval, Captain Philip 147
Perseverance, HMS 175
Phillips, Captain William 137, 147
Pickersgill, Richard 177
Pistolet Bay 151
Pitt, William, the Elder 7, 9, 12–13, 34, 77–8, 94, 121, 130, 133
Pitt, William, the Younger 66
Pitt Harbour 170
Pitt's War *see* Seven Years' War
Pittsburgh *see* Fort Duquesne

Placentia 114–15, 129, 157
Plymouth 26–7
Point de Levis 85–7, 89, 92
Point Pleasant 108, 113
Point Riche 140–1, 155, 158, 179
Pomone (Fr) 102
Porcupine, HMS 84, 86, 88, 100, 102–3, 106
Port au Choix 179
Port au Port Peninsula 177–8
Port aux Basques 168
Port Dauphin 54
Port Morien Mine 71
Port Saunders 179
Portland, HMS 148
Pownall, Thomas 74
Price, Walter 157, 163
Prince, HMS 20
Prince Edward, HMS 47
Prince George, HMS 148
Prince of Orange, HMS 77, 80, 101
Proby, Captain Charles 34
Prussia 7, 9–10, 12
Pulliblank, Edward 179

Quebec 8, 10–11, 13, 39, 66, 70, 72, 74–81, 83–6, 89, 91–105, 107, 134, 142, 179
Quiberon Bay 13, 179, 184
Quirpon 134, 136, 138–9, 146–7, 149, 151–2, 154, 158

Racehorse, HMS 100, 103, 106
Raissonnable, HMS 148
Ramea Island 167
Ramezay, Major de 93, 98
Rardon, Timothy 164, 170, 173, 187
Red Bay 125
Red Hat Mountain 157
Red Island 177
Repulse, HMS 106
Resolution, HMS 175, 178
Restigouche River 104, 134
Regnier, Claude-Louis-Francois 140
Richardson, John 120–1
Richardson, William 187
Richmond, HMS 87–8, 90, 97, 101, 103

Roberts, Charles 157, 163
Robson, John 46, 80, 101
Robuste (Fr) 113, 115
Roche, John 147
Rochester, HMS 106, 110–12
Rodney, Admiral Sir George 107
Romney, HMS 29
Rose, HMS 185
Rossant, George 187
Royal Navy 17, 41, 58, 123, 125, 129, 144–5, 149
  charts 62, 125
  clothing 113
  enlistment in 14–15, 17–18, 74
  prize money, allocation of 37
  promotions 190, 192
  provisions 26–7
  punishment 103–4, 152
  recruitment 14–17
  wages 41
Royal Society 60, 69, 126, 167, 169, 183–5
Russell (GB) 88
Russia 7, 9–10
Ruthven, Captain John 134, 137

Sable Island 106
Sacred Bay 151
Sagona 161
St Albans, HMS 28–9
St Barbe 158
St George's Bay 177
St George's Harbour 177
St George's Island 113
St John's 11, 96, 107, 113–18, 120, 122, 127, 129, 137, 139, 142–3, 147, 149, 154, 170
St John's Bay 179
St John's River 158
St Lawrence Harbour 157, 160, 166
St Lawrence River and Gulf 11, 51–2, 63–4, 70, 73–4, 79, 81–3, 91, 93, 97–8, 101, 104, 106, 110, 112, 121, 129, 134, 138, 157, 172
St Nicholas 91–2

St Paul Island 168
St Pierre et Miquelon 127, 129, 133–5, 137–9, 141–2, 146, 157, 160–1, 172, 174
Sally (schooner) 136
Saltykov, Pyotr Semyonovich 9
Sanderson, William 2
Sandwich, fourth Earl of *see* Montagu, John
Saunders, Admiral Sir Charles 9, 21, 76–81, 84–6, 89, 91, 93–5, 97–9, 107, 144, 179
Savage Bay 154
Saxony 8–9
Saxton, Captain Charles 134, 147, 158, 165
Sayer, Robert 183
Scarborough, HMS 172
Schomberg, Captain Alexander 102, 105
Scorpion, HMS 93
Scotland 43
Scott, Alexander 98
Scourge, HMS 175
Scurvy 17, 24
Seahorse, HMS 90
Seven Years' War 7–13, 33, 42, 81, 106, 124, 127, 129, 141, 190
Shag Island 178
Shag Rocks 178
Shepherd, Andrew 147, 152
Ship Cove 162, 167
Short, Richard 77
Shortnell, Morris 157
Shrewsbury, HMS 118, 141
Signal Hill 117
Silesia 7, 9, 12
Simcoe, Captain John 46–8, 54, 62–6, 73–5, 80–1, 93
Simcoe, John Graves 47, 62–3
Simms, John 173
Simpkins, James 173
Skottowe, Thomas 2, 17
Smart, Edward 136–138
Smith, Captain Isaac 41, 173–6, 187
Smith, John 173, 187
Smith, Thomas 157, 164, 173

Snook, Morgan 160
Solar eclipse (1766) *see* Cook's Eclipse
Solebay, HMS (1742) 4, 11, 39, 41–5, 193
Solebay, HMS (1763) 147, 154
Spain 10, 12–13
colonies 10
Spitfire, HMS 124
Spruce beer *see* beer
Spy, HMS 137, 146–7, 163, 165
Squirrel, HMS 80–2, 86–7, 90, 93
Staithes 2–3
Stamp, Richard 147
Stanford, Lieutenant William 165–6, 180
Stephens, Sir Philip 125, 129, 131–2, 144–5, 172, 185, 187, 192
Stirling Castle, HMS 21, 84, 89
Stringer, Zachariah 164, 170
Surridge, James 173, 178, 187
Sutherland, HMS 84, 86–7, 90, 92, 96, 106
Swallow (Boston) 103
Swanton, Commodore Robert 102
Syren, HMS 114–15, 118

Tahiti 184
Tamar, HMS 114, 132, 134
Ternay, Charles-Henri-Louis d'Arsac de 54, 113, 115, 117–18
Terpsichore, HMS 132, 134, 137
Test, Edward 133
Thames River *see* Bay of Islands
Third Carnatic War *see* Seven Years' War
Third Silesian War *see* Seven Years' War
Thompson, Captain Samuel 134, 147, 158
Thurot, Francois 44–5

Three Brothers (GB) 3
Three Sisters (GB) 88, 173
Thunderer, HMS 124
Townshend, Brigadier General George 89, 92–4, 98–9
Transit of Venus (1769) 183–5, 190
Trepassey Bay 133
Trident, HMS 101
Trinity 158
Trinity House 40–1, 125
Triton (Fr) 29–31, 38
Tryal (GB) 185
Tulliken, Colonel 118
Turner, John 180
Turner, Robert 164, 170
Tweed, HMS 126, 132–5, 137–8, 146–7, 149–50, 178
Tweed's Harbour *see* La Poile Harbour
Two Brothers (Fr) 112

Unfortunate Cove 152, 155
Unicorne (Fr) 115
Utrecht, Peace of (1713) 129, 140

Valentine (GB) 185
Vandome, Abraham 173
Vanguard, HMS 102–3
Vaudreuil, Marquis de 83–4, 93, 104
Vauquelin, Captain 55–6, 86, 100, 102
Vincent, John 173

Walker, John 3–4, 14–15, 37
Walpole, Horace 13
Walpole, Sir Robert 12
Walsh, William 147, 157, 163
Wapping 14
War of Austrian Succession 7, 15, 19, 42, 52, 76, 81
Wardale, Frances (cousin) 124, 189

warfare 10–11, 149
Washington, George 8, 16
Weazle, HMS 175
Webb, James 136
Weir, Alexander 187
Wells, HMS 165, 170
West, Nathaniel 92
West, Admiral Temple 21, 24–5, 34
Western Squadron 10
Westminster, Treaty of (1756) 12
Westminster, Treaty of (1758) 13
Whately, Thomas 142
Wheelock, Captain John 46, 80–1, 85, 93–4, 105
Whitby 3, 14
White, Joseph 95
White Bear Bay 167
Whitmore, Edward 51–3
Wilkinson, Captain Andrew 180–1
Wilkinson, Thomas 103
Williams, John 164, 170
Willoughby, James 157, 163
Willoughby, John 164, 170, 172
Wilson, Henry 67–8
Windsor, HMS 28
Wise, Richard 48, 125
Wolfe, General James 48, 51–3, 55, 58, 61, 64–6, 70–1, 77–81, 85–90, 92–4, 97–100
Wood, Alexander 89
Woody Point 179
Wyatt, William 46

York Harbour 136–9, 158, 178, 180
Young, John 147

Zephyr, HMS 146–7, 158–9, 165, 168, 170